The Steep Places

Norman Angell

THE STEEP PLACES

The devils ... went into the herd and behold, the whole herd ran violently down a steep place into the sea, and perished in the waters.

—From the Gospel of St. Matthew

HARPER & BROTHERS

New York and London

1-8

TABLE OF CONTENTS

PART I

The Human Factor:
The Danger and the Hope

The Human Factor: The Danger and the Hope

WE HAVE been abundantly warned of a danger threatening human life over wide areas of the earth. There threatens also, as the result of measures designed to avoid that danger, peril to the liberties and ways of living which we—particularly in the United States and Britain—hold dear.

It is not the purpose of this book to enlarge upon the physical danger, nor to discuss the external facts of the political situation, except in so far as that is necessary in order to indicate the changes in human behavior, the ideas and scale of values, which that situation demands if we are to survive in a free and humane civilization. It may be true that we cannot "change human nature" (whatever the phrase may mean) but the simple record of the known past shows how much we can change human behavior and ideas.

If we are to retain unabated the passions and violences which have marked the tribal, national, religious, revolutionary, political, social, and economic conflicts of the past—and which still mark some of the present—we shall not be able to maintain democratic governments; nor a democratic world authority sufficiently stable and powerful to control the new weapons and enable us to escape mutual destruction. We are likely then to turn to totalitarian methods. This is the challenge which Russia throws down to the West.

The obviousness of danger sets up a general call for better understanding between peoples. This book insists that that better understanding with others cannot be achieved without a better understanding, first of all, of ourselves; of the motives which have caused every one of our nations to contribute to the difficulties in which mankind now finds itself entangled.

To the extent that we understand how we were led into the

3

errors of the past, we improve the chance that we shall avoid repetition of them in circumstances that may make them still more disastrous. That is why certain of those past errors have been given somewhat detailed examination in the pages which follow.

First as to certain facts of the present. Since the end of the war four events, any one of which taken by itself would be as portentous and overwhelming as anything in history, have occurred simultaneously. They are:

1. The coming of atomic weapons of war.

2. The dissolution of the British Empire accelerated by the economic crisis at its heart in Britain, a crisis so severe as to amount to threatened collapse of the country's economic foundations.

3. A very great increase in the power of the Russian Empire, marked by actual extension of territory, or political control and domination, in both Europe and Asia, and by a diplomatic factor new in the policy of modern states: the use of ideological allies in the form of tightly organized and disciplined parties within nations which might be disposed to resist Russia's political or military expansion. The basis of this new diplomatic system is the wide appeal of a doctrine of which Russia is regarded as the power spearhead and political instrument.

4. The arrival of the United States as a world power, possessing as it does industrial, economic, and financial resources unequaled by any other nation. These resources are prodigious at a moment when other nations, yesterday great powers, are today eliminated (e.g. Germany, Japan) or so grievously exhausted by two world wars as no longer to be able to fulfill their international roles of the past (Britain, France, Italy). Even Russia, greater in population, military power, and, perhaps, potential material resources than the United States, looks to the latter for material aid. The United States has already taken over (as in Greece, Turkey) some of the functions fulfilled by Britain in that "British Century" which lasted from Waterloo to the outbreak of war in 1914.

These events are interrelated. The industrial resources of the United States made possible the manufacture of the atom bomb;

the fact that the United States is the dominant power in the New World and has these resources is due in part to that British imperialism which began with the defeat of the Armada, making possible the settlement of the Pilgrim Fathers in North America; which continued with the pushing back of France from the valleys of the St. Lawrence, the Ohio, the Mississippi in the eighteenth century; enabled Jefferson at the beginning of the nineteenth to warn off Napoleon from the establishment of Louisiana as the basis of a French Empire in the New World by threatening him with the alliance of the United States to Britain; continued also when, at British suggestion and with British support, Monroe blocked the American plans of the Holy Alliance (headed by Russia); and continued, of course, in the present century when Britain embarked upon two wars which later the United States was to recognize as her wars also, aiming at a purpose indispensable to American security.

The result of the power exercised by the English-speaking peoples during four hundred years has been on the whole to strengthen the influence of that form of society in which the state is regarded as the instrument of the individual and his welfare, as against the influence of that form of society in which the individual is regarded mainly as the instrument of the state, an end in itself. The English type of government and society has left its impress very deeply on the United States, Canada, Australia, New Zealand, South Africa, and to some degree on the parliamentary institutions of India, Burma, Ceylon, and on the colonial societies of the West Indies and Africa, growing rapidly toward that independence which the Dominions have already achieved.

The power of the democracies of this type has been out of proportion to the size of their territory and material resources. The extent of the territory occupied by the United States on the Western Hemisphere is very greatly exceeded by that of the Latin republics. (Brazil alone has a greater land area than the United States.) The population of Latin America is now not much less than that of English-speaking America. Yet the wealth and power of the latter far outweigh that of the former. The twenty Latin-American republics all put together could not possibly have played the wartime role of the United States, nor provided the wartime allies with the military help and the postwar world with the economic help, which the one republic of the north has done. This should be no occasion for vainglory. It is a phenomenon which we should, however, examine. For the sources of strength in the Western world are matters which may concern us very deeply indeed in the immediate future. Britain's position in the world has presented some similar phenomena in the immediate past, as when a small island, at a time when its population was not much more than that of greater New York today, brought under control a whole subcontinent on the other side of the world (with now four hundred million people) and held it and governed it for two centuries.

Such events should interest us if only because something of this art of maintaining authority over very wide areas and over many peoples of very divergent cultures will have to be acquired by the projected international body—the United Nations or another—if purposes like the effective control of atomic weapons with the necessarily far-reaching inspection and policing are to be achieved.

It is a curious thing in this connection that while there have been many explanations of how it came about that a very small Britain should have conquered a vast India, there seems to have been no attempt to explain why the reverse should not have happened— why a vast India or China should not have conquered a small European country like Britain, or a whole group of such countries. After all, China and India possessed elaborate civilizations when the Britons were woad-painted savages, and when Rome brought them under the control of its empire. The matter has more than academic interest in view of the sharp decline in the relative power of Europe and of the democratic societies of which it has been the source; their failure to deal with the tendencies to disunity, divisiveness, and fragmentation; and the relative success with which Russia—at whatever cost of freedom—manages to restrain such divisive tendencies in the areas under her government or domination. It is not in those Russian-dominated areas that we find the civil wars, the underground movements, the mutual massacres of rival religious groups, the threatened governments, that are so much in evidence elsewhere. Despite the harshness of methods employed by Russia in a round dozen nations which have so rapidly fallen into her orbit, she has within those nations powerful allies—more powerful than the United States can find in China or Greece, or Britain in India, or Palestine, or Egypt. The expansion of Russian totalitarian power is welcomed by parties—often small, but always disciplined and tightly organized—and by sections of the progressive forces everywhere in the world. Neither the United States nor Britain has such supporters, though the government of Britain is now a socialist government. It makes no such appeal to the revolutionary forces of the world as does the Russian dictatorship. And it is altogether probable that the coming of the atomic bomb will tend to strengthen the favor with which dictatorship is so often regarded. The argument is likely to run that if dictatorship alone can prevail over passionate disruptive differences then it may be the only alternative to atomic extinction.

The failure of the sporadic attempts of the Western democracies to create an international authority capable of checking aggression and violence stems in part from a strange unawareness or unconsciousness of the real nature of the motives which move men and nations; and of the prime function, therefore, which such an authority should fulfill. For a generation or two it has been fashionable to repeat that what we want above all, and first and last, is peace. But what we have actually done has proved, again and again, that this is not true. The event has revealed that what we want first of all in international relations is the nation's survival, the secure right to live under the institutions of our own choice, even if it means sacrificing peace—and, in Britain's case, nearly everything else. The truth that we put security before peace is proven by the fact that when the right to live our own lives is jeopardized by the possible domination of alien power we abandon peace and provoke war; as we have done twice in one generation. If our real intention had been plain to ourselves so that we could have made it plain to the potential aggressor earlier than we did, he would not have gambled on not being resisted.

This confusion as to the order of our vital purposes explains in part the tendency which has characterized public opinion both in America and Britain, the tendency to be internationalist in wartime, or when war or crisis threatens, and isolationist in peace. Association with other nations for the purpose of making war, once it has started, seems the most natural thing in the world. It is then self-evident to all that in order to defend ourselves effectively we must be prepared at times to defend others, in order that we shall not be isolated, defeated in detail, by having potential allies picked off one by one so that the enemy can sooner or later concentrate his whole power upon us. When war looms, lend-lease seems as "natural" as Neutrality Acts do in peacetime.

But this reversion to isolationism in peace involves repudiation of the only method by which power can be used to prevent war, the method, that is, of making it clear beforehand that we will indeed oppose aggression if it is attempted, even against others. Only so can power be used as a deterrent of war. The fact that we have failed in the past thus to maintain a policy which might prevent war, and used our power instead merely to win wars once they have started, is of disturbing significance in the atomic age when civilization can no longer be preserved by "winning" wars; only by preventing them.

But such policies can only be maintained if it is clear, first of all to ourselves, what we shall do in the event of aggression which has not yet arisen. It was not clear to us before either of the wars we have already fought. It is not clear now with respect to Russia, though the confusions differ from the preceding ones.

After a period in which even the slightest criticism of the Soviet system was regarded by many liberals and progressives as sheer sacrilege, *lèse majesté*, we have run into a state of mind in which we regard communism as the main enemy to be fought. Yet one of the purposes of the war just finished, fought in conjunction with Russia, was to vindicate the right of nations to live under the system they preferred, which included the right of Russia to be communist. If now we are to set out upon a crusade forbidding any nation to adopt the communist form of socialism we shall almost certainly disastrously fail; justify Russia's suspicions of the West, present her with good cause for war; divide the West still more deeply by "polarizing" opinion, pushing it into two rival extremes; and confuse and frustrate what should be the underlying purpose of our policy. Our efforts should not be to impose some particular system on any nation, should not aim either at introducing the Russian system

into the West nor the Western into Russia, but should be to find
the means by which two or more very different systems can live
together in the same world. We should fight, not communism, but
aggression.

Powerful elements in Britain and France (more powerful in
France than in Britain) are now advocating a policy of virtual nonresistance to the expansion of Russia.[1] The policy is defended,
even by noncommunists, on grounds already indicated: atomic war
means extinction for a mainly urbanized people like the British, or
a largely urbanized people like the French. Although—runs the argument—life under communists may be pretty grim, there will be
a chance, so long as the people go on living, to soften its worst features; but no chance for anything if they are all dead. The feeling
behind that argument is widespread at present. Liberals and progressives particularly decline to be disturbed by the Big Bad Wolf,
or the Big Bad Bear. But in the light of repeated experience we
have to ask how they will act when the Big Bear has become bigger;
and has come nearer.

Will they behave like those who supported so ardently the Neutrality Acts, or the appeasement policy; who applauded the Oxford
Oath, or joined the Peace Pledge Union and then, when aggression
was at the door, became belligerent? Shall we do as we did on two
previous occasions: change our policy when the risks become visible, and decide at the eleventh hour to resist; resist by fighting a
war which our power, used earlier in different fashion, might have
prevented?[2] To answer this—and the question concerns particularly

[1] A resolution presented at the 1947 Labor Party Conference demanded that
the Service Departments (War Office and Admiralty) be instructed to frame
their estimates and make their strategic dispositions on the assumption that
Britain need not prepare for self-defense against the USSR or the United States.

[2] An American historian of the year 1937 relates: "Thousands of students in
New York recited an American version of the Oxford Oath, proclaiming 'I
refuse to support the government of the United States in any war it may conduct.'" The newly formed Peace Pledge Union of Great Britain, which stood
for the principle of the Oxford Oath, had already in that year a membership of
considerably over a hundred thousand. But more important than these expressions of pacifist opinion was the view of governmental and military and naval
circles that though the country would be right to defend itself if attacked it
would be wrong to fight for any collective principle: to "die for Danzig." In
the event, it was not attacked and it fought, if not for Danzig, for Poland.

the progressives and the leftists—we must settle in our own minds, before alien power is on top of us, what value we really attach to the things we talk about so much, our "way of life," our freedoms, all the things we said we were fighting for in two world wars.

The decision not to resist Russia at all may conceivably be the best available policy. (That is discussed in the pages which follow.) But obviously, its success will depend upon following it out to the bitter end. And that we are not likely to do unless we have faced fully and starkly beforehand our real feeling about national independence and the real nature of communist government, the kind of life that men lead under it. And we all know that anything like objectivity in judgment in regard to Russia and communism seems a psychological impossibility. Yet the worst possible policy would be to assume (without real examination either of the external facts or our own feeling about them) that we shall not resist; and then discover at the eleventh hour that we cannot stomach what the policy demands; and decide to fight. This would correspond to the kind of conduct which produced World War II. It would be certain to produce World War III.

The failure would come less from refusal to face the facts of the international situation, or of communism, than from refusal to face the facts of our own natures.

In the last analysis the problem is one of adjusting deeply rooted subjective impulses to life in a society which technology changes more rapidly than we are able to change our behavior. It is so much easier to deal with the physical material of the external world than with the forces within ourselves which come into conflict with the needs of the highly complex, interdependent, and vulnerable society which science has brought into being. We follow in pursuit of our conscious ends a behavior bound to defeat those ends; and fail to see the relation between the behavior and the defeat.

Thus the Western nations have set before themselves two main objectives: security for their national way of life, and economic welfare. The first purpose demands, as already noted and as the event has so abundantly demonstrated, collective international action; co-operation with others for defense against aggression. (A policy of each his own defender invites aggression by facilitating defeat in detail, as we have already seen.) The second purpose (of economic welfare) in an economically interdependent world demands removal of barriers to effective economic intercourse. The strong, sometimes fierce and violent, impulses of nationalism have made it virtually impossible so far to apply these necessary means to those conscious ends. After the first World War popular nationalist feeling in America dictated a retreat into isolationism, despite all that Wilson and his administration could do; peace treaties in Europe far from attenuating economic nationalism made it very much worse. At least ten thousand miles of new tariff barriers were erected. The first task of newly acquired independence is usually to set up new economic barriers against neighbors. The Irish Free State did so; India (already then beginning to acquire fiscal independence) did so in 1922. It is likely that the two new Indias will do it against each other. Welsh and Scottish nationalism seem to be taking a new lease of life in the acrimony and bitterness that usually mark nationalist philosophy. Britain having liquidated so much of the empire may now begin, if this nationalist trend continues, to liquidate herself and get back to the heptarchy. It is not the road to security or welfare. But it is the road along which easily aroused and ill-disciplined impulses so often push us.

National security and welfare are most often betrayed by those who have the most passionate feeling about national interest: the nationalists and the isolationists. Their passion prompts them to apply policies which destroy the thing they would preserve. To passion add irresponsibility. It has become a commonplace observation that men acting in the mass show a degree of irresponsibility of which they would not be guilty in the conduct each of his personal life. (Very few of those who make up a lynching party could or would do as individuals what they do so readily as a group.) Even in personal affairs instinctive acts of self-preservation are often a sure road to self-destruction, as in a theater fire. The instinct of self-preservation which prompts a rush for the doors will usually destroy those who obey the instinct. For such situations in normal daily life we have managed to inculcate a degree of personal discipline which makes it possible to bring the first thought under control of the second: "If I do this, others will; if others do, my individual act won't save me."

But in politics—particularly where national, party, or doctrinal feeling is involved—this kind of discipline is commonly repudiated, and powerful vested interests exploit and develop the more irrational factors of conduct as against the more responsible and rational. Popular newspapers of enormous circulation (and corresponding revenues) inflame the crudest chauvinism; trade unionists from a sense of loyalty stand with the union "right or wrong"; and politicians of all parties feel "in the interest of the party" that it is necessary to pander to instincts which run counter to the nation's real welfare. Indeed the politician implies, usually, that the group or mass decision, with all its irresponsibility, has in it some divine quality: "The Voice of the People Is the Voice of God"; "Fifty Million Can't Be Wrong." We are called upon to make this Century of the Atom Bomb the Century of the Common Man, the Underprivileged, the man who is the victim of a society so ill contrived that he has not had the advantages in education, training, leisure, health which less common men have had. It is a curious reading of human nature which suggests that a generation, threatened as this is from lack of political wisdom and responsibility will find salvation by handing the direction of things over to those who have been the victims of social injustice and educational deficiency and by assuming that their decisions cannot possibly be mistaken. Their right to decide their own fate should be unquestioned, if we are not to drift to a new slavery. But an indispensable part of avoiding that fate is to recognize that the mass, the People (even when they are not Germans or Japanese) may so easily be utterly wrong, and that it is our business to find the causes of their repeated errors and some cure for at least the worst of them. The greatest service we can do the Common Man is to abolish him; to enable him to abolish himself by ceasing to be a common man.

The national, or party, or doctrinal obsession—loyalty if you will —commonly stands in the way of applying the scientific method to social and political problems, even to the extent to which the physicist in the laboratory or the judge in the law court manages to do so.

The refusal to apply that method is not usually conscious, though the refusal is evident enough in commonplace daily experience of testimony on political subjects. Thus two witnesses, both honest and sincere, both meaning to tell the truth, go to Russia, or China, or Palestine, or Greece, or India; travel over the same ground, see precisely the same things—and on returning give flatly contradictory testimony. Where one sees freedom, another sees slavery; where one justice, another injustice. Still more, of course, is this true of parties directly concerned: the communist sees democracy, where the social democrat or the free enterpriser sees its destruction. Where one sees a given object as white, the other sees it as black. In the conflicts of Hindu and Moslem, Jew and Arab, Jew and Briton, Arab and Briton, trade unionist and employer, CIO and AFL, each accuses the other of being the enemy of right and justice, color-blind, fact-blind. The same words—"freedom" "democracy" are used to indicate opposite things, so that they come to lose all common meaning; and human testimony nearly all value.

This is the most blood-curdling discovery, or rediscovery, of our time: the ease with which the public mind—made up of your mind and mine—can become thus color-blind and fact-blind; blind it may be to some yawning gulf beneath our feet, like that into which the civilized, educated, cultured German people walked twice in a single generation, driven by doctrines of race and nationalism, as earlier torturers in Inquisition dungeons, or in Holy Wars, or on jungle altars of human sacrifice were driven by religious doctrine; or as we see men driven to massacre in India or in Palestine today.

Now, not only does the generally accepted moralist attitude toward these passionate conflicts not help us; that attitude is to some degree the direct cause. To get peace and order and freedom from violence, says the moralist, you must do justice. Violence and crime and hatred are the outcome of unjust conditions. The implication is that "justice" is something in itself self-evident; and that failure to do it must be the result of conscious wickedness on someone's part, a refusal to do what the offender knows to be right; and that the recipient of justice will recognize it as such if he gets it. But the whole issue arises, not because of bad moral intention, nor from any repudiation of obligation to do the right thing, but because men differ sincerely and passionately as to what the right thing is. We are confronted with the need not of bettering moral intention but of bettering judgment, the kind of judgment which can weigh, not plain Wrong against plain Right, but the merits in a conflict of two rights.

These various conflicts that surge about us have one outstanding feature in common: the unshakable conviction of each group that since it is so plainly and unquestionably right, its opponents must be not merely mistaken but willfully wrong, knowing that they sustain an evil cause, and their motives interested, selfish, criminal. There is ample evidence to show that despite the mixture of motives which prompts most human action, all parties alike in the cases mentioned act under the impulse of a sense of right, of eternal justice; sure that any doubt or question of their cause would be craven unfaithfulness, betrayal of comrades, treason. There is general acceptance of a code in which objective examination of the facts, if they tend to weaken faith in the "cause," ceases to be a virtue and becomes simple disloyalty. To the average German drifting twice toward war, it would have been as base to question Germany's mission ("the truth is that which aids Germany") as for a Japanese to question Japan's; as for an Arab to doubt the righteousness of making Palestine an Arab state; as for a Jew to question the righteousness of making it a Jewish state; as for the average communist today—in or outside Russia—to doubt the infallibility of Marx or Lenin; or to believe that heretics to that faith can be moved by any motive than that of capitalist avarice or be anything but "fascist beasts" worthy only of liquidation.

These things are illustrated vividly in two cases: Russia and Palestine.

In Russia we have the story of men aflame with deep passion for social justice, determined to establish a new society from which ancient injustices, wrongs, poverty, and oppressions should be abolished; an order truly free and humane, where all should be equal, all comrades.

Well, we know the result. Its details need not be indicated here. But the point which concerns us most in the present context is that that result, in tragic and complete contradiction of all that was intended, was not due to an absence of feeling for justice and right.

Not only were those responsible for modern Russia moved by those motives, but the abominations which now mark their regime—the police terror, the purges, the chattel slavery of the forced-labor camps, vaster even than the camps whose stench poisoned the air in Nazi Germany—could not probably be maintained unless those who maintain them had persuaded themselves and the Russian people that they were measures justified by a necessary and holy war against the enemies of mankind. They are as convinced on that point as the Inquisitor was convinced he did the will of God.

Two strange facts stand out in relation to the (unintended) result of the Russian Revolution. Most available evidence indicates that for the Russian people as a whole the revolution is still glorious, still represents the dawn of a new and beautiful world. Most of the Russian people would fight to the death to defend it against the assaults of the oppressed and poverty-stricken wage slaves of the United States or Britain or Western Europe. We usually dismiss this feeling of the Russian people as explained merely by the powerful machine of indoctrination operated by the Moscow rulers who are by its means able to control the mind of the Russian people. But that does not explain a second fact. Many in every country of the world, not excluded as are the Russians from access to knowledge about the outside world, take broadly the same view as the Russian people and regard the result of communism in Russia, not as a warning, but as an inspiring example to be followed. Everywhere there are considerable movements which look to Moscow for their lead: in France and in Italy they may perhaps come to power.

From Russia turn to Palestine, the land whence have come three great religions based on the principle of love, equality, brotherhood. The problem is to form for a land so sanctified a government in which two closely related branches of the same Semitic race shall be able to co-operate. But the attempt has produced hates more intractable, more violent, bloody, murderous than anywhere else outside of India at the moment of writing these lines. Neither of the two branches of the race which inhabits the country will agree to the political ascendancy of the other. The Arab declares he will fight any government dominated by a Jewish majority, the Jew, any dominated by an Arab one; each (after millennia of exhortation to live as brothers) making demands for domination which he would indignantly reject if made by the other. Both fight Britain, which is accused by the Arab of favoring the Jew and by the Jew of favoring the Arab. Both Jews and Arabs are deeply divided among themselves.[3]

Given a situation of that kind, what does it avail to say to the rival protagonists: "Stand by your convictions; insist on justice though the heavens fall." To inflame a "passionate sense of justice" in men unable to judge the merits of an opponent's case is to increase the risk of injustice. What is needed is to put some feeling behind the kind of obligation which is so seldom recognized: the obligation to be impartial, to be intelligent, to give the opposing case its due. Not only is such an obligation usually unrecognized in the mind of the patriot, the party man, the doctrinal partisan, but to act upon it would be regarded as heresy, disloyalty, treachery.

The resulting chaos is such that dictatorship may come to seem preferable. The few remaining centers of Western stability are threatened: in France, the main pillar of Western continental Europe; in Italy; in the whole Mediterranean area.[4] Upheavals at one point tend to affect all. Whatever the settlement in Palestine, its repercussions will involve the Arab and Moslem worlds, Britain, the United States, world Jewry. Similarly with conditions in India (where, after two centuries of unity, ever increasing disintegration accompanies appalling massacres) and in China, which after nearly

[3] Among organizations very active in the United States is "The American League for a Free Palestine." "Free" in this context means a Jewish state governed by what is at present a third of the population, against the will of the remaining two thirds. The Arabs also demand a "free" Palestine, meaning a state governed by the Arab majority. Both use the same word, with all its emotional appeal, to describe contradictory and mutually exclusive purposes.

[4] In a radio address of August 8, Mr. Mark Ethridge, Member of the UN Balkan Enquiry Commission said: "Britain's distressed condition contributes to the unrest and insecurity of a continent which has always regarded her as a stabilizing influence. . . . The military men responsible for our security certainly cannot look with equanimity upon the fact that if Greece falls to her communist minority under the Red-starred guerrillas and politicos . . . the Dardanelles will be finessed, the Near East flanked and the Eastern Mediterranean dominated.

forty years of civil strife, war-lordism, famine, corruption, seems as far as ever from unity, peace, order. These two areas, containing nearly half the population of the earth, are contiguous to Russia, who does manage, by an iron rule unequaled in its severity, to maintain the unity of a vast empire which for three centuries has steadily grown, and which within the last five years has brought within its power nations heretofore regarded as Western. If anarchy, the absence of stable government, persists throughout Asia and creates a political vacuum, it would seem inevitable that Russia, with its extremely efficient and somewhat oriental methods of repression, should move in as Britain and America move out.

The whole situation raises a question as to the validity of the proposition, so commonly accepted by the Left, that doctrinal and ideological conflict, having in the Leftist view economic roots, will cease so soon as the economic problem is solved and that therefore the first and fundamental task is to establish the right economic system.

Surely strange confusion is here involved. It is true that when people are dying of famine, doctrines can matter little: their first need is an economic system or method that will bring them food. So be it. But who is to run the system? It can only be done by a government that has power (say) to move food to the most needy areas; to keep it out of the hands of robbers, to see that ships are unloaded, trains run, and perform many similar tasks. China has often failed in them; there may be similar failures now in India. A revolution which aims at economic transformation must first of all accomplish a political, not an economic, task; it must create a government, the indispensable tool of the economic purpose.

It is here that the trouble arises. Who is to govern whom? In the passions which surround the answer economics are forgotten in those ideas, ideologies, doctrines which are a much more obstinate source of conflict than opposing interests. The Jew is right when he tells the Arab that a Jewish state would raise the Arab standard of life. The Arabs are as unmoved as were the British by the arguments that they would have saved themselves immeasurable hardship and prolonged poverty by submission to Hitler (or by making with him the same kind of deal Vichy France did); or as unmoved as Jinnah's followers when they are told that a united India would deal with its economic problems better than one divided between Pakistan and Hindustan; or as unmoved as in the past the Europeans have been by the entirely true argument that political unification along the line of the United States would make Europe a more prosperous place. But if it is obvious that the economic failure in Europe and Asia must be explained by the political failure, and that economic improvement is dependent on the political, it is nearly as obvious that political improvement is dependent on some management of the psychological forces which prompt men to act collectively as they do in politics, and to interpret the facts as they do, one seeing facts which are not present, another failing to see those that are.

What we witness in this complex of rival passionate convictions producing insoluable situations is something like this: Men see a truth, or part of a truth, tear it away from the larger living body of which it should be a member, isolate it, put it into a watertight compartment, and then with deep passion proclaim it as the single guiding star by whose light alone we should travel the difficult road ahead.

Thus the protest against British imperialism, which has for so long been part of very genuine emotions in American politics, has doubtless been prompted by a profound sense of right: no nation should govern others, or impose its will upon them by force. Such a principle is regarded as an eternal verity, absolute, never to be compromised. Yet the American nation could never have existed at all if it had been guided simply by that single light. The men who began this nation—and whose story, with strange contradiction, is made an heroic legend of saintly pilgrims and pioneers—came to a country which was not theirs, imposed their will upon its people, seized their land, and in the end virtually wiped away those who had originally lived upon it. But that was only the beginning of the way in which "absolute and eternal verities" had to be set aside. The nation could not have existed if those who made it had failed to impose their will, not merely on the Indians, but upon fellow-European invaders, Spanish, French, Dutch, and, later, Mexican. When the southerners came to regard the Americans of the North as alien and hostile and to demand the right to live as an independent nation themselves, then under the leadership of a great and noble figure, vindicated by history, the North imposed its will upon that would-be independency, so that to this day some southerners say: "We are a conquered people." But now this single principle that no nation should govern another is suffering further violations: Americans are at this moment governing and imposing their will upon Germans, Japanese, Koreans, Pacific Islanders, and will probably continue to so for a very long time. Americans might see their institutions utterly destroyed unless they were willing thus to be guilty of this degree of imperialism.

We are not faced in these matters by hypocrisy or sham morality. We are faced with a habit of thinking which proclaims as the whole truth principles which are only part of it. It is a dangerous habit.

The tendency to give to certain political and social theories the attributes of religion is analyzed later in these pages. That analysis does not suggest we can or should eliminate such feeling from the codes by which we live. It does recall the simple historical fact that religious emotion has proved itself again and again to be subject to curious perversions, perversions from which have sprung at times cruelties, ferocities, abominations more evil, perhaps, than from any other manifestation of the human spirit.

In a previous age very learned theologians were profoundly convinced that different churches—Protestant and Catholic, say—could not coexist peacefully in the same state. This conviction plunged much of Europe into some of the bloodiest and cruelest conflicts it has ever suffered. The event proved the learned theologians to be wrong. The modern theologians of the Marxist faith now insist that the whole world must be socialist and capitalism destroyed if peace is to be preserved. This conviction about capitalism is a far greater obstacles to peace than the existence of capitalism itself. It is a doctrine which, added to the already disruptive and divisive influences of nationalism, constitutes one of the weaknesses which may make more difficult the already very difficult task of liberal civilization in maintaining itself against all the pressures of totalitarianism. To that must be added the fact that to make either socialism or free enterprise an exclusive doctrine or faith by which the world is to be saved or lost is pretty certain to make insoluble the economic problems of our time. For solution is to be found in a judicious synthesis of the two, an expedient eclecticism; a refusal to regard either as a panacea.

It may be argued, of course, that the foregoing survey makes altogether too gloomy a picture. Perhaps it does. No man can tell. But when we have to make provision against a danger, the course of wisdom is to take all likely developments of it into account, not to minimize it. If the danger proves less than we thought, no great damage is done, and we can rejoice. If it proves greater than anything we made provision for the result may be destruction.

But what provisions are called for? What policy?

We must, of course, build up the United Nations and make it strong enough to cope with all these dangers. (The present writer is one of those who believes that ultimately some world authority is the only true and dependable solution, and has labored during a long life toward that end.) But, obviously, we cannot build up a world authority along United Nations or other lines so long as the deep and bitter divisions just outlined continue in all their passionate ferocity; or so long as Russia and the Russian-dominated world remain unshakenly convinced that the West is bound shortly to collapse; and that for Russia to tie herself in with it would endanger, alike, Russia's own security and all hope of future security from atomic destruction, of prosperity, and of welfare for the common people.

There are few truths at this moment more vital, more indispensable to the prevention of a third world war with all its atomic horrors than this: *a greater unity of the non-Russian world is not the alternative to an effective UN and the inclusion of Russia therein. It is the indispensable condition of UN success and the inclusion of Russia.* And this remains true even if, as a stage toward world order, Russia for a time ceases to be a United Nations member.

The failure of the Western nations to create a stable international society, some central authority capable of maintaining peace, is an old story. Europe has not managed it since the Roman Empire gave a peace that lasted between two and three hundred years. But to the instability of international life, industrialism has now added increasing strains within the life of each nation; an increasing friction and failure in the co-operation of organized economic groups —capitalist, worker, one kind of trade union with another, trade-union with socialist government, as in Britain. And, once more, Russia alone of modern governments is able to deal effectively with these internal conflicts. She does so by means of severities of which democratic governments of the West are (as yet) happily incapable. But she finds a solution.

To appreciate the nature of the difficulty, we must note the tendency of industrial society to become increasingly collectivist or socialist, even when it calls itself capitalist. The trend is less marked in America than in Europe, but it is inevitable everywhere. The kind of world in which we live could not go on without a great deal of government control over the economic processes which bring us our food, our water, our light, which clean our streets, maintain our sewers, restrain the hoodlum, and give an eye to the solvency of our banks. In Britain, conservative and traditional of habit, a socialist government came to power in 1945. Although (contrary to general belief) it did not secure a majority vote of the electorate, it did secure a large majority in Parliament and has carried through sweeping measures of socialization. Most of these measures have received the approval of the Conservative Party in their recently published *Industrial Charter*.

A curious feature, moreover, marks the collectivist or socialist method: the more it fails the more it has to be applied. If, for example, a disastrous runaway inflation or critical semifamine shortages were to occur in France or Britain, remedial measures could only be found, at least temporarily, in more government action, more socialism. The justification for the extreme measures voted by the British Parliament in the summer of 1947 was that conditions had reached a dangerous crisis. The crisis may well have been due

—much of it certainly was—to causes quite other than the socialism already applied. But when that failed to cure, still more had to be imposed. A Conservative government would have been obliged to do about the same things.

But there is another feature of a managed economy or a planned society which raises immediately the question of compulsions which may become indispensable if life is to go on. If the conflicting claims of organized groups cannot be settled voluntarily, by consent, give and take, then compulsion will increase. If freedom has value, then the need for fair public judgment, for sound interpretation of the facts, becomes more acute as society becomes more planned. However cruel the automatic decisions of the older laissez-faire society, the "laws of supply and demand," they were at least automatic. Decisions were made for men by impersonal forces, regarded almost as belonging to nature, and which did not therefore excite anger and passion. (If you are stopped by the river or the mountain, that is not "oppression," provoking anger. If you are stopped by "government," it is oppression, provoking hatred, and you fight.) Decisions today, in a planned society, have to be made by men—often by tired men sitting as a committee in a cold room (if the committee happens to be an English one) compelled to decide on incomplete and unbalanced evidence, knowing that any decision which satisfies one group may be regarded as a flaming grievance by another; and knowing also that that other may be a group of a few hundred in a key position (winders at a pit head, meat porters, stevedores) who can paralyze the life of whole cities, of half a nation; and who will not therefore easily submit to what they may regard as injustice. Yet if they cannot be persuaded, if they are so passionately convinced of their rights as to be unreasonable, they must be forced— or the community's life could not go on. And to force decisions on large numbers of men demands powers of coercion; society becomes to that degree less free.

If class consciousness, or opposing doctrinal predilection, is so fierce as to throw groups into such bitter rivalry that voluntary cooperation becomes impossible, then the case for totalitarianism and dictatorship is complete and unanswerable. Government must say what is fair and enforce it by its power.[5] If trade unions must always disagree, not merely with capitalist employers or a capitalist government, but with one another and with a socialist government, then agreement of some kind, again, must be imposed—as in Russia and Russian-dominated societies. A temper of reasonableness, the absence of the "class war" psychology, are the indispensable conditions of freedom.

This need for "reasonableness" is thus more vital in a socialist than in a bourgeois society. In a bourgeois society railway shareholders may get what they regard as insufficient dividends; or none. They do not normally, as a means of carrying their point, bring the nation's railways to a standstill. The workers who regard their wages as insufficient sometimes do. A socialist government is likely to have less trouble with its professional groups, the middle class, whose position on the whole gets worse, than with manual workers whose position on the whole gets better. Where a trade union controls indispensable materials or services, it can, though only a small minority, dictate the policy of a government. The French General Confederation of Labor has done it more than once. If a conservative government came to power in Britain and the miners should decide to go a bit slow and take things easy (even a labor government has found them "difficult") they could make the life of Britain under such a government impossible; could declare that no conservative government should hold office. They are in a position to impose a one-party government along communist lines. (Incidentally communists are very influential in the National Union of Mine Workers; its secretary is a communist.) Even a socialist government would not like to be at the mercy of so small a pressure group and would need to take steps to see that a minority of half a million

---

[5] And thereby probably came into conflict with trade unions as heretofore operating. At the Labor Party's 1947 Annual Conference, Arthur Deakin, General Secretary of the Transport and General Workers' Union, declared: "We will not agree that regulation of wages belongs to the government. . . . The Trades Union Congress has rejected and will continue to reject this interference with the liberty of the individual." Or, he might have added, with a power which has belonged heretofore to the trade unions, a power which, with the regulation of wages, would be taken over by the government. Deakin gave blunt warning of "strife and conflict within our ranks" if the party ever adopted such a policy.

men did not dictate to a nation of nearly fifty million. But what steps? The men would have to be controlled, "directed." Even the United States, not in England's parlous condition, is beginning to learn something of the difficulty of "controlling" trade unions. "You cannot put half a million men in jail" says the Englishman or the American, closing the discussion. But it does not close the discussion in Russia. If half a million miners, or for that matter two or three million peasants, fail to co-operate in the plans of the government, those millions are not merely jailed; they may be jailed under conditions which amount to their "liquidation"—in forced-labor camps. Russia has found a solution in one way for problems which we must solve in our way and which will quite certainly demand measures of moral and intellectual conditioning we have hardly begun to consider.

It ought not to be necessary, but it is, to point out that the foregoing really does not indicate on the part of the writer some underlying predeliction for fascist dictatorship. It does indicate a preference for understanding the real nature of the forces we have to meet if we would preserve our freedoms; for understanding the strength and not only the weakness of the enemy.

We of the West have very rightly rejected the dictatorship method of ensuring the necessary disciplines and collective action. But the harder way, the democratic way, in which responsibility rests with the individual (who professes to control the state) demands on his part much higher moral and intellectual standards than are needed in a society where the government relieves the individual of his responsibility for decision. Not only have we not taught the need for that higher individual discipline, we have in a thousand ways repudiated it. Some of the ways in which we do it, the fashionable theories which encourage irresponsibility, are dealt with in the pages which follow.

In the way of the greater unification, peace, and strength of Western civilization, stand obstinate barriers, not material or geographical, but moral: ideas rooted in separatist nationalism, now further complicated by theories of an inevitable class war and beneficent revolution. But even more than the specific ideas of national sovereignty, class war, abolition of capitalism, proletarian dictatorship as obstacles to the co-operation of Western nations which have different social and political institutions, stand the methods of thought and interpretation we apply to social and political fact.

This book insists upon the possibility of political behavior more rational than that which gave us a second World War which could have been avoided, but does not pretend that it will be easily achieved. To achieve it we must profit by past errors and past successes, and to do that must recognize them. We must try to discern why we did this, did not do that; why the right thing we did late could not have been done earlier. It is *not* easy to be wise after the event, to profit by it. But it is necessary.

If our political judgments are to be guided by experience at all, and our social theories checked by the event—as a physicist would check his hypotheses in the laboratory, or a man engaged in medical research be guided by his controlled experiments—we have to take into account the successes of a given social or economic order as well as its failures. We need to explain the successes in order that the underlying forces may be applied perhaps to the cure of some of the failures.

Yet during the last few decades so much of our reforming intelligentsia has been absorbed in eloquent denunciations of the badness of our existing Western civilization, and in dwelling upon what is wrong with it, as to leave the impression that nothing is right with it. Only in the East—in Russia, in Asia, or in Africa—may we look, it seems to be suggested, for lessons and for hope. Yet surely a democratic society like that which has existed for so long in, say, Switzerland, and for some generations in the Scandinavian states, has a few lessons for us, and is in truth rich in those goods that men everywhere have aspired to—personal freedom, individual dignity, a widely disseminated material welfare; richer perhaps than anything shown in antiquity or non-Western lands. In the much criticized society of the United States itself, despite the depression, the cartels, the economic royalists, the wickedness of Wall Street, the Ku Klux Klan, the lynchings, the long prophesied collapse, one fact still stands out: more people enjoy a greater material comfort in greater free-

dom than has ever been known in history before, or is enjoyed anywhere else in the world. The point has been touched upon briefly
already: the Common Man, more of him, enjoys a higher standard
of living than anywhere else, and America has been able, out of her
abundance, to come to the aid of the Common Man elsewhere in
the world, where he has no such abundance, where indeed, in so
many cases he suffers from dire scarcity.

What accounts for the capacity of America to do this? Not merely
just the natural resources of a new and unexhausted world. The wide
lands to the south of the Mexican border, stretching all the way to
Cape Horn, have immense resources also. The standard of life in
most of that vast and generally rich territory is very much lower than
it is in the United States. Nor is the wealth of the United States and
its successful distribution to be accounted for merely by efficient
government: other countries perform some of the functions of government better. (The comparative statistics of crimes of violence may
give a hint of what some of those functions are.) What, then, is it
that makes the abundance in this one corner of the earth, and which
does not exist in similar degree elsewhere?

We have no commonly agreed explanation, largely because those
who most concern themselves with these matters—the promulgators
of social and economic theory—so often ignore the fact, and indeed,
by implication so often deny it. They avail themselves of a familiar
psychological phenomenon, namely that what men already possess
they are apt to value lightly, and to value very highly what they do
not yet possess. The distant pastures are the greenest. Before men
possessed the right to vote they were ready to die for it; when they
get it, a large proportion simply do not use it—especially if it rains
on election day. Mussolini and Hitler had, and communist leaders
have, little difficulty in persuading many in democracies that the
right of political opposition, of access to the facts, is mainly a
bourgeois sham of little real value, beside all the things that an
uncontrolled dictatorship can achieve for the Common Man. In
truth the disparaged political freedoms are beyond all price, even
for economic ends. But the tendency to overlook and undervalue
what has been achieved, in favor of the glamour of what is promised,
has enabled left-wing forces to persuade those who have many
comforts (e.g. Americans) that they have few; and to leave the

impression that those who have few (e.g. Russians) have many—or at least are better off than the wage slaves of Western capitalism.

There is, of course, a further explanatory fact: in Russia indoctrination is so persistent (and effective) that the whole population are missionaries for their experiment, with the ardor of missionaries. We have not similarly conditioned our people for a society of Freedom. Every schoolboy in Russia is familiar with the doctrine of Marx and can recite its catechism. It gives the youngster a plausible, understandable, even if fallacious, explanation of the how and why of communist society. What proportion of the pupils turned out by the schools of the United States and Britain have any corresponding understanding of the method of freedom and democracy; the need of it as an instrument of an efficient and prosperous society—and of worthy human beings? Compare the number coming out of Russian schools made familiar with Marx with those coming from schools of the English tongue who are familiar with, say, Mill and his incomparable masterpiece on liberty. Incidentally the declamations of a Patrick Henry are no substitute for reasoned expositions of freedom as a social method.

The needed type of political rationalism was commoner, perhaps, in the generation of the Founding Fathers than it is in ours. Their work gives a hint of the answer to the question: "What accounts for the unique wealth of the United States?" They saw to it that the thirteen colonies, instead of breaking up into many sovereign governments as Latin-American colonies were to do a little later, made themselves into a single Union, a fact which included among other advantages peace between the states (broken only once), and the largest free-trade area in the world; which in its turn made possible larger-scale production in industry than anywhere else. Had the local patriotism of each colony been such that, having acquired independence from Britain, they demanded independence from each other; if the Confederacy had been able to make good its demand for independence and self-determination—if either of these things had happened, we can be sure that there would not have been the immensely powerful United States we know to play the role it did play in resisting totalitarianism; and in restoring afterward a war-broken world.

Here we have one indication, at least, of the lines along which we may develop the vast potential power of Western civilization. The principle which made possible the creation of the United States out of separate colonies must be extended—not necessarily applying it in the precise way in which it was applied between colonies. These, after all, had lived ever since their establishment under a common crown, and had given allegiance thereto; were inheritors of the same kind of law and culture. New adaptations of the method then applied will have to be found. The British Commonwealth may have lessons to offer in that connection.

But unification of itself will not be enough. The United States has developed the wealth and power it now possesses by virtue of policies it has since abandoned, its questionable example in so doing having been followed by the British Dominions. The fact illustrates the curious way in which we have lost freedoms we once possessed, and are unaware of the loss—or its significance.

The other day Mr. Bevin said he looked forward to the time when he could go to Victoria Station, ask for a ticket to any place in the world, pay for it, and go there. He seemed to speak of this as an unrealized utopia to which the world might one day look forward when it had firmly established its planned socialist economy. The remark was suggestive in that it gave no hint that those features of the future utopia would be merely a return to conditions which actually did exist in the time of Mr. Bevin's youth. Until the end of the first decade of this century a man could travel around the world without a visa, without a passport; having stood in no queues at consulates, signed no papers, taken no oaths, without having given the nationality or Christian names of his grandparents. He neither needed permission to leave his own country nor permission to enter another. This present writer, having as a youngster decided to emigrate to America, bought a ticket and did so; he walked ashore in New York with no questions asked or answered; took a job as a farm hand, entered a variety of occupations varying from cowboy and miner to newspaperman, had to join no union, and finally returned to Europe with the same freedom with which he had left it.

This, it may be retorted, was a bourgeois freedom; that the working class shared none of its benefits. Nothing could be more untrue.

When conditions for a worker became intolerable in Europe—when famine struck Ireland or discrimination against Jews in Eastern Europe—the victims at least possessed the freedom which permitted them to move, literally by millions, into the empty spaces of the New World. (A man could cross the Atlantic at the end of the nineteenth century for nine dollars, which sum included his food during the passage.) Today, in this Century of the Common Man, one of the most appalling and shameful of all its shameful spectacles is that of the displaced person—the uprooted human being, the common man expelled from the land where he and his forebears have lived it may be for untold generations—Finns, Esthonians, Lithuanians, Ukrainians, Poles, peasants from East Prussia, Yugoslavs unpleasing to Tito—who still, after years of hopeless waiting, rot behind the barbed wire of the DP camps. They number, it would seem (figures from Russia are unobtainable), about a million. A bill before Congress for the admission of four hundred thousand at the rate of a hundred thousand a year has failed of passage at the date of writing, despite the efforts of a small group of valiant Congressmen. With all our planning, national and international, for the welfare of the common man, great masses have less hope of rescue from intolerable fate than they would have had a century since. In the benighted age before 1914 America could take over a million immigrants a year and never know that she had done it. The unplanned society solved without friction a numerically far greater problem of "displaced persons" than that which our more planned society of today finds all but insoluble.

One of the results of our collectivist society is a panic fear of freedoms which we once possessed. We seem to feel that if the freedom of movement which existed in the unregenerate nineteenth century were restored, that if people could move to and fro like that, society would fall to pieces. But when we possessed that freedom, society did not fall to pieces. It was more stable than it is now.

In the comparison of the new with the old conditions, several details are worth noting. One is that many immigrants into the New World came from czarist Russia, notably from Russian Poland. There is no escape today from Russia under its government of Socialist Republics. That age of relatively free movement for the common man was the much condemned age of British imperialism, when an all-powerful British fleet dominated the seven seas and when the Dominions still retained something of their colonial status. They were more open to immigrants then than they have become as independent states—some of them under labor-socialist governments. This last point has its importance, for the reason that though there may be some substance in the argument that the restrictive measures in the United States are due to the filling up of the once empty areas, this can hardly apply to Australia, New Zealand, Canada, South Africa. The situation is the more tragic—and the more ridiculous—because the economic interest of these last named countries urgently needs more population. Yet it is an assumed economic interest, that of preventing unemployment, which has stood heretofore so largely in the way.

There are signs now that a wiser policy is beginning to emerge in the Dominions. (An Australian official has just declared that his country needs a million new immigrants as quickly as she can get them.) We should seize every means of encouraging this tendency. It is far more closely tied in with the purposes for which America fought two great wars than is generally realized. The acceptance by the British Dominions of a freer migration policy is closely related to a future balance between the power of the democratic societies and the totalitarian power which presses, with increasing weight, upon them.

It is common just now to talk of "Britain" as finished, to assume that British power in the world of tomorrow can be disregarded. But if by Britain we mean the British Commonwealth, the British Communities established all over the world making today a world encircling group, the notion does not correspond to the facts.

The overseas British Commonwealth—exclusive, that is, of the home Dominion of Great Britain, and including only Australia, New Zealand, South Africa, Canada, the probable future Dominions of the Rhodesias and the West Indies—has today a larger population than the United States had at the close of the Civil War. The United States had then just emerged from one of the bloodiest struggles of history up to that time. It was racked by internal strains of the bitterest kind, including a race problem that is still unsolved. Its physical resources were not any greater than those which are today embraced within the British Commonwealth, if they were as great. Yet that population of thirty million was to become, within the lifetime of men who fought in the Civil War, a country of a hundred and forty million, the richest as well as the most powerful nation in the world.

Moreover, the British Union today has advantages which the American Union at the death of Lincoln did not possess. The development of transport and intercommunication is such that Ottawa or Cape Town or Melbourne are nearer to each other and nearer to London than Washington was to San Francisco when Lincoln died. The means of production, the mechanical power which can be put into the hands of a worker, are many times greater today than they were in 1865. On the face of it, therefore, the physical means of survival exist. If they are not utilized—and they may not be —it will not be due to physical obstacles but to moral and intellectual ones.

But if the thirty odd millions living in the overseas Dominions today duplicate the history of the thirty millions who lived in the United States of Lincoln's day we shall, in the lifetime of men now living, see the emergence of an English-speaking world of three or even four hundred million souls. Such an agglomeration, if it had any sort of unity or cohesion, would have immense powers of attraction to those on the periphery—to the Latin-American nations of the New World, to the smaller democracies of Western Europe. Democracy would not then be broken by its internal strains, its nationalist fissures.

But it will depend on a return to some of the freedoms we once possessed and have since sacrificed—among them a greater freedom of migration.

When we talk, as we so often do, about demonstrating the superiority of the democratic over the totalitarian method, and when we imply that totalitarian vetoes stand in the way of organizing peace, we cannot simply disregard this issue of the displaced person on one side of the world and so many empty or relatively empty spaces held by the democracies on the other. Here is a policy which it is entirely within the power of the democracies of the two New Worlds to apply—the new world of the Americas and the new world of the antipodes and so much of Africa.

If we of the democracies are really determined to prove to the common people of the earth that the democratic West can do better than communist Russia, that our systems are based upon a better standard of human needs and social morals, here is the opportunity. It is an act of policy making for the peace of the world, which does not wait upon the consent of the Soviets, and which they cannot veto.

To take the road of salvation here suggested may mean a reversal of some recent tendencies and a stocktaking of accepted ideas. It would mean on Britain's part a recognition that her problem is less economic than political. If the evolution of the Commonwealth had been such that Britain today were part of that unity to the extent, say, that the state of New York is part of the economic unit of the United States, the life and death elements of Britain's problem would not exist. If the Commonwealth, instead of making six or seven separate nations, were composed of states in a federal system some-what along the lines of the American Union with such tariffs as did exist applying only to the Commonwealth as a whole, it would constitute, then, an economic entity comparable to the United States.

It is true that when, in the past, attempts have been made to shape development along those lines, they have been indicted as crude imperialism, as the attempt of British monopoly finance to retain its hold. There may be some truth in the charge, just as western states in America today are apt at times to proclaim bitterly that they are the financial serfs of the East. But no one would suggest that the West secede, as the agricultural states of the South once wanted to secede. Such a cure, however much the West may suffer from the financial imperialism of the East, would bring more pains than the disease. The fiscal independence of the Dominions has not made easier the problems of that Western civilization of which they have become so important a part.

We should have done better to be skeptical of the Marxist theory that imperialism finds its taproot in monopoly capitalism. The facts are against the theory, as a few modern economic historians have shown. But even if it were true that the economic motive plays a large part in political imperialism, the present behavior of Russia would indicate that imperialism of a very harsh type can exist without capitalism, that other motives than those of capitalist profit play their part.

Democracy and freedom have never been easy of application to politics. The only two remaining great powers, or states which might be great powers, that have managed to apply the democratic method successfully are the United States and the British Commonwealth. There are other nations who have been more successful than the English-speaking peoples in the working of democracy, but they are not, and cannot be, powers. There are other states that are or might become great powers (particularly in Asia), but they are not democracies. Any possibility of preserving freedom "in the Western sense" will demand the initiative, leadership, and close but not exclusive co-operation of the English-speaking peoples.

This is not because these peoples are possessed of any quality of racial superiority (alike in Britain and the United States they are as mongrel as any in the world), but because the hazards of history and geography thrust that role upon them, as their contribution to Western civilization; just as another kind of contribution has been made by the Greeks in intellectual method, another by the Romans in law—still with us—and in political organization, and the greatest of all, possibly, by the Jews in their system of ethics. Recognition of the contribution made by these three peoples does not involve any claim of racial superiority for Greek, or Italian, or Jew. Similarly, recognition that parliamentary government has been most successfully worked on principles and habits which English-speaking peoples have especially developed involves no claim to racial superiority. To deny or ignore the fact is likely to cause us to overlook or discard an instrument of co-operation we have been driven again and again in war and crisis to use, and which, had it been used more fully, could almost certainly have prevented the second World War. It may be indispensable in the prevention of a third.

PART II

Human Nature in the Atomic Age

CHAPTER I

The Old Errors Have New Dangers

THERE is nothing new in the fact that nearly the whole world should be enveloped in bitter conflict, civil war, fear of foreign war; and that many lands should know famine, suffering, oppression, insecurity, chaos. All that is familiar. Any long period of peace over any considerable areas of the earth is a rare exception to a general rule. Nor is it new that a civilization should be in process of disintegration, as that of Western Europe very visibly is at the moment. Roman civilization, which once covered Europe, and gave it the longest period of peace it has ever known, also broke down, and gave place to what we call the Dark Ages. Nor are the cruelties, violences, and ferocities which mark the clash of religious and national groups, such as we see in Palestine and India, anything new. That behavior is as old as history.

Nevertheless there are certain new features in today's conflicts and social disintegrations. One of them—that arising out of the creation of the atomic bomb—is dramatic, visible. Atomic weapons have put into our hands instruments capable of destructions and devastations so much greater in degree than anything man has heretofore used in warfare, as to be different in kind. We are rapidly approaching the time when war, if it comes in the old form of nation against nation, will involve the reciprocal annihilation of the contestants. Self-propelled and guided missiles which can be sent from any point on the earth to any other point, carrying atomic explosives, gain daily in accuracy and effectiveness. The pleasures of belligerent nationalism, which were formerly relatively harmless pleasures from the point of view of human society as a whole, have suddenly become suicidal.

But there is another new feature of our modern society, less visible and dramatic in its immediate effects, of which men are less

37

conscious perhaps than of the threat of atomic destruction, but which may nonetheless become as pregnant of human misery.

The condition of things in Britain at this time should give a hint of the nature of this new force of destruction—destruction of human welfare. For the British have suddenly had brought home to them the realization that a great society may without the aid of bombs sink into a state of collapse which bombs, when they were actually falling, did not produce. The people of Britain are in imminent danger of finding themselves without the most elementary needs of life—adequate food, shelter, warmth, clothing—and of being unable to say how they shall be supplied. The cause is no mystery. Warnings have been uttered by those disturbed at the possibility of the kind of thing which has now happened; but they have had little effect on policy.[1] The fifty millions more or less in the British Islands have heretofore been fed largely by an elaborate process of world exchange which used to be described as that of turning coal into bread by the alchemy of industry and trade. The machine which did it is running down; and the people concerned do not know how to keep it going. Man's mechanical ingenuity—which is very great— here fails him. For not merely must this machine, like others, be run by men, this particular one is made up of men, moved by impulses, emotions, passions. We need a type of understanding, of moral and intellectual discipline, wisdom, in short, for which knowledge of matter and practice in its management seem to give little assurance. Our mechanical ingenuity, particularly in contraction of distance, has brought into being a world so closely integrated, so small, so interdependent in its parts, and consequently so vulnerable, that only some considerable social and political wisdom—not mere mechanical skill—can keep it running smoothly and prevent self-destruction. The story of this century, with its two world wars and their results, proves that modern man has not so far acquired that wisdom, and that he has, contrariwise, embraced doctrines which militate grievously against his doing so.

The prospect of atomic destruction seems, so far, to have made little difference. It certainly has not diminished very much the

[1] For one such warning see the author's *If Britain Is to Live*, Nesbit, London, 1923.

tendency toward conflict, whether between nations or between classes, parties, races, castes, outcasts and religions, within nations. Our progress toward agreement in the peace settlement is slower after this second World War than it was after the first.

One reason, among several, for the failure of the atomic bomb to "bring us to our senses" is that our senses have been dulled to the nature of this new menace because we have been told so often in the past that war would "end civilization." Heretofore it has not done so. It is true that by the beginning of this century it had been demonstrated (but not generally believed) that in our modern world (whatever may have been the case in earlier times) victory in war could bring no economic gain, and indeed result in nothing but economic disaster, a proposition all too painfully proved by the condition of victorious Britain today. But we have seen many great wars which did not end civilization.

The Thirty Years' War was, among wars of the modern time, exceedingly destructive. Yet Europe recovered from it. Its close, indeed, marked the beginning of a new era of relative religious toleration. The Anglo-French wars of the eighteenth century and the beginning of the nineteenth extended over much of the world, into America and India, as well as to the continent of Europe. Yet their close marked the beginning of great economic and social development in Britain itself, and of the growth of democratic institutions throughout the world. In the New World the bitter and bloody war between North and South did not prevent, subsequently, a vast economic expansion over the United States as a whole. Wars and revolutions in the Latin American republics were for a century, at least, a constant feature of their politics. But Latin America survived, though the endemic political instability probably cost more suffering than the Civil War in the United States. The world survived even the first World War, though it marked perhaps the beginning of the end. Only in this second World War has Western civilization been deeply and visibly shaken. All of which has helped, doubtless, to immunize us from taking too seriously the talk of the destruction and extinction of civilized life, and partly explains why the menace of atomic war has had no very great effect upon our political habits or way of thought.

This is in keeping with familiar experience in other fields. We accommodate ourselves to threats of annihilation continued for any length of time, much as people who live over a volcano that might at any moment engulf them forget its existence; just as Londoners in the blitz, even when they heard the bombs falling, went on with their jobs as usual.

When belief in everlasting hell-fire as punishment for wickedness was all but universal, wickedness still flourished, even among believers. The theory that such a threat would of itself deeply influence human behavior left too many things out of account. The very genuine fear of war which marked the years of appeasement (and of American Neutrality Acts) should warn us that an indiscriminating fear of war may help to bring it on. Had we been less afraid to challenge the aggressors when they were weak instead of waiting until they were strong—Japan back in 1931 before Hitler's rise to power, Italy when she began war on Ethiopia, Germany in the matter of Spain and the Rhineland—the chances of peace might have been increased (putting the case at its mildest). We hated the thought of war in those days. But the emotion did not always prompt the policy most likely to prevent it. It usually prompted the least likely.

The knowledge that the hell-fire of the atomic bomb may easily one day become a satanic reality will not of itself tell us what to do about it; what policy we should pursue either at home or abroad to make control of it dependable; whether we should favor a Western Bloc or a United States of Europe; what we should do to reach agreement on Germany, to help compose the struggle within China, or those within India, or Greece, or in Palestine—all interrelated questions which bear on the future of the international organization we will somehow have to build up. Least of all will the fear of the atomic hell-fire tell us how we may reach agreement as between the West and Russia without sacrifice of the values we have fought such costly wars to cherish and preserve; nor throw light on the question whether understanding and co-operation between Britain and the United States will help or hinder co-operation with Russia.

Heretofore we have accepted complacently enough as quite in the natural order of things the violences which have usually characterized the clashes of history. Historians innumerable have argued that while it is true that these conflicts, including the revolutions, have been marked by cruelty and terror, you cannot make omelets without breaking eggs, and the omelet of progress, runs the argument, has on the whole justified the broken eggs of the civil wars, the revolutions, the executions, deportations, repressions, purges.

Whatever validity this argument may have had in the pre-atomic age, it has obviously lost much of that value in ours. For the costs of war, internal and external, will not be temporary, as in the past. They are likely to be such as to end urbanized civilization as we know it in Western Europe and America, and leave things to be carried on by the peoples who have greater space for dispersal. The bombs which quite certainly would finish the New Yorks and the Londons could not finish a population dispersed over the vast spaces stretching between, say, Stettin and Vladivostok; or wipe out the innumerable villages of China or of India, where for ages in any case famine and plague have taken as many lives as the bombs might take. Though, of course, biological warfare might be a better instrument of extermination for the jungles and the steppes.

It comes to this: if the same passions which have usually in the past marked the clash of rival ideologies—political, economic, social, religious, nationalist—are equally to mark those of the future, we shall destroy ourselves, or accept totalitarian dictatorship as the alternative. The world could afford those zealotries, bigotries, fanaticisms, in the pre-atomic age. It cannot do so in ours. Passion our world may still need. But not the passion which explains the readiness of men to go to war or to make revolutions by violence; nor passion put behind the particular conceptions which lead to those things.

The older zealots, who were so ready to rack and burn and torture, guillotine and liquidate in order to dispose of doctrinal opponents, did not possess the means of instantaneous, widespread, complete extinction. The new do, or will do very shortly.

Yet those old fanaticisms and ferocities have been a feature of man's story ever since he has had a story. Why should we suppose that he will now suddenly stop behaving as he has always behaved?

(Change will have to be relatively sudden, for the time is so short.) Change will not come by virtue of the "natural" forces within men. The "natural" forces, given free play, will prompt in our day the behavior which men have shown in all their days. Indeed the kind of doctrinal passion which gave us the Inquisition, the religious wars, the revolutionary terrors, the wars of the nationalities, now threaten us in the clash of rival social doctrines, to be fought, so many learned folk insist, as the inevitable "war of the classes." We must have the mood and temper of war in the social field, we are told, in order to give men the necessary energy to destroy the evil system of property, which must be blasted, the same authorities insist, before men can achieve economic liberation. In the circumstances of a country situated as is Britain, this mood could destroy us though never a bomb fell among us.

CHAPTER II

Survival in the New Age

THE British are apt to take pride in the fact that they "muddle through"; that their mental processes are not always very logical or symmetrical. And indeed there is sometimes virtue in this. But a Frenchman—after watching a debate between an English cabinet minister and a French one—remarked to the present writer: "I think you English believe your stupidity to be a gift of God. It may be. But it is a gift that must not be abused."

In July, 1940, all those throughout the free world who could appreciate the inner meaning of the drama of human events were holding their breath. A New Attila had swept over Europe and had most of the nations of that ancient continent at his mercy. He stood, as the world outside Germany knew, for very evil things. If he triumphed, the world would have found itself forced either to accept those evil things, submit to their imposition, or spend immeasurable effort and vast treasure, twisting its desired way of life, in continuous efforts at resistance. To this extent all Western civilization was at stake.

In all Europe, one small nation stood up against the flood, a nation which had already suffered terrific blows, had lost its armor, and had to start rearming almost from scratch while the bombs rained down upon it.

Nearly all intelligent people everywhere agreed that what Britain was setting out to do could not be done; that, instead, she would have to follow France in making the best bargain she could. But the impossible thing was done: as Britain had done such things before, against Napoleon, against eighteenth-century France, against Spain's Armada.

It was not just courage (these pages later insist) that enabled her to do this in 1940. Other nations have courage as great. A quite indispensable factor in her success was a capacity for national unity, for agreement by people of all parties and opinions on what was most important, and a capacity to work together for its achievement. There was little of the bitter, unbridgeable divisions, hardened by suspicion, partisanship, implacable doctrine, which had made national unity in some neighboring countries so difficult. Perhaps a certain wise stupidity, or slow-mindedness, did account for this: so many British people just did not understand some of those curious theories which so excited foreigners—dialectical materialism, or what not. Thus a House of Commons had a Communist Party composed of one member, while that of the Chamber of Deputies across the Channel had over seventy. The English have been skeptical of theories and political blueprints. If an institution or a method worked and gave results, it did not much matter if it spoiled the symmetry of some neat doctrine. Thus the nation which possessed the most democratic system in the world, so far as its practical results were concerned, had kept its monarchy and a hereditary House of Lords —things which theoreticians elsewhere often find shocking.

And the wise stupidity became a magnificent stupidity after the fall of France. Intelligent people all over the world demonstrated clearly that Britain was already defeated, that it just was not physically possible for her to continue resistance. They proved it; knew it. But the British were so stupid they could not see the proof, and, so, did not know it.

But, as the Frenchman warned, this magnificent quality must not be abused. The temper which served so well in war may be fatal in peace.

Ever since the labor government took office it has issued warning after warning (notably in the February 1947 White Paper) that unless the British people agree to do certain things they "may never rebuild the foundations of national life." This is a quotation from the Paper which the London *Times* described as "the most disturbing statement ever made by a British Government." The things which, the government kept on reiterating, alone could save Britain were: increased individual production in mine, mill, and factory; surrender of present claims for shorter hours of work; the introduction of foreign workers on a very considerable scale; still further increase of exports, still stricter limitation of imports; close co-operation with employers; renunciation of wage increases which might damage exports or threaten inflation. All of which meant that any relaxation of controls or of austerity was out of the question.

Within a few days of the publication of the White Paper the secretary of the National Union of Mine Workers saw the Prime Minister and expressed his opposition to nearly every one of these conditions, particularly the introduction of foreign labor in any quantity. The miners' representative reasserted the demand for a five-day week (disregarding the government's view that this would cut production); insisted that the austerity of the rationing be relaxed by special supplies of sugar, fats, fish, prefabricated houses, goods for miners' wives; demanded increased wages in the form of income-tax reduction, free transportation. (Other industries facing such new sacrifices as two million workers put on to night shifts began to wonder what the general effect of granting the above demands would be.)

The reaction of the miners was, after all, in keeping with a general attitude throughout industry as a whole, an attitude expressed in a long succession of unofficial strikes, a continuance of absenteeism, and similar manifestations. It is not in the least surprising that this should be the result. For the pleas of the labor government were in flat contradiction with the general trend of labor propaganda this last thirty years. However little it may have been intended, the net effect of leftist indoctrination has been to leave the impression that for a man to produce his maximum is to do some mate out of a job; that labor-saving machinery may make profit for the capitalist but inevitably increases unemployment; that any addition to the number of workers today means unemployment tomorrow; that there is no such thing as community of interest between employer and employee; that the whole economic system is wrong and that therefore the sooner it collapses the better. Let that doctrine seep and soak into a man through his adult life and he is not going suddenly to turn around and base his whole behavior on contrary assumptions. The truths which the labor government is now attempting to bring home to British workers are truths which nearly every labor candidate on the platform, and much of the leftist press, has disparaged as minor, irrelevant, or opposed to the socialist-labor scheme of things; or simply as capitalist falsehoods. After a whole generation of that kind of evangelism, the worker is now told that if socialism is to be successful, he, the individual worker, must produce more than he has ever done before; must work in close co-operation with his employer, who is no longer to be regarded as his enemy (80 per cent of the nation's industry is still in the hands of private employers); must make the utmost use of labor-saving machinery; must by every device cut down the number of hands required for a given job; and —crowning disillusionment—must introduce a new and heretofore unheard-of form of dilution, acceptance into his trade of large numbers of foreign workers, Poles, Italians, Lithuanians, Germans. ("Tomorrow," remarked an old trade unionist, "it will be the Chinese again.") If these things are not done, he is told, then not merely must the worker surrender any idea of improved conditions, he must face the fact that the very foundations of the nation's life, the possibility of sufficient bread for his children, will collapse. It is not quite what the socialist propagandists led him to expect when the day of victory should dawn for a socialist government.

An American observer[1] traveling throughout industrial Britain just after the publication of the White Paper, and interviewing day after day workers, their wives, their employers, trade-union officials, government officials, comes to some suggestive conclusions:

The men's leaders are still fighting old battles . . . they tell you of 1922 when the long slump began. . . . They tell you their people are better off now. The leaders know that all-out production is essential but say that the men are not convinced. . . . The enemy is still the boss. The objective is to keep the boss from getting the best of them. . . . Labor, government and representatives agree that if the present crisis had come under a Conservative Government there would have been a revolution. The workers would never have believed that it was not an employers' plot. The British are not in the habit of talking lightly of revolution.

The same observer notes that the employers, too, are still fighting old wars, still complaining about the workers' cussedness and slacking. He adds:

[1] Michael Hoffman, the New York *Times*, February 24, 1947.

While many employers see the general economic situation more clearly than the workers, they are helpless to influence the men and are politically impotent. Nothing is more likely to make the British workman doubt the reality of the country's danger than to have the employer tell him about it. "We've been fooled too often," the men say. For too many years the only result of the economic policy favored by the employers was unemployment and misery.

The conclusion which the visitor to Britain drew was this:

Nothing but an early and profound change in the attitude of the British people toward the problem of national survival can prevent the present crisis from becoming a steady slide into conditions of poverty unknown in the Western world in modern times.

That is a view that any visitor to Britain could hear privately expressed by Britons of all shades of political opinion in a position to know the realities of the country's economic position.

Three points need to be kept in mind if the foregoing is not to be fatally misinterpreted. They are these:

1. The catastrophe to which the reporter, whose conclusions have just been indicated, refers is not inevitable. Britain need not drift to a coolie standard of existence. There need be no permanent decline; Britain is not necessarily on the way out.

2. The arguments deducible from the facts, and outlined in this book, are not arguments against socialism in the sense of a largely planned and centrally controlled economy. Socialism in that sense is inevitable, and the worse things get the more socialism we shall be compelled to apply. But the fact that socialism is inevitable does not mean that it will succeed. It may come, and fail to produce a tolerable standard, as, so far, it has failed in that respect in Russia. It may fail from causes irrelevant to the old socialism v. capitalism debate: a sliding of the non-British world into such chaos that foreign trade becomes impossible; a chaos to which too severe a reduction of British commitments and ill-managed liquidation of the empire may contribute.

3. If we are not to sacrifice our freedom in order to get bread—and then perhaps not get the bread—or to sacrifice welfare in order to keep our freedom, then certain leftist errors in the approach to this problem must be avoided. They are here indicated.

To overplay a bit the attractions of a given reform or necessary change may be an indispensable part of the democratic process, and excusable enough. The inherent inertia of a stable society, a people's laziness and indifference, has to be overcome, and without the kind of zeal and enthusiasm which minimizes the difficulties and overstresses the benefits, nothing very much would get done. With that no political realist would have much quarrel.

But that is not the fault for which the British are now paying. It is something much more fundamental. The effect of so much socialist propaganda—especially where it leans to the Marxian view—is to undermine personal and individual responsibility, including responsibility to the community of fellow workers by insisting that all the trouble has been due to an evil system and will be cured by a new economic constitution. The government in Britain, for instance, is now trying to instill into the worker a sense of responsibility for keeping the national economy going by old-fashioned virtues of work and order. But he had been led to believe that the first need was not to work harder but to bring the capitalist system to ruin, having done which the new order would arise on those ruins and all would be well. It was not the intention perhaps of Fabian socialism to produce that attitude and mentality. But to a war-weary people, impatient and frustrated, the notion of bringing about a new heaven and a new earth by fighting a tangible enemy, the "master class," is more attractive than to keep the existing machine running by hard daily work; even though it be changed while it is running.

Socialism, if it is to be voluntary, unforced, undictated, that is to say the instrument of free men, demands an understanding of the reasons for those things which governments like the British are now asking of the worker. If they are not understood, the attraction of violence and dictatorship will grow. Yet violence and dictatorship cannot, in the case of Britain, produce even the measure of success they may have had in Russia.

It was noted in the previous chapter that not until the second World War was Western civilization visibly and deeply shaken. It was thus shaken because for a long time it had been paying for its material progress by becoming immensely more complex and interdependent and so more vulnerable; its mechanism more difficult to understand (an expert like Keynes can spend a lifetime studying one section of the mechanism and at the end find himself in serious disagreement with other well-trained experts). Its management obviously demanded moral and intellectual qualities which mere technology has done little or nothing to develop.

Much has been written of the changes wrought by the industrial revolution; of the oneness of the world of our generation. But relatively little attention seems to have been paid to the question how we may adjust certain habits of mind and a scale of values developed by life in one kind of world to life in quite another kind of world.

Consider this particular contrast:

In the time even of our great grandfathers, whether in Europe or in America, each village was self-contained, self-sufficient. If impassable roads suddenly cut it off from the outside world the village life, or life on the remote farm, went on much as before. Its water came from its own wells, its food from its own fields, its clothing woven from the wool of its own sheep, its fuel from the forest, its light from candles made at home. The outside world might have drifted into chaos: it made little difference. Unemployment, overproduction, monetary maladjustment, inflation, deflation would have been for the most part meaningless phrases to a household where the daily tasks were more than the household could perform, where the producer was also the consumer of the goods he produced, where he and his family were their own market and where he could adjust consumption to production and vice versa. The processes of the economy were visible to those who lived by them, and relatively under their control. The people might be tyrannized by a feudal lord or a squire. But in that case the source of their misery was known and seen and the very antiquity of that way of life (anything from five to ten thousand years in China and in parts of India) shows they knew how to keep the tyranny within the limits at least of survival.

There was nothing very idyllic about it, and we could not return to it if we would (though the poets did call it Merrie England and it showed a lustiness of life which its Chaucers and Shakespeares and Elizabethan adventurers knew how to express). The point is that its problems, such as they were, were within the scope of men's imaginations. The world they had to deal with was mainly the world they could see and touch, which could be brought home to each through his own individual consciousness.

Compare that with the picture of the modern community dependent for its very life—thanks to cheapened transport and division of labor—on some community situated perhaps on the other side of the world; one group producing coal, which it cannot eat, another producing butter or eggs, which it cannot burn. If these two communities are cut off from each other, then one starves and the other freezes. And they may be cut off though the roads are not physically blocked. The process of exchange may have been brought to a standstill owing to things which have happened in another part of the world, from causes which those who suffer from the paralysis do not even know about and cannot understand. The cottage light, which originally came from candles made at home, now comes from a power station where there is a jurisdictional strike, of the merits of which the cottager is ignorant. Much of the food originally produced in the English village now comes from Buenos Aires or Chicago, where a lockout has stopped its production; or a truck drivers' dispute keeps it piled up in the factory. The clothing once made by the farmer's wife out of the farmer's wool now comes from factories closed because they cannot get coal, or cannot pay for the raw cotton which comes from America, owing to a high American tariff which makes it difficult to turn Scotch whisky or Sheffield cutlery into dollars; all these factors complicated by monetary inflation, political unrest in Asia, by wars of powerful countries whose population has somehow become hypnotized by psychopathic dictators drunk with the fanaticism of insane doctrines. The harassed citizen who suffers by it all has to decide—in his spare time—what decision, as a voter, he ought to give about it.

The economic machine by which a country like Britain lives—involving problems of maximum industrial production, exports which must compete in foreign markets, banking, insurance, transport, foreign loans and investments—has a complexity which obviously again and again baffles the experts. (They are repeatedly in disagreement as to what ought to be done.) Yet it is the non-expert, the layman voter, who has to make the final decision and decide between the experts. It is as though a man who had acquired a motorcar but had never seen the inside of one had to decide what had caused it to break down.

However little he might know about the matter, there are, nevertheless, certain things he would know, assuming that he had ordinary common sense. He would know, for instance, that he could not know what was wrong, and would be a fool to have violent half-baked opinions about it; that in choosing between mechanics who differed as to the cause, he would be thrown back upon the record of each in dealing with such cases, or his own judgment of character. He would know, further, that it could serve little purpose to lose patience with the damned thing and use a crowbar—though he would know that it is quite easy thus to get senselessly angry even with inanimate objects.

Yet strange as it may sound, the lay voter, occupying in relation to the socioeconomic machine above described, the position of the car owner, is assured by demagogues the world over, not merely that as owner he has the right to decide concerning the final disposition (which of course he has), but that he can by some sort of magical insight make the technical decisions too, and indicate the treatment for cures of the malady. (Is not the Voice of the People the Voice of God?) And there are plenty to assure him that to use the crowbar of revolution is precisely what is needed ("we must blast the foundations of the old society," a giant intellectual of the left puts it); and that to use that crowbar effectively he must be very angry indeed. Counsels of this kind are extremely common, as we all know. The temper of the class war, if not the war itself, is urged as indispensable, and the example of Russia is held up as proof of how successfully the crowbar of coercion, revolution, and dictatorship can be used to solve the characteristic problems of this country.

Yet, apart from innumerable other considerations there is one supreme difference in the circumstances of the two countries which should make it plain that a method which may be workable in the Russian case could not possibly work in Britain's.

Russia is, or might be made, the most self-sufficient country in the world, stretching as it does across half the world; underpopulated, rich in almost every natural resource, particularly the sources of food. It has a highly centralized autocratic government exercising its power over relatively primitive peoples, who for the most part in all their history have been accustomed to autocracy, and have come to accept it as in the natural order of things. The resources from which the population could live are all within the power of that one central and powerful government.

In nearly every one of these particulars the case of Britain differs fundamentally. She has not within the power of her government the resources indispensable to the life of her people. The process by which she lives is largely a process not under her control at all. The livelihood of her people depends upon elaborate world-wide co-operations which they have no power to impose, and can only keep going by bargain with and the voluntary agreement of foreign governments or peoples. In Britain, no government, whether social-ist or conservative, can force foreigners to buy her goods or to sell theirs; it cannot by the power of its legislation or its planning im-pose the conditions upon which the exchange shall be made. A British government might be given the fullest powers of control, planning, nationalization, develop the completest managed econ-omy anywhere in the world, and still a great part of the economy by which Britain secures even the essentials of physical existence, would be outside her control altogether.

This would not be true, or so true, of a more self-sufficient coun-try; one with unlimited foodstuffs and raw materials of its own. It is true of Britain. This does not invalidate the case for socialization. Rather the reverse. For not only will a large degree of socialization be indispensable in any case, but the greater the scarcity the greater the degree of socialization which will be necessary. But it does in-validate the theory that Britain should adopt an attitude of hostility to "capitalist" nations like the United States; would become cor-rupted or "enslaved" by entering into economic arrangements with them; that she could live by confining her economic contacts to so-cialist states (the greatest of which cannot at present prevent grave famine among its own people).

If Britain must "export or die," then that means that she will export mainly to capitalist countries or die. She will live, if at all, out of the surplus of capitalist economics. For if they do not produce a surplus over and above bare subsistence, they cannot buy British goods or send Britain what she needs. The United States, Canada, South Africa, Egypt, and other African states; Argentina, Brazil, other Latin-American countries; Spain, the Near East, the Arab world, India—none of these at present is socialist or even very socialistic. Survival for Britain will depend on her being able to find means of effective co-operation between a "socialist" and a "capitalist" economy, not merely establishing a precarious *modus vivendi* but discovering means of close and mutually profitable economic co-operation. If Britain proceeds on the assumption that close relations with a "decaying capitalism" are not to be encouraged; and if her foreign policy generally is to be based on certain assumptions which seem to animate a good deal of leftist ideology, it will all end by making the already desperately dangerous position of the country impossible.

Given the prevailing disregard of fact, the assumptions commonly made in our political thinking, the danger of a divided and disrupted people, unable to apply any policy of remedy with sufficient thoroughness—then difficulties would be as great under a conservative as under a labor government. A socialist opposition could be quite unrestrained in its criticism, and would be led by a natural process to make the most of class war; to which suggestion the mood of the workers would once more become receptive. A conservative government in the face of scarcity would be compelled to resort to about as many controls as a socialist government, though, being less hagridden by doctrine, it might recognize that efficiency of administration had become far more important than any large general social theory, and be in a somewhat better position, perhaps, to mobilize administrative talent. But the feeling for a revolutionary change of "system," of society's whole economic constitution, would become stronger than ever and produce the familiar situation in which policies on both sides tend to run to extremes, in which middle parties become submerged, and there ensues a bitter struggle between the extremists of the right and those on the left.

Even under a labor government there have been veritable epidemics of unofficial strikes, sometimes paralyzing in their effects, indicating a drift to the left of the government. A labor government has been able to use the army to get indispensable goods into the hands of the people. There was some criticism and opposition from the workers. But if a conservative government had employed the army to break strikes, the political opposition, as well as rank and file of trade-union workers, would have combined in a passionate uproar, with charges of fascist militarism; and then indeed we might have been faced with something like a revolution.

The labor government has not solved the problem of incentive; it has removed the old one of hunger and starvation if a man does not work; it has not found an adequate new one, as the unofficial strikes, the absenteeism, and indeed the frank comment of government leaders and the pleas they make sufficiently prove.

As indicated previously a British or American government cannot put five thousand men in jail. But the Soviet Government can send fifty thousand—or five hundred thousand—into forced-labor camps and does; and the security of the government is not shaken in the very slightest. (The Russian writer Kravchenko, who as an engineer under the Russian Government had continually to call for workers, puts the numbers in forced-labor camps, including death camps in the Arctic, at about twenty millions. The consensus of opinion seems to be that it does not fall below ten millions nor rise above twenty or twenty-five millions.) The deportations of the Kulaks ran to hundreds of thousands, probably to millions. Deportations from the Baltic States have been on a similar scale.

But that only raises another question.

Why no revolts? Partly, of course, the efficiency of the all-pervading police system; partly because the natural leaders of revolt —the old Bolsheviks who brought the October Revolution to success and were conscious of the extent to which the present regime has repudiated its objects and ideals—were liquidated in the purges. But the main reason for the absence of revolt, and it is the one which should concern us most, is that the Russian people don't want to revolt. For they believe themselves fighting an enemy bent upon the destruction of their fatherland and their religion. Give a people an enemy, a doctrine, and promise of a future paradise, and you have furnished them an opium which will make them forget the conditions in which they happen to be living. Those who in the Hindu-Moslem riots of the last year or two managed to slaughter some twenty thousand people did not do so as protest against the appalling conditions in which both live; those conditions were forgotten in their hatred of each other. Even if we assume that these hatreds were exploited by scheming people behind the scenes, the fact remains that the passions had to be there before they could be exploited. Of course Hitler profited by anti-Semitism. But he did not and could not create it; it, or similar phobias, exist the world over in lesser or greater degree. That kind of intolerance, "herd instinct," sometimes excited by difference of race, more often by difference of doctrine, has its roots deep in the human heart.

The Soviets have given to the Russian people a religion[2]—Marxism, Sovietism, call it what you will—and if they can keep that alive (which their control of the modern instruments of public opinion will almost certainly enable them to do) and the slogans acquire something of the sanctity which Biblical texts do to a Bible reading Protestant, they will be able to do three main things: (1) persuade the Russian people that their system is the best in the world, deserving for its defense any sacrifice which may be called for; (2) induce them to remain blind to the deficiencies of their present life, its lack, not merely of freedom, but of the most elementary needs and comforts; (3) perpetuate fear and hatred of a wicked capitalist world bent upon the destruction of the Fatherland of Socialism.

Herein lies the danger of what one may call the doctrinal solution of our problem of incentive; the indoctrination of political or economic dogma which includes the creation of scapegoats, enemies,

---

[2] There is grim irony in the fact that a government which could proclaim religion to be "the opium of the people" has itself employed the opiate of a doctrine more thoroughly than such means of government have ever before been employed. H. A. L. Fischer in his *History of Europe*, published shortly before the outbreak of the second World War, has this passage: "There is this novelty in the soviet system. A living religion is enforced by the massed large-scale propaganda of a scientific age, by machine guns and airplanes, telephones and telegraph, printing press and film, broadcasting and the regimentation of all the arts. A hundred and sixty million human souls are by a gigantic system of governmental pressure hermetically sealed against the invasion of unwelcome truth. All previous experiments in tyranny recorded in human annals pale beside this colossal achievement."

witches, which a people are taught to suspect, fear, hate. By it Stalin and Tito get things done—but by coercions which would have made the blood run cold in the veins of any ordinary Western man in the nineteenth century (including any ordinary German). It was not so long ago, we may recall, that a single act of legal tyranny, like that against Dreyfus, set the world ablaze. Ten thousand, or a million, such acts do not cause a flicker of interest today. They have become a recognized political method. So we are getting on. Leftist idealists in the West today either ignore or deny or hotly defend the methods used in Russia. The difficulty of finding any solution for low *per capita* production may induce those idealists tomorrow to defend similar methods for Britain, being careful, of course, to begin with the doctrine first and let it engender the mood of war, the class war. It might succeed. But it would be the end of free and humane civilization in Western Europe, as it has already ended for the time being in Eastern Europe.

In an earlier chapter it was pointed out that Britain's problem in 1914 and again in 1939 was not to get peace. She could have had peace by submission to Germany and acceptance of the kind of society that might have ensued from her domination of Europe. So now. Britain's problem is not merely to find the means of feeding her people, but to find the means of doing it without turning the country into a prison or a barracks where men are conscripts—industrial conscripts—all their lives, living in servitude, to their employer the state; not less servitude because such euphemisms as "direction of labor" are used.

The Labor Party has fought steadily to avoid the choice of the Stalinist methods; wants no liquidation of the bourgeoisie; takes pride indeed in the fact that its support derives largely from the middle classes, has sought class co-operation rather than class war.

But it has been very much under fire from its own left wing, especially in its foreign policy which is tied in so closely with domestic policy. A new version of Little Englandism has been taken over. There are insistent demands not merely for complete withdrawal of all British forces from Malaya, Egypt, Greece, Palestine, Malta, Cyprus, Gibraltar, but equally insistent opposition to Britain's place in these areas being occupied by the United States, from whose policy Britain should in any case, insist the critics, dissociate itself. This is virtually the policy proclaimed by the British Empire Communist Congress held in London early in 1947. The Communist Party takes little pains to disguise the fact that the vacuum created by the withdrawals of Britain would be filled by Russia, along the lines adopted in Poland and the Balkan countries. Given such a situation, Britain would be entirely defenseless—as defenseless as at the end of the war were Poland, Hungary, Rumania, Yugoslavia, Bulgaria. A British Communist Party might well then be the only party that could guarantee peace (thanks to its intimate relations with Moscow) and at the same time be in a position, thanks to the spell or lure which communism exercises over the minds of a mass rendered neurotic by hardship, anxiety, exasperation, puzzlement, to enforce the necessary disciplines on labor—by the Stalinist methods.

Even if that result did not ensue at any early date, the rapid liquidation of the empire, and dissociation from the United States, would intensify the conditions likely to produce it. The elaborate, intricate processes of world trade described a page or two back, by which alone Britain can maintain a decent standard of life, demand a sufficient degree of peace and stability for trade and exchanges to go on. Whatever the sins of "British imperialism" (and they have been great and many) it managed in the hundred years which followed Waterloo to maintain a world-wide order which was not seriously broken until two world wars had bled Britain white. The dissolution of a great empire necessarily sets up deep disturbance. As one authority is withdrawn there is bound to be conflict between those who hope to take its place. Parties or groups formed to promote particular doctrines or theories of society see their opportunity. (And the most ruthless and fanatical are likely to come out on top, at least for a time.) This inevitable unrest does not easily settle down. The collapse of the Roman Empire produced chaos in Europe for a thousand years. Chaos did not then, in terms of human survival, so much matter, for the reasons already indicated: every village could support itself. Pirates came and looted and slaughtered, but in between whiles the village lived on. The food was at its doors. It is not at the Briton's door today. There comes a point when dictatorship and the suppression of all freedom will be preferred, gladly, willingly, to misery, pestilence, famine. To live under the aegis of Russia, or a Russian-sponsored government, would not then look so bad.

CHAPTER III

Opinions, Not Facts, Guide Men

TO SAY that men's conduct is guided, not necessarily by the facts, but by their opinions about them, which may or may not truly interpret the facts, comes near to being a truism. Yet this near-truism embodies a direly neglected truth which lies at the very foundations of the difficulties with which we are wrestling. If forces within the minds of men prompt them to turn away from the facts, our first job is to find means of overcoming the subjective obstacle which prevents the truth from being seen.

Men desire welfare and intend by their policies to promote it. Yet the policies they have pursued so often and so long (as in the case, say, of the economic fragmentation of Europe by its tariff barriers) successfully defeat their intention. The antagonisms which now devastate the world are not for the most part antagonisms due to any inevitable or necessary conflict of material interest, such as might arise in a world which could not, whatever the effort or ingenuity, produce food sufficient for its population, so that if A was to live, B had to die. Material interest would then truly be in conflict. But the problem we now face is not due to any inevitable scarcity. Rather has it arisen because A and B, both starving or hungry, reject the co-operations which could produce abundance for both. They reject the co-operations, not because they do not desire welfare—their motives may be genuinely economic—but because they mistake the means by which welfare might be achieved, a misinterpretation commonly due to emotions such as those which lie behind nationalism or xenophobia or old habits of feeling and thought, as when workers persistently refused to ease the manpower shortage by permitting the use of foreign labor. Their fears of unemployment produced the thing they feared. "Bourgeois" and capitalist behavior has been no less irrational. Quite a number of capitalist economists have pointed out what shockingly bad guardians of capitalism capitalists have so often proved to be.

At the base of our problem lies the need of improving men's interpretation and judgment of fact, especially in the collective decisions of politics where personal responsibility is lessened. We must somehow become more aware than we usually are of the emotional forces which send our judgments astray, wildly sometimes, as in the case of the German public, causing wars we can no longer afford or, within the borders of the nation, economic paralysis which may involve the collapse of our civilization.

How may we get a sounder general public opinion? Merely to say "education" says almost nothing. The Germans were the most highly "educated" people in Europe—a matter with which subsequent chapters deal. It is more relevant to ask how this or that new social system will affect a people's way of thought, the soundness of its public decisions, and diminish or render less destructive the passions or obsessions which seem to threaten public sanity. To assume that men cannot behave rationally is to give up the ghost and to assert something that experience does not support. Some men and some nations show more of reason and reasonableness than others (some more, for instance, than the Germans showed).

An oversimplified materialistic interpretation of history and human nature has only succeeded in confusing this issue. To assume that a materialistic interpretation of conduct need regard only the external factors of soil, climate, geographical situation, is to neglect half of even the material factors. Certain facts within the nature of man himself which determine or influence his judgment—emotions which have their basis in physical fact like the adrenal processes— are also material. There can be no true picture of man's relation to the external world unless included in that picture are the psychophysical forces within himself, which deeply affect his interpretation of the external world. Freud was a materialist, as well as Marx; though Freud took into account certain material origins of human behavior which Marx did not.

The main tendency of progressive and leftist thought of our time is to insist that the irrationalisms of the public mind, which are obviously so dangerous, can only be remedied by a change in the structure of society. Thus a modern professor of psychology insists that inevitably capitalists should think as capitalists, workers as workers, Arabs as Arabs, Jews as Jews; that conflicts "will never be resolved by compromises, or attempts to 'change human nature' on any individualist basis" and that "no amount of purely intellectual understanding will bring about any change in the direction of men's activities. . . . The only way to bring about the human nature we want is to plan scientifically the kind of social and economic environment offering the best conditions for the development of human nature in . . . a direction which spells freedom from group conflict and freedom for personal development."

There is surely confusion in such a proposition. Arabs will cease to think as Arabs, capitalists as capitalists, workers as workers when society is scientifically reshaped. Who is to do the reshaping? The scientific planning and the reshaping will of course have to be done by Arabs, Jews, Moslems, Hindus, Americans, Britons, capitalists, workers, and if it is impossible for them to think and behave, other than as their group environment dictates, the planning is not likely to be scientific and the conflicts will go on.

The error here is to overlook the fact that men's minds are themselves elements of the social environment; that to plant a new idea, start an intellectual or moral fashion, interpret interests in a new way, is to change the environment. And Marx himself is the supreme illustration.

In his recent life of Marx,[1] Leopold Schwarzschild has this passage:

In one way or another the most important facts of our time lead back to one man—Karl Marx. It will hardly be disputed that it is he who is manifested in the very existence of Soviet Russia, and particularly in the Soviet methods. Even the orthodox Marxists who regard the influence of personalities on the course of history in general as negligible and that of "objective forces" as decisive, commonly make an exception in this case. Without Marx there would have been no Lenin, no Communist Russia. But, indirectly, Marx is also responsible for the other totalitarian states, since all of them, rivals of Soviet Russia though they may be, are at the

[1] *The Red Russian*, Scribner, New York.

same time imitations or variations of the Soviet model. And, after all, it is because of Marx that the rest of the world has for years been obliged to sacrifice one after another of its liberal traditions to the necessity of self-preservation. There can be no doubt that our whole life would be very different if Marx had never lived.

We cannot, it is true, explain man's conduct without considering the material facts of his external environment—climate, raw materials, coal, minerals, geographical situation—all in their turn playing their part in determining his economic system, his way of earning his living. But quite clearly these are only part of the story, one-half of the equation. The other half is, once more, man's own mind, the way in which he interprets those things of the external world. And that way of interpretation is largely the result of inherited skills, skills which begun, it may be, by some fortuitous discovery can be imitated almost unconsciously, as we adopt accents of speech and tones of voice. The North America of the United States and Canada, which now supports a hundred and fifty million souls at the highest standard of living ever achieved for such a mass of men anywhere in the world, or in history, is the same North America, embracing the same deserts and forests, in which, for about twenty thousand years, less than a million primitive men (some authorities have put it as low as a quarter of a million) found only the means of semistarvation and fought each other in deadly wars for the meager resources of the hunting grounds. The Europeans who replaced the original Indians did not bring a new climate or a new soil, new external conditions; nor a human brain which differed physiologically from that of the Indian. What the European brought was a new way of thought in using the soil and the climate as a means of sustenance, new skills in the use of thought as a tool for the achievement of that end. And but for the coming of that new technique of interpretation the indigenous inhabitants might have gone on for another ten or fifteen or twenty thousand years as they had gone on for some such period before. (It took thousands of years for the Stone Age man to make changes—like putting his stone hatchet at the end of a stick—which his descendants learned from the European in a generation, or a week, or an hour.)

The economic determinist would insist, perhaps, that the tribal wars of the Indians were economic, representing the "inevitable" struggle for life, for raw materials, food. But when there was no more tribal warfare in the territory which is now the United States and Canada, the means of life became immeasurably more abundant for a vastly greater number of people, proving that the wars were not the inevitable result of a natural scarcity. (Incidentally, the economic system by which a hundred and fifty million live in abundance, where originally half a million nearly starved, is the capitalist system. That of the Indian tribes so constantly at war was communistic, without bankers or bondholders or armament-makers to sow the seeds of war.)[2] The root of the constant wars of the European "tribes" today is economic only in the sense in which the wars of the North American Indian nations were economic. Could the wars of the European tribes cease, the raw materials or economic gains for which they fight would be abundant for all concerned. The obstacles which stand in the way are not in any ultimate sense economic, or physical, but psychological; psychological both in the sense that the nationalism embraced in the term "economic nationalism" is a psychological phenomenon, and in the sense that the intellectual failure to grasp the advantages of co-operation over conflict is due mostly to the nationalist emotions which obscure the objective facts and distort rational judgment concerning them.

The twenty-five nations of Europe which have clashed so often over what we commonly call economic questions have done so because they are separate nations, not, say, States of a Union, as in North America. It is in this political fact of nationalism, and the emotion which it engenders, not in any necessary total shortage of material goods that we shall find the final explanation of Europe's relative poverty as compared to the standard in the United States. (Incidentally, such features of economic nationalism as protective tariffs are directed toward keeping out goods, not toward getting them.) Europe as a whole would be economically benefited if the "economic" barriers were abolished, producing a unit comparable to

[2] The Marxist might argue, of course, that in nineteenth-century America capitalism was in its "constructive phase." But the Communist Manifesto which would have abolished it was issued a hundred years ago.

that of the forty-eight states of North America. The United States itself, however, provides illustrations enough of economic nationalism. Michigan will accept the competition of low-paid Negro labor in Alabama as a matter of course, because Alabama is part of the nation, but if the competition comes from Canada or Mexico, it will be resented and a tariff demanded. Yet, again, if Canada became part of the American Union, the same goods, the entrance of which into competition with American goods is now deemed to do the United States an economic injury, would enter quite freely, and the American public would deem it no injury. But they would be the same goods.

Where economic considerations are really uppermost, agreement is usually easy because the common advantage of co-operation then becomes obvious. Even when men pursue consciously what they believe to be their economic interest, rejecting as they think all sentiment, the question whether their opinion of their interests, their interpretation of them, does indeed correspond to the facts will depend upon whether their judgment is twisted by the sort of emotionalism which we have been discussing. And quarrels which may start in economics may soon enter the region of feeling and passion, in which the economic is forgotten. A Kentucky mountain feud, or a similar one on the Indian northwest frontier, or in Corsica, which began with a quarrel about the ownership of a pig, may go on for generations and involve the loss of twenty or thirty lives. Yet even the Kentucky mountaineer does not place the value of a pig above the value of a son's life. But he does place the indulgence of his passion of retaliation above the lives of all his sons, and, which is a suggestive part of the phenomenon, the sons concur and readily give their lives in the quarrel.

All this has added importance because for a generation or more influential writers have questioned whether good political judgment on the part of the multitude much matters, or is possible; whether the time has not come to replace the method of popular discussion and public decision by the decisions of a small minority of enlightened men of revolutionary temper, using dictatorship as the means of imposing their verdict. Influential, if not numerous, sections of "advanced and progressive" opinion the world over believe that such a time has come; that the method of continual public discussion between the government and an organized political opposition has been proved ineffective in the achievement of needed social results; that it has become merely a method by which an exploiting privileged class retains its power and defeats the purposes of the people. This view, as the following pages show, is by no means confined to the Communist Party. (In the past, of course, a contempt for parliamentary and public discussion has been a favorite theme of the extreme right, which repeatedly insisted that these "talking shops" should be shut up.)

In the short run, at least, the method of dictatorship has a great deal to be said for it. We adopted it in some degree for the purposes of the war, and if we are to regard social reform itself as mainly a war against a privileged class, then it is almost inevitable that dictatorship should be adopted for this war, the war of the classes, also.

But it raises a question almost never discussed, which this book suggests is ultimately the main question, and the one therefore to which attention is very largely addressed.

It is this: What will be the effect upon the character of the national mind, the temper of its political judgment, its capacity for deciding by reason, an impartial weighing of the facts, if organized political opposition and its accompanying free discussion are eliminated? And what will be the effect upon the minds and characters of the men who form the governing dictatorship? Upon the bureaucracy through which it will be obliged to work? It seems to be assumed that the effects of a new economic constitution for mankind will be limited to the mechanics of economic administration, the production and distribution of its goods; that the purpose of a political opposition is simply to secure the representation of minority views as to the terms of the new distribution of wealth. But, after all, the effect of the habit of discussion, upon the way men's minds work, upon their capacity to weigh opposing points of view, to give a reasonably impartial and detached judgment of the facts, is as important as any narrowly economic benefit which might result from the new system. For the way of thought determines everything, including, finally, the economic result.

Merely to indict public emotionalism, and plead for reason, would indeed be a futile business. Sometimes thought is clearer and straighter when it is driven to its task by feeling, by passion. Without emotion men won't be stirred even to exercise reason. Our purpose is to direct emotion into the right channels, particularly to put it behind a sense of the moral obligation to use reason. We need keener realization that unless we take the trouble to find out what truth is we cannot tell it, and unless we have found out what justice is we cannot do it. The finding out is difficult. If we pretend that it is not, that carelessness in either task is venial, we shall betray alike truth and justice.

We must apply to the understanding of some of the secrets of the human mind and heart the same skill and patience, and, it may be, the same intellectual methods that we have applied to the secrets of the atom and of inanimate nature. There is already a science of psychology engaged in that task. But it is a science in which the doctors differ and hardly within the reach of the layman-citizen preoccupied with the mundane tasks of daily life in a difficult period, yet who, nevertheless, has final responsibility for public policy. What are the traps into which he is most likely to fall? How may he learn to avoid them?

Some warnings, at least, may be given him. They are here uttered.

CHAPTER IV

Moral Passion for Immoral Causes

THE nature of the problem which faces us is well illustrated by two contrasting paragraphs from the writings of Professor Harold Laski, who has been so ardent an exponent of the view that by socialism alone can the world be saved. Both the passages contain suggestive truths, though in varying degrees. In his book, *Faith, Reason and Civilization,* Professor Laski writes:

> The solemn truth remains that in the Soviet Union more men and women have had more opportunity of self-fulfillment than anywhere else in the world . . . it is the only nation which . . . knows without doubt that its people move to the control of their own destiny. . . . If therefore it be accepted that our own time bears a profound resemblance to the era in which Christianity was born, it seems to me that we are entitled to conclude that the regeneration of values which the new faith effected, after no doubt a long and bitter struggle, is more likely to be secured in our own age by the central idea of the Russian revolution than by any alternative principle we are in a position to choose.[1]

Throughout much of the book indeed the moral forces behind the Russian Revolution are presented as comparable to those which marked the coming of Christianity.

As a statement of what is really happening to the Russian people, or to Europe as a whole, the foregoing passage will be regarded with some doubt. But as testimony to what has been happening in Professor Laski's own mind it is not questionable at all; it is first-hand evidence of something very important. For it is indicative of what has been happening to certain groups all over the world. Whether the control of the minds and souls of the Russian people by the little inner circle in Moscow can properly be described as

[1] Pages 57-8.

self-fulfillment and spiritual liberation we may doubt. But we know this: what has been happening in Russia (and to this extent Laski's generalization is sound) has inspired revolutionary groups everywhere with an almost mystical Messianism, though more akin, perhaps, to the temper which underlay the amazing military conquests of Mohammed than to the nonmilitary conquests of the early Christians. It is a Messianism which prompts the members of communist and fellow-traveler groups to consecrate themselves utterly and completely to their common cause, and prompts a selfless dedication which has extended on numberless occasions to the willing sacrifice of life itself.

On behalf of what? Not of socialism. The social democrat offers socialism even though it be evolutionary, and in country after country has successfully lifted the standard of life thereby, lifted it, incidentally, far above the Russian standard; in Britain itself, in most of the lesser states of Western Europe, in New Zealand, Australia. And development in those countries along those lines of social democracy continues to go forward. But the social democrats, again as we have seen, are included by the communists among the class enemies, or at best as either the lackeys or the dupes of the enemy. The communist, as is known, usually hates the social democrat much more than he hates the capitalist. Why? What causes these groups to reject the more humane method of change for the more ruthless, the revolutionary with all its risks of hate and bloody violence?

The reasons are not far to seek. If the social democrat, or the democratic socialist, succeeds, his success will do things to the communist, which to the passionate adherent of any faith are extremely painful things. First, however little the communist himself is likely to have his faith disturbed by a fact he will have an uneasy feeling that the fact may shake the weaker brethren. And no man likes to have his pet theories exposed to those risks. It will prove that the transformation of society can take place by means other than civil war, the "class" war and the maintenance of a war psychology; prove that the "capitalist" will not necessarily "fight with tooth and claw invoking all the furies of hell," as Trotsky prophesied the English capitalist would, rather than surrender any considerable part of his wealth. And it will prove that dictatorship—in which some communists hope, perhaps, to do the dictating—is neither inevitable nor necessary.

For those who have keyed themselves emotionally for battle, who have a sense of grievance perhaps against life, against society, and would have found in the battle an emotional relief—for these it is not at all satisfactory to find there is no enemy. The discovery would bring frustration, dismay. And they continue to seek theories which will give some color to their belief in the existence of the enemy. It is emotionally so much easier to fight than to think; to indulge passions of retaliation than to put honestly to oneself the question whether our retaliation has in fact justification, a question which may be a genuinely puzzling one, of difficult intellectual decision.

These very simple psychological truths are familiar to anyone who has been much in touch with revolutionaries and has kept any detachment of mind at all. This writer recalls some incidents of early association with Irish, socialist, and Indian revolutionaries. An Irish woman once said to him: "I will listen to you no longer. If I do, I may lose my hate of the British, and the thing which has given my life a purpose, endowed it with feeling, color, romance, is that hatred. If I lose it, my life will lose its meaning." A young laborite, very critical of the labor hierarchy (he is so still, as one of the active rebels in the labor ranks), said once in impatience of labor's methods: "If, when labor comes to power, it has the guts to bump off a dozen of the fattest Tory capitalists, and imprison a couple of hundred, I shall believe it means business; not otherwise." And the Marxian socialist had his battle cry: "Those who are not with us are against us." Put such expressions together—and they may be heard endlessly in any intimate gathering of the revolutionary left —and you get some notion of the underlying mood and motive. Those who voice these sentiments want violence and retaliation because it would be emotionally a release; they want the silencing of critics because criticism is a reflection upon their infallibility; they want the exercise of unqualified power because the possession of power is an ancient and universal human appetite. There is nothing strange or new in such conclusions. They are enforced by the history of every religion, every revolution.

But see where it may lead—and Professor Laski himself has told us. In addition to the book entitled *Faith, Reason and Civilization,* which approximates the inspiration coming from Moscow to that which came from Judea at the beginning of the Christian era, Professor Laski has also written, as Chairman of the British Labor Party, in the pamphlet[2] designed to support the party's refusal to permit affiliation of the British Communist Party, the following:

The Communist Parties outside Russia act without moral scruples, intrigue without any sense of shame, are utterly careless of truth, sacrifice, without any hesitation, the means they use to the ends they serve. . . . The unstated purpose of all their thinking is the need for crisis, in order, when the battle has been joined, to establish the dictatorship of the proletariat. . . . Once they were as a party admitted to affiliation they would wreck the Labor Party by undermining its morale and direct the energy of a secret minority within the greater movement from turning into one more instrument, not of working-class power in Great Britain, but of subservient devotion to the dictatorship of the Communist Party in Moscow. . . . Rigid orthodoxy of aim is, among communists, remarkably combined with elasticity of method. The hero of one week becomes the traitor of the next. A left-wing deviation today may become a necessary dogma tomorrow. The only rule to which the communist gives unswerving loyalty is the rule that a success gained is a method justified. The result is a corruption both of the mind and heart, which is alike contemptuous of reason and careless of truth.

Compare this passage with the one from Professor Laski previously quoted, for both contain a measure of truth, and it is the degree of truth in each which makes the two together of such tragic import.

The above was written of the British Communist Party. But the same kind of verdict is passed by everyone who examines with any detachment any Communist Party anywhere in the world, as may be gathered from some further evidence in a later chapter.

A careful account of the nature and activities of the United States Communist Party was recently made in the magazine *Life*[3] by Mr.

[2] *The Secret Battalion: An Examination of the Communist Attitude to the Labour Party,* by Harold J. Laski. The Labour Publications Department, London, 1946.

[3] July 29, 1946.

Arthur M. Schlesinger, Jr., the historian. His verdict duplicates in almost every respect the above description of British communists. But Mr. Schlesinger enters a little more scientifically into the nature of the moral impulse which the communist obeys, and his psychological analysis is valuable in this context. He says:

Party discipline is not, for the most part, a matter of making people do things they do not want to do. The great majority of members, for reasons best understood by psychiatrists and dictators, *want* to be disciplined. The party fills the lives of lonely and frustrated people, providing them with social, intellectual, even sexual fulfillment they cannot obtain in existing society. It gives a sense of comradeship in a cause guaranteed by history to succor the helpless and to triumph over the wealthy and satisfied. To some it gives opportunities for personal power not to be found elsewhere. Communists are happy to exchange their rights as individuals for these deeper satisfactions; and absorption in the party becomes in time the mainspring of their lives. The appeal is essentially the appeal of a religious sect—small, persecuted, dedicated, stubbornly convinced that it alone knows the path to salvation. To understand the communists, you must think of them in terms, not of a normal political party, but in terms of the Jesuits, the Mormons or Jehovah's Witnesses.

Once fully committed, adds Mr. Schlesinger, the communist's world becomes totally the world of the party. The clause in the party constitution forbidding "personal or political relations with enemies of the working class" does not have to be invoked often, for most communists voluntarily cut out their nonparty friendships and activities. One member, explaining why he had made the party the beneficiary of his insurance policy, said, "The reason I did that was, in the first place, I am not married and have nobody to leave anything like that to, and in the second place the Communist Party is more in the world to me than anything else is." Mr. Schlesinger goes on:

The total assimilation of the individual to the party creates selflessness and consecration. Like a platoon isolated behind enemy lines, the communists perform marvels of daring at their leaders' word, each acting as if he embodies the impersonal force of history. Their fearlessness has impressed thousands of workers with the invincible determination of the party.

But the price of enjoying such intimate relations with history, adds the observer, is an intensive personal supervision "which can only be duplicated in a religious order or in a police state." Gossip becomes a form of healthy criticism and party dossiers go into the minutest detail of private lives. Most members accept this all-encompassing control. In the end they become so involved socially and psychologically that the threat of expulsion strikes them as excommunication would a devout Catholic. It is enough to keep them in line long after they begin to develop intellectual doubts about the infallibility of Russia.

The USSR is much more than a very great military state—beyond any question in many important respects the greatest in the world today. It has also become the headquarters of this new faith, as Rome became the headquarters of the Christian faith. The new gospel has devotees as sincere and self-sacrificing as the early Christian martyrs who perished in the Roman persecutions; and leaders as ready as was Torquemada to rack and torture on behalf of the true doctrine. Moreover, its inquisition (in the shape of an OGPU, or an NKVD, or however the organization of the movement may be designated) is more omnipresent, and much more efficient than the old, because possessing more effective instruments both of coercion and persuasion. Commanding, as the Russian state does, all the means by which the people learn anything whatsoever— the facts of the world about them, social developments, political and social philosophy, anything taught through the medium of schools, books, press, radio, films—it is able completely to shape the mind of the people, to make sure that they shall think and feel upon any question precisely as the government desires. And, of course, if you have the means of controlling completely what a person shall know, you have the means of controlling what he shall think, how he shall feel; and so, how he shall act.

That the Labor Party pamphlet from which quotation has just been made did not distort the character of the moral outlook of the communist is shown by the writings of Lenin and by Stalin's adaptations of them. Lenin taught that noncommunists should be regarded as enemies with whom the communist should consider himself permanently at war, and toward whom he should adopt the methods of war. "We must be ready to employ," Lenin wrote, "trickery, deceit, lawbreaking, withholding and concealing truth."[4] And again: "We can and must write . . . in a language which sows among the masses hate, revulsion, scorn and the like toward those of different thought."[5]

It is important, however, not to forget that the men who adopted this attitude were not Diabolists, trying to throw the cloak of philosophy over evil self-indulgence, like degenerates engaged in some Black Mass. The pioneers and leaders of the Russian Revolution were in a sense what one of their biographers has called them, "saints," men utterly self-sacrificing, prepared to give their lives (and take those of others) on behalf of a cause which they believed to be that of mankind. Lenin's code, as reflected in the words just quoted from him, is the moral code of war; a code adopted toward the enemy by every one of the combatants in both world wars. The communist believes that he is engaged in the greatest of all struggles, the class war against a redoubtable enemy, the capitalist bourgeoisie; and that if he renounced those means of deceit and deception all good soldiers employ, then he would be beaten and the cause of The People would perish. The very essence of communism is the inevitability of the class struggle which is to go on until "history has fulfilled itself in the classless society," the transition to which can only come through violence, revolution, absolute and unswerving adherence to the party line.

If all this were just the rationalizations of a criminal gang, a sort of super Capone mob, it would be of no particular danger. But, as Professor Laski so truly insists, it is a faith, a creed, which has been gaining steadily in power at least since the Communist Manifesto of a hundred years ago.

Nor would the communist state of mind be so dangerous, perhaps, if it were confined to communists. But the underlying assumptions obviously animate a large part of the left who would repudiate the accusation that they were communists. Among those assump-

----

[4] *The Infantile Disease of Leftism.* Max Eastman, who has translated much from the Russian, notes that in the American translation, "trickery and deceit" were changed to "strategy and adroitness," "withholding and concealing truth" to "reticence and subterfuge."

[5] *Krassnaya Letopis*, No. 7, Leningrad, 1923, p. 233.

tions are that mankind is to be saved only by a new economic constitution; that under the influence of this new constitution the antisocial part of man—his primitive jealousies, resentments, the dislike of those who differ from him, the desire to have power over them, his pugnacities, all those qualities of mind and spirit which have entered into his ferocious cruelties committed in the name of Jesus or Mohammed or Rousseau or Marx—all this, or as much of it as need concern us in the organization of society, will melt away once the new system is achieved, "the" revolution completed. Once grant this as an act of faith, then anything done on behalf of the revolution and the system it is to inaugurate can be justified.

Few of those very far on the left boggle at this conclusion.

One of the mildest and gentlest, as well as one of the ablest of the leftist intelligentsia, Mr. H. N. Brailsford, puts it all very bluntly in his book *Property or Peace*, a title which sufficiently indicates the theme: capitalism is the cause of war. "War in the modern world," writes Mr. Brailsford, "is the outgrowth of the system of property. . . . Socialism offers in the modern world the one sure road of escape from war. It alone can arrest the logical movement by which property generates it."[6]

Mr. Brailsford demands intransigence, fanaticism, as indispensable:

Our goal of order and peace can be reached only by a relentless concentration on the single purpose of abolishing private property in the means of life. It asks from us the hardest of all things for intelligent men to concede—a deliberate narrowing of ourselves, a set fanaticism that will neither pause nor capitulate till its central purpose is achieved.[7]

The coming of the atom bomb (to say nothing of the behavior of the socialist fatherland in its international relations) does not seem in the least to have attenuated this attitude on the part of the leftist eminences. Professor Laski, addressing a large audience in New York on the subject of the bomb, reasserts the thesis he has been maintaining for so many years: unless the capitalist order is utterly abolished throughout the world, the capitalists will indubitably use

[6] Page 261.
[7] Page 245.

the bomb. "There is no middle way," he declared. "Free enterprise and the market economy mean war; socialism and the planned economy mean peace. All attempts to find a compromise are a satanic illusion."

Other leaders of the labor intelligentsia emphasize the necessity of dictatorship. Mr. G. D. H. Cole, Reader in Economics at Oxford, writes:

If any party sets out really to change the fundamental basis of society it must feel assured of its own prolonged continuance in power and against the undoing of its work by the opposite party. But under the parliamentary system it can never have either of these assurances, for both of them are plain denials of parliamentary democracy. I find it impossible to believe that any country will ever achieve socialism by parliamentary means, though parliamentary methods may avail to carry it a certain distance along the road. For socialism involves a radical change in the basis of society such as could not possibly be carried through to the end piecemeal, or in the face of all the checks and balances of a neatly adjusted parliamentary system.

If then socialism is to come, I believe it will involve transitionally some form of dictatorship and when it is over a system of administration more closely resembling Sovietism than parliamentarianism.[8]

Mr. Cole goes on to explain that this does not postulate either violent revolution as a means nor communism on the Russian model as the instrument. "Different countries," he goes on, "with widely different economic and social conditions will need to work out their own salvation each in its own way. No one can prophesy what the way will be." But the way must, in Mr. Cole's view, include, even in Britain, dictatorship and, after dictatorship, "a system of administration more closely resembling Sovietism than parliamentarianism."

All these declarations are of most praiseworthy honesty.

But questions arise. How long is "transitory"? The dictatorship of Moscow was to be transitory. Indeed the whole state was to "wither away." It is part of the doctrine of the more thoroughgoing socialists that men once possessed of property will never surrender the privileges it gives, except by force, a fact which may,

[8] *The Cole Outline of Modern Knowledge*, Gollancz, London, 1931, p. 736.

against the will of socialists, compel violence in reply. But the small inner club which governs Russia has control, not merely over all the property of their country, but of all the men. Their power extends not merely to inanimate things, as in the case of the capitalist, but to the lives of men and women—who have no say in the disposition that shall be made of them; shall not be allowed even to know the facts upon which the ruling autocracy makes its decisions. Any attempt to discuss those decisions, to suggest any fundamental alteration of the system which gives this autocracy such limitless power, is an extremely dangerous thing, and may invite the kind of fate which became so common in the great purges. It is true that those who live under this new form of freedom can be conditioned by a process of indoctrination to welcome it; to defend it with their lives against any who might disturb it or change it. Which strange fact itself raises the ultimate question: what is the new "transitory" dictatorship going to do, not mainly to the property of men, but to their minds, their characters, their capacity for weighing one good against another?

We have already noted in another connection how very little the facts will affect the party line and the rigid discipline with which it will be followed.

Recall one particular episode of what might be termed the moral history of communism during the last decade. In March, 1939, the guaranties given by Britain and France to Poland made war by Britain and France upon Germany probable. It was assumed that Russia would be part of the resistance to Germany. In that period the war which might come was proclaimed as the people's war, in which the communist, the socialist, could take glorious part. It was all in accordance with that process of history and the dialectic of materialism about which the Marxist can be so positive and so infallible. Thus we find *Daily Worker* (New York) editorials running in this vein:

> . . . talk of American "isolation" while the bandit Hitler goes about his robberies in Poland becomes real assistance to the nazis in the present drive, and is a guarantee that should fascism succeed this time, the injury to American security will soon be felt. We should never forget that the fascist dictators have already begun the second imperialist war, and that they are striving to expand the present conflicts into a world war directed

against the leading democracies: the United States, France, Great Britain and the Soviet Union . . . [August, 18, 1939].

The people of Poland, whose national independence is in imminent danger from the threats of fascist aggression and Chamberlain's appeasement schemes . . . realize the firm position of the Soviet Union in uncompromising support for their freedom and independence . . . this support will be continued and further strengthened. . . . [August 23].

Note the date of this last communist editorial. It is August 23, 1939. This was the day upon which the Molotov-Ribbentrop pact was signed but had not yet been published. When it was published, note the effect:

Our country cannot become involved in the quarrels that lead to the present conflict; America must actively seek an opportunity for a decisive intervention for peace, to follow up and co-operate with the energetic peace efforts of the Soviet Union [statement by Browder, September 2, 1939].

The switch was to be emphasized a day or two later:

. . . we wish to place on record our firm accord with the stand of the President of our country against American involvement in the war, or in the rivalries and antagonisms which have led much of Europe into chaos. . . . [letter to President Roosevelt by Foster and Browder on war crisis, dated September 11, 1939].

. . . this is an imperialist war in which all the wreckers of small nations, from Hitler to Chamberlain, are vying for the domination of the world.

Mighty and unruffled, the USSR stands as the main bulwark of world peace, the defender of small nations, and the champion of human rights and progress [editorial; the Capitalist Press and *Pravda*'s editorial on Poland, September 16, 1939].

Thus the war which for years socialists and progressives the world over had been urged to regard as a people's war for liberation, a war against the imperialists, a war for the democracies of the United States, France, Great Britain, and the Soviet Union, became in twenty-four hours a war against the people for imperialism on behalf of Wall Street and the bankers for the purpose of bolstering up capitalism. And it thus remained for twenty-two months. All over the world groups of men of deep and sincere conviction insist that the war is just a manifestation of the conflict of rival imperialisms, that no issue of importance to humanity is involved, and that the triumph of Germany over France and Britain is something to which the workers of the world can be completely indifferent; Britain's effort something they should sabotage. This view is supported with long and elaborate sociological, historical, economic arguments, invoking all the intricacies of dialectical materialism, Marxism, capitalism, socialism—for communist leaders the world over are usually highly educated, learned, erudite. Even the rank and file include in almost every country writers, scientists (names will occur to anyone in England or America familiar with the personnel of the Communist Party); fellow travelers include in both countries a very large part of the leftist intelligentsia. They are extremely passionate in the assertion of these conclusions and in violent language condemn those who do not accept them as fascist bandits, corrupted by the influence of capitalists, defying a truth so obvious that any plea of sincere error as distinct from willful wrong must be denied them.

Then, suddenly, once more at twenty-four hours' notice, another complete somersault. The exact opposite of all this learning represents the truth. The real interpretation of the historic forces, the dialectical materialism, the economic determinism, leads now to exactly contrary conclusions. The war against Germany is not a conflict of two capitalisms; not a manifestation of the imperialist rapacity of Wall Street or Churchill's bankers. Churchill is not the instrument of the exploiters of downtrodden colonials. Contrary to all that has been proved with such irrefragable logic for nearly two years, the Western Allies are fighting against evil forces, which, unresisted, will spread over the world. Britain and the United States are the instruments of human freedom, and the defeat of Germany is a major interest of mankind.

The foregoing moral phenomenon should be regarded in the light of these considerations:

1. Communists, and those associated with them, pride themselves above all upon being rigidly scientific. They have their own science of history and human behavior based on what is very positively asserted to be established fact, and material fact at that, uninfluenced by such human weaknesses as sentiment.

2. Repeated examples reveal, however, that the hard scientific fact and the cold intellectual analysis may point positively and without doubt to one conclusion on Monday and positively and without doubt to the opposite conclusion on Saturday. Which would seem to imply either that the scientists were blind on Monday and opened their eyes on Saturday or became blind on Saturday to what they saw so clearly on Monday. And these changes, be it noted, applied not to a few men gathered around a table in Moscow but to millions all over the world. Behind each change goes the same type of passionate conviction.

3. Such changes do not apply merely to the twists of Russian foreign policy. They apply equally to the meaning of words—democracy, freedom, dictatorship, a free press, basic human rights. For a long time democracy in the Marxist world was dismissed as bourgeois fiddle-faddle, which serious men need not worry about. But of late it has become a valuable and splendid ideal. But it is to be found only in Russia. So with dictatorship. The whole Russian people (so even observers very friendly to the Soviets, like Mr. Edgar Snow, tell us) are convinced that the American and British people live under intolerable dictatorship (Lenin took broadly that view). In Russia, on the contrary, the people, the proletariat, dictate; in Britain and America the "master class." Similarly with a free press. It is in the capitalist countries that the press is shackled. In Russia it is free. (The Russian constitution says so, and explains why.)

4. Passionate conviction lies behind each of these views, however much one may contradict the other. The conviction is not likely to be pretended by the millions; it is much more likely to be sincere. Though the change of "line" may be initiated in Moscow the emotional support is self-generated, spontaneous, and goes beyond the confines of the Communist Party.

5. It is the relative ease with which the passions of millions can be manipulated in this way, irrespective of logic, fact, event, that constitutes perhaps the most disturbing feature of the phenomenon.

Concerning the last of these points it is to be noted that the ready swing of feeling from one position to an opposite one reaches far into many leftist groups. The view, for instance, that the form of democracy in Russia is truer and sounder than the form found in the Western capitalist states was, during the interwar years, the view of most of the leftist intelligentsia in the West. Until practically the eve of the war the Lenin-Stalin theory that the one supreme cause of war was capitalism; that capitalism was at the root of territorial expansion; that since such aggression arose from the need for capitalist profits a socialist state could not possibly generate it—all this was held with practical unanimity by socialist parties of every color and brand. Yet when war came, Britain and America were usually described by the left as "the peace-loving nations." But now comes a somersault not unlike those we have seen in the case of the Communist Party. Much of the American left now reassumes the earlier position, that Britain, prompted by her imperialism, is the criminal. Witness, among other evidence, the books of Ralph Ingersoll, Elliott Roosevelt, Louis Adamic, and a good many of their colleagues, all of whom disclaim the quality of communist or even fellow traveler. Arthur Schlesinger, Jr., reviewing Elliott Roosevelt's book writes:

The thesis of this curious and lively little book is that Franklin Roosevelt, anticipating a mortal struggle between Great Britain and the Soviet Union, regarded Britain as much the greater menace to the world in which he believed. . . . He reports—in direct quotes—the President's consistent and detailed suspicions of British perfidy. Churchill figures as combined buffoon and villain, endlessly scheming—generally to the detached amusement of the President and his son—to divert the United States from the war against Germany to the war against Russia. Hearing the British military and naval leaders on board the *Augusta*, Elliott found himself wondering—this was before Pearl Harbor—"whether it was the British Empire's purpose to see the nazis and the Russians cancel each other out, while Britain grew strong." Stalin makes a reassuring entrance at Teheran, something like the wise old uncle from Australia in the Horatio Alger books. "Listening to Stalin's quiet words, watching his quick, flashing smile I sensed the determination that is in his name: Steel."[9]

[9] The *Nation*, November 2, 1946. Mrs. Eleanor Roosevelt, in her foreword to this book (*As He Saw It*), remarks: "I am quite sure that many of the people who heard many of the conversations recorded herein interpreted them differently." Mr. Sumner Welles, in his own account of some of the same incidents (at which he was present), interprets them very differently and gives documentary proof as justification for his very different interpretation.

Even Mr. Henry Wallace is led at a great mass meeting in New York to warn the American public against the dangers of British imperialism, i.e. the expansion of British territory and power. New York C.I.O. unions organize the picketing of Churchill with great placards proclaiming "Churchill Wants War." Comparing all this with what was believed and felt during the war, the changes are only less remarkable than those of the communists in the matter of "imperialist wars." And on the British side the leftist ranks of the Labor Party are telling us in all seriousness that the United States, which made possible by its help the survival of communist Russia, is now bent upon war with Russia in order to save the system of Wall Street and enable the "thugs of Detroit"[10] to make a Roman holiday. The switches are a little less crude than those of the communist proper, but they reveal a similar intellectual character.

It is impossible, of course, to look into other men's minds (it is often impossible to look into our own),[11] but whether the leaders of communist and leftist thought believed equally firmly each succeeding phase of the party line, the significant thing is that they obviously believed that their followers would take each new belief seriously. And it is the rank and file, the neophytes, the recruits, with whom we are, after all, more concerned than with the leaders. For it is through the rank and file that the leaders acquire power. If the masses, whose opinions it was the purpose of the propagandists to shape, had resented or had been revolted by the rapid changes of doctrine, the whole object of the propaganda would have been lost. Obviously they were not nauseated or revolted. Their minds presumably have been so conditioned that what was truth yesterday, supported by elaborate argumentation and complete sincerity, can become in forty-eight hours evil falsehood, "filth spewed out of a foul nest of fascist bandits" (a quotation). We are forced to the conclusion that communists as a whole throughout the world are

[10] Mr. Tom Driberg in the House of Commons: "I must warn the Foreign Secretary that . . . the people of this country will certainly not follow him now or in five years' time against Soviet Russia in partnership with the barbaric thugs of Detroit or the narrow imperialists of Washington and Wall Street."
[11] Once at the close of a very impassioned piece of oratory by Aristide Briand a friend asked him: "Were you really sincere in what you said?" Briand replied: "How should I know?"

quite capable of believing one thing one week and the opposite thing the next, and being as ready to kill for one belief as for the other.

The creed so marked has adherents all over the world.[12] What can happen to the mind of civilized men brought under the hypnosis of some centrally directed "line" even a Western people like the Germans have proved to us. But Hitler's world organization of "cells" was amateurish and trifling compared to that which world communism boasts. The Hitlerian ethic did not possess the atom bomb. The new totalitarian ethic will almost certainly possess it.

Our job meanwhile is not to hunt out communists and penalize and punish them. That sort of martyrdom is bound to give them new life and drive them dangerously underground. Our job is to find out the secret of the spell, the lure, which prompts men racked by miseries to turn to a method least likely to effect a cure; why communism has such strong appeal to ardent youth, deeply sincere reformers, to the underprivileged, to the discontented, as well as, it must be added, to the failures, the paranoiacs, the psychopaths.

Many of these have no particular doctrine perhaps. But many a nationalist who fought and gave his life in the war, or in one of the underground struggles, had no clear doctrine or theory of nationalism. He was just caught up by it; by something which has its roots in a tribal atavistic impulse. It is nonetheless very real and very deep. And part of the genius or the luck of the new communist Vatican in Moscow is that it is able to combine this atavism of what Trotter called the herd instinct with a doctrine and theory which can make its appeal with little more than a few unexamined slogans.

It goes beyond any problem of Marxist leftism. In 1939 a group of lads, little more than schoolboys, members of the Irish Republican Army, declared war alike against Mr. De Valera and Great Britain, much as the Irgun Zvai Leumi in Palestine (who, incidentally, state that they model themselves on the Irish underground) have declared war both against Britain and many of their fellow Jews. The Irish lads, who knew that they were probably giving their own lives,

[12] "In most of the world, effective popular leadership is in the hands of persons who are sympathetic to Soviet communist doctrines and who turn to Moscow for moral support. The communists have strong positions in India, in China, in most colonial territories, in Latin America, the Arab States and in Western Europe." (John Foster Dulles, New York Press, January 18, 1947.)

did not hesitate to throw bombs into civilian crowds in Britain, killing people who had no more to do with Ireland's grievances than the ancient Assyrians; and they had no moral doubts whatever. The IRA had a doctrine, passionately held, but it had little to do with any facts. The history of Ireland, its relations with Britain, its position in the war, the rightness or wrongness of neutrality, the place of the Protestant Reformation, the conditions which had produced a Belfast or a Protestant North—about these things they were satisfied, doubtless, to accept a few catch words. But those catchwords were sufficient to drive them on to gladly accepted risks of shameful death. But whatever it was that caught them up, all the evidence would seem to show that the forces which moved them exist in far greater measure in the appeal of revolutionary leftism to the young, the active, the discontented, the imaginative, the passionate, the fanatical, the self-sacrificing. Something similar is to be seen in the ferocities of the civil war in China, the Palestinian terrorism, the struggle in Poland, in Yugoslavia, in Greece, the mutual massacres of Hindu and Moslem in the Indian cities; and even perhaps in the struggle of white and Negro in the American South.

The stock reply whenever attention is called to the dangers of ideological fanaticism in our time is that such violences would not be dangerous but for poverty. "Communism will be no menace," writes R. H. S. Crossman, "once the world outside Russia has been made a decent place to live in." He goes on to imply that when the world has been shown that there is something better than either communism or free enterprise, the danger will have passed. This, he adds, is the heart of the matter. Unfortunately experience proves that it is not. The heart of the matter is not merely to show the fact, but to get men to see the fact and act upon it. The other day, at a public meeting in New York, two men stood on a platform telling us of conditions in Russia, whence they had just returned. Both were educated, intelligent men; and they flatly contradicted each other, to such an extent that one comment became general: they could not be talking about the same country. This spectacle has been repeated daily for years in the world's press outside Russia giving diametrically opposed reports even on questions of fact.

On a recent notable occasion Mr. Henry Wallace said this:

We must demonstrate that we can raise the standard of living faster and to higher levels than can Russia.[13]

It would seem that in Mr. Wallace's view that has not been done by a country where real wages are many times higher than in Russia.

Poverty of course on occasion accounts for savage and irrational policies. But the worst fanaticisms and irrationalisms of history have not been the result of poverty. The church which created the Inquisition and the very sincere men who imposed its sentences were not driven by poverty; the multitudes who acquiesced and supported the church did not do so because they resented their poverty, but because it is "natural" in men to dislike those who do not share their doctrinal convictions. It is doubtful whether the young IRA terrorists were any poorer than the Free Staters. Some of the worst extremists in Palestine happen to be well-to-do middle-class young men. The poorest and worst treated group in India are the untouchables. It is not they who provoked the Hindu-Moslem massacres.

Clearly, what we call the Russian enigma is more than Russian. It is an ancient problem of human society taking a new form, not only in Russia but in the West as well. To dismiss its appalling implications in this age of atomic destruction is not to be realistically immune to hysteria. It is to close one's eyes to the ugly facts of the actual world about us; and within our own natures.

Yet to look only at the dark side is to get an untrue picture, especially if, as the foregoing would indicate, the danger arises so largely from noble motives put to the service of evil ends. By what means can it be brought home to those who would serve mankind that they have become, from originally good motives, the servants of evil?

What of education? Longer school periods? Access to the universities?

[13] Speech at the Hotel Commodore, New York, April 12, 1946.

CHAPTER V

Educated Defiance of Fact

THE present generation is the most literate and scientific which has ever existed, with greater knowledge and more means of disseminating knowledge—books, libraries, schools, universities, newspapers, radios, films—than mankind has ever previously possessed. It is also a generation more perilously threatened by the results of unreason than any which has preceded it.

Events reveal in this connection not merely the failure of learning, in the sense of erudition. We have set at naught repeatedly in our policies the commonplace knowledge derivable from the facts of daily life about us, the plainest facts of our own experience.

Indeed it is true to say that the second war of our generation could have been avoided if the average citizen in Britain, France, America had applied to the guidance of policy the knowledge which for the most part he already possessed. John Citizen did not need to know more; he needed to make better use of what he already knew.

Which is a somewhat devastating reflection. For if the average voter can disregard the knowledge he already possesses, he will be able as readily to disregard new knowledge which more schools, longer school years, more university training, more printed matter, books, newspapers, radios, might convey.

We recognize this particular failure in the case of the Germans, and how devastating the consequences can be. If the highly literate and educated German people, heirs to centuries of Christian culture, having given to the West some of its greatest physicists, philosophers, religious reformers (and to Britain part of its Reformation and its royal house) could nevertheless follow a psychopathic ignoramus into policies, not only utterly destructive of the welfare and freedom of their nation, but also of appalling savagery and barbarism, it was not from lack of scholastic or academic erudition—the Germans excel in those things[1]—nor because facts and knowledge of more commonplace kind had been in the past less available to the Germans than to others. The German public which accepted Hitler and acquiesced in his policy was a public which had had, up to that time, access to the relevant facts as freely and amply as those facts were available to the French or British or American publics.

If the Germans adopted such theories as the responsibility of the Jews for Germany's plight and her right to exterminate them, and if this theory led to the abominations of the mass killings, it was not because "the facts about the Jews" were less available to Germans than to Englishmen or Americans. The Jews were as familiar to the Germans as to the rest of the world. Indeed, Hitler did not secure acceptance of his policy by a process of submitting the facts, the evidence, but by a process of so selecting facts as to stir obscure but fierce atavistic instincts and passions which made sound or even sane interpretation impossible. In this, as in the long list of cases dealt with in these pages, men were not guided by the facts but by their interpretation of them, an interpretation which caused, not merely in the Jewish issue, but in other profound issues of civilization, devastations and miseries beyond description.

We have in the German phenomenon the clear demonstration that nearly a whole people, very mixed in its racial and cultural composition, can go utterly and dangerously wrong in its political judgments; can share, or be made to acquiesce helplessly, in errors that result in ferocities and barbarisms of which a universe might in one way or another become victim. Though this phenomenon gives warning of the existence within the human mind, within all of us, that is, of dreadful forces of unreason, it is for the most part dismissed as a manifestation of some special evil in Germans as a race or a nation—coming near to acceptance of the German "race" theory of inferior and superior "races." But this theory, so commonly accepted on the Allied side, that the atrocities and abominations are

---

[1] A German student once said to the present writer something like this: "My professor is a very learned man. You can take to him a quite simple matter; and in ten minutes he will have made it completely incomprehensible."

due to some special "German" wickedness, this, too, is something denied by the plainest facts of universal knowledge. The German failure is a universal one, varying only in degree. Japanese behavior has been as bad in some respects as that of the Germans. The Chinese are a refined and courteous people, and are the inventors of particularly elaborate and complicated forms of judicial torture. The organization which has come nearest to duplicating the horrors of the Gestapo or the German or Japanese or Russian concentration camps, or the tortures of the Chinese magistrate, was an organization of the Christian church. The wars which have come nearest in atrocity to the wars waged by Japanese and Germans were the religious wars of the sixteenth and seventeenth centuries into which entered also deep religious convictions. Equally ferocious were the earlier Holy Wars of the followers of Mohammed, Prophet of Allah the All-Merciful.

The German phenomenon is proof that the power of a nation— probably any nation—can become a force threatening mankind. Civilization as a whole at the close of the first World War was confronted with an old problem: how society may protect its members against criminal or fanatical groups. It has done this within the national frontiers by using its collective power for the defense of each, thus confronting the criminal or fanatic with a force he had little temptation to challenge because it was overwhelming. This simple truth in the mechanism of society is revealed in our everyday experience of the world about us. But we were quite unable to apply this common knowledge to the most urgent need of civilization. Even at the close of the first World War the Allies were passionate enough in their condemnation of Germany, but that passion did not prompt the measures of co-operative and collective defense which might have prevented Germany, or any other aggressor, from becoming once again a menace to mankind. The Allies quickly forgot their animus against Germany in renewal of their animus against each other. The power for mischief of any criminal or fanatical nation to menace her neighbors resided, and resides now perhaps more than ever, in the divisions among those neighbors, their incapacity to combine to meet the danger. Germany was a small fraction of the power of Western civilization as a whole, a mere 5 or 10 per cent. If in any society a criminal 10 per cent can threaten the more law-abiding 90 per cent, it is because there is something wrong with the 90 per cent. If we heard that the criminal gangs of Chicago were, under Al Capone or a successor, taking charge of the Illinois state government and going on from that to the conquest of other states, aiming obviously at the White House, the historian would be little concerned to animadvert on the wickedness of Capones. What the historian would want to know would be how it came about that a hundred and thirty million were so little able to fulfill the first function of organized society—defense against lawless violence—that they were faced with the danger of a small criminal gang becoming their master.

The truth which we failed to perceive at the close of the first World War, a failure which gave us the second war, is a truth so simple that it lies at the very basis of all organized society. We failed to see that any secure defense must be collective; that it is impossible to defend ourselves unless on occasion we are prepared to defend others. If we repudiate this obligation, if we say that we will act only for ourselves and the rest may go to blazes, then immediately there arises the situation by which Hitler profited; he can take us one by one. Ten men can easily overcome a hundred if each of the hundred remains isolated, each separated from the rest. For in that case the ten do not face a hundred. They face only one, one at a time. If we refuse to hang together, then obviously we can be hanged separately. The supreme right of all, the right to existence, to life as a nation or an individual, without which no other rights have value, this right must be defended collectively, by an organized society, or it cannot be defended at all. This is still in the order of first things to be put first.

If the public rejected Wilson and the international co-operation he urged in 1920, and adhered obstinately to isolationism (culminating in the Neutrality Act some sixteen years later), but accepted Truman and his internationalism in 1945, it was not because the knowledge of the facts was not available at the earlier date (Wilson urged them with passionate intensity and a proportion of the American public agreed with him); nor because the Americans lacked sufficient schools or newspapers or libraries or universities (they had about as many when they passed the Neutrality Act as when they began to do the very things the Neutrality Act was designed to prevent them doing). If Neville Chamberlain adopted in March, 1939 (in the guarantees to Poland), the policy of collective defense which he and the governments preceding his had rejected in the long years of appeasement, it was not because the facts which justified the policy were hidden (for years a large section of the British public had accepted the conclusion from them which Chamberlain finally drew). Indeed, it is possible to say of the history of the interwar years that, if the truths recognized late had been recognized somewhat earlier, or if those who did see the right policy earlier had been more numerous, the second World War need never have occurred.

Consider this bit of recent history.

In the late summer of 1940 an eminent and at one time very popular American, distinguished in a certain field of technology, educated, sensitive, high-minded, honest beyond most who have much contact with politics and the public mind, began a political campaign, addressing great meetings in Chicago, New York, and other cities of America. Listening to him (as this present writer did), it was obvious that the speaker did not like the job he was tackling and that he was doing it from a real sense of public duty. Colonel Lindbergh (for he was the campaigner in question) had visited Europe a year or two previously, had met the heads of states—including the heads of the German state—had lived in England, was a military man of training and distinction, an expert on the subject of the most modern form of warfare, that of the air.

And he had decided that it would be disastrous for America and the welfare of the world if the United States aided or encouraged Britain to maintain her then difficult, precarious, touch and go resistance to Hitler.

Lindbergh was moved largely by moral considerations which are important to examine because they are all but universal, deeply affect Britain's position in relation to world opinion, and particularly affect her relations (as we shall see presently) with the United States. The war had arisen, Lindbergh explained, out of "an issue which is one of the oldest and best known among men; one which had caused conflict in Europe ever since European history began, which would go on causing wars until it was rectified." Germany's effort was a blundering but fundamentally justified one to correct a basic injustice which had cursed mankind. In aiding Britain, all America did was to perpetuate this injustice which cried aloud for remedy. Here are some passages of his speech:

There is a proverb in China which says that "When the rich become too rich and the poor too poor, something happens." This applies to nations as well as to men. When I saw the wealth of the British Empire I felt that the rich had become too rich. When I saw the poverty of Central Europe, I felt that the poor had become too poor.

The cause of this war is that Britain owns too much of the world and Germany too little, and wars will go on until this profound and fundamental injustice is corrected.

When he pronounced the words, "Britain owns too much of the world and Germany too little," the audience, on this particular occasion one approaching twenty thousand, broke into applause which shook the building, and it was quite evident that his proposition had touched heartstrings. He had drawn a picture which already existed in the minds of the audience: an opulent, bloated John Bull, owning a vast estate, while starvelings clamored at his gates, a condition which demanded a preliminary and indispensable act of justice, lacking which nothing else could be of much value: there must be a redistribution of "property" between the nations.

Lindbergh had made it clear that he was not using the term about ownership of property in a general sense, applying more to political power than to actual wealth; he was, as his actual words quoted above indicate, very specifically dealing with actual wealth, the ownership of goods.

In the picture which he drew and the obvious meaning which he attached to the words he used, he was no solitary figure. He stood for a point of view all but universal, not merely among Britain's critics, but actually among so many Englishmen themselves. In a book now half a century old, I have shown by page after page of quotation from contemporary political literature that this is a view of the struggle between nations accepted very nearly the world over as an axiom, a statement of the case so obviously true as not to be worth discussion at all. It is true that today a very sharp distinction has to be made. Economists and specialists who have studied this particular aspect of the relation of economics to war no longer talk in terms like those employed by Colonel Lindbergh. But the lay public, that lay public which includes Congressmen, members of Parliament, editorial writers, columnists, radio commentators, writers of books on the general cause of war, heads of states, politicians— all these would agree with the statement of the case made so repeatedly by Lindbergh. A year or two before his particular campaign the subject had come up apropos of the proposal to impose sanctions against Italy for her projected conquest of Abyssinia, and in the discussion of Germany's need for colonies. At the time of the Ethiopian crisis Mr. Leland Stowe, a foreign correspondent then attached to the New York *Herald Tribune*, a very distinguished journalist, addressed a gathering of the business elite of Chicago and expressed a view of the Abyssinian crisis which paints the precise picture that Lindbergh painted. Mr. Stowe said:

It seems to me there is just as grave responsibility on the shoulders of the British Government, which possesses in the world more than it ever needs to have. . . . And it has never offered to give up even ten thousand square miles to satiate either Germany or Italy in order to prevent the next war. . . . In reality, in this conflict Abyssinia is just a bone. There are two dogs after this bone, and one of them is the dog of British imperialism, which is very well fed and very fat, and the other is the dog of the newly born Italian imperialism, which is very scrawny and very hungry. That is the final issue. That is why it may lead to another war.[2]

Writers even more distinguished in the field of economics, of international affairs, authors of books like Mr. Frank Symonds' *Price of Peace*, highly praised on two continents, adopt precisely the same general propositions as Mr. Stowe. Mr. Frank Symonds wrote:

It is a matter of life or death for Germany and Italy, as it was for Japan, to break the blockade which is throttling the economic activities of both.[3]

[2] Address by Leland Stowe to the Executives Club of Chicago, October 18, 1935.
[3] The *Saturday Evening Post*, October 5, 1935.

The Italian ambassador in Washington at about that time crossed the *t*'s, and dotted the *i*'s, repeating almost the words just quoted.

At that time one of the publications of the American Foreign Policy Association, which exists to put the facts of the international situation before the American public, explaining a chart showing the difference in possessions between the "Haves" and the "Have-nots," said:

> The war to end war failed to solve the economic problems that had been its root cause. . . . The chart shows why England has built up a great empire of colonies from whom she can import the things she lacks and to whom she can send surplus population and production. . . . Germany is densely populated, produces little wheat, many potatoes, some coal, a little steel, practically no oil and no cotton. She now has no colonies.

A little before this time an American judge of a state supreme court wrote:

> The tentacles of England extend everywhere from Halifax to Jamaica, from London to Capetown, from Gibraltar to Siam, and these tentacles have a sensitive power of suction. . . . From India, from Australia, from South Africa and from Canada, her sons return laden with the profits of newly developed regions. Proprietorship of those regions is thus bringing back its gains.[4]

The reader will note the use of the word "proprietorship." During the debates in Congress over the war-debts problem arising from the first World War, it was more than once suggested that Britain could settle her debt to America by "selling Canada to the United States." Senator Hatfield, who made the suggestion in the Senate on November 26, 1932, explained that Britain had so great an estate that she could afford to part with some of it, and that, like every landowner in debt, John Bull should settle his debts by the sale of some of his property. It is the Lindbergh picture.

In no popular comment on that picture could one discover the faintest realization that Lindbergh was using words that were either a defiance of simple and obvious fact or had no meaning whatsoever. But if one could bring that indictment against the particular audi-

[4] *Facing Europe* by Judge Bausman.

ence who so thunderously applauded Lindbergh, one also had to bring it in only slightly less degree against the learned authors, newspaper writers, columnists, commentators, politicians, Congressmen, who had discussed the desirability of Britain "selling her property of Canada" to the United States, of "granting Italy" ten thousand miles or a hundred thousand miles of territory whereon she could grow raw material, or giving back to Germany some of those colonies which Banker Schacht had said were a life-or-death matter for her to own.

For the truth is simple and visible: Britain does not own her empire at all; it is not her property. She has governed and governs a rapidly decreasing area of it. But she owns none of it. Nine-tenths of the moral indignation of Lindbergh and his audience was due to a crude confusion between the meaning of the word "own" and "govern."

The fact, as distinct from the myth, does not rest upon difficult and dubious analysis of statistics. Any citizen of elementary-school education, with any knowledge of the commonplace facts of the world about him such as might be gathered from the reading of the daily newspaper, is perfectly aware that the farms and fields and factories in Canada, Australia, or India, or Jamaica, are held by the people who hold title to those properties, not by the person we describe as "John Bull," the people of Britain. At the time that Senator Hatfield made his suggestion about the transfer of Canada to the United States I tried to point out to some friends in Washington that if Canada became a state or a number of states in the American Union, there would be no transfer of property from one group of owners to another. There would be a change of government which might be good, bad or indifferent; but, setting aside altogether the fact of Canada's political independence now registered in the Statute of Westminster, and even assuming that Britain could give political title, which, of course, she could not, how would there be a transfer of property, since the people who owned the property would be transferred with the property itself? And I recall still how hotly this proposition was disputed by men of education and intelligence (several of them journalists), who insisted that of course "America" would be richer by the acquisition of all that wealth, unable, it would seem, to grasp that the "America" which would then own the wealth would be an America including Canadians, the present owners of the wealth. It was quite without result that I tried to show that a hidden magician at work in their minds was juggling with words in such a way as perpetually, by a sort of intellectual three-card trick, to hide the simplest and most obvious truth from them.[5]

I have sometimes tried to shock Americans into realization of this absurdity by putting to them this proposition: if the whole of the British Empire, including Britain, were transferred to the United States, no ordinary American, speaking broadly, would gain a pound, and no ordinary Englishman lose one. The proposition has usually been treated as a sort of catch; that it just could not possibly be so. Yet, of course, it has been put to the test of experiment on a world-wide scale. For Britain did "lose" a whole empire when the thirteen colonies gained their independence. But the loss did not mean that Britain's economic advantage therefrom was also lost, for her trade with the new independent state quickly became greater than had been her trade with the thirteen colonies.

Indeed—and alas—there is no need to resort to a supposititious case to illustrate the fallacy of "ownership" of empire. In this year of glory, 1947, the third year of Britain's greatest victory in history, with her enemy at her feet, her empire, her "estate" still in being, at least for the moment, what has happened to the "owner," the obese proprietor who has so much, too much, of the world's wealth? What has happened to the picture drawn by Colonel Lindbergh, and by so very many learned folk who tell us of the vast wealth which "British capitalism" knows how to extract from the exploited slaves of the empire? Well, this bloated landowner goes short on food, warmth, shelter, clothing, light for his homes or his streets. With all that "property" and all those "slaves," why the penury and the misery? Why indeed.

[5] Of course there may be advantages in enlarging the administrative area, as a city may find it advantageous to take in an outlying suburb. But this does not mean that the city now "owns" the suburb, or that there has been a transfer of property. Indeed the advantage to be derived from the union of independent areas depends on there being no "ownership" on either side. If Canada were to be incorporated into the American Union it would mean that Canadians would partake in the "ownership" of the United States, as United Staters would that of Canada.

When an eminent professor tells us with complete assurance that no single cause of war is greater than the revolt of colonial peoples against their imperialist oppressors, one wants to know which world war of the last century and a half has so arisen. Certainly not the wars made by Germany twice in a generation (to say nothing of the earlier wars). Germany was not in 1914 a colony subject to imperial masters; nor was she in 1939; nor was Japan in 1931, when she began the war against China, nor in 1941, when she began that against the United States. Certainly the wars made by the Italians against Spain, against Abyssinia, against France and Britain were not revolts against colonial status. Italy was not a colony. The Italians, whose king was emperor of Ethiopia (the native ruler of which country had found refuge in imperialist Britain), were hardly colonial peoples struggling against oppressive foreign domination.

These are misinterpretations which badly obscure the nature of the problem facing us. The present writer has had some experience of the way in which this happens.

In the spring of 1941, France having collapsed nearly a year before, Britain was hanging on by the skin of her teeth, fighting both Italians and Germans. The situation was such that at any moment we might get the news of the capture of the Suez Canal and the junction of German and Japanese forces in the Indian Ocean. It was at that juncture of the war that the present writer found himself in contact with American university students, both as lecturer at an American university and as director of an organization for the study of world affairs. Questions of the freest kind from students were encouraged. The nature of most of them was more than a little startling. The question whether the British Commonwealth could hold out—the question, that is, whether the German-Japanese combination would win the war then in progress and become the dominant power of Europe and Asia alike, of the Western as of the Eastern world—this question was not that which provoked the most enquiries, which seemed uppermost in the minds of most of the students, or seemed to stir emotions most readily. The drama which then hung in the balance did not fix their attention, which ran far more to Britain's offenses of appeasement in Spain, to her oppressive colonial system, the alleged hostility to Russia, the Cliveden set, the caste system (in England). Would Hong Kong be returned to China? Would Canada be liberated and become a free republic? But above all, India. Would India be made free, and when?

These questions were not without interest, and one respected the concern of these youngsters for those whom they regarded as the underdogs of the world. But if that explained the order of their interests, one wondered that they were concerned so little with the question of what the position of those underdogs would be if the Axis triumphed; and what the position of their own country would be if henceforth its way of life was to be guided not by what the American people preferred but what would best defend it against the designs drawn up in Berlin or in Tokyo. This would not be independence. It was a curious scale of values which at such a juncture put Hitler, his conquest of Europe, his alliance with Japan, and his pact with Stalin in the background, and Gandhi, British oppressions in India, the caste system (in England), and the sins of British imperialism generally in the foreground. It was indeed the more curious in that the United States had lived, ever since she became an independent state, cheek by jowl with the British Empire in Canada, and the fact had never been notably a menace to American security. Nor indeed had the fact that Britain had governed India for two hundred years been in any sense a threat to the United States. Of which more in these pages presently. As to India, that country, with all its grievances, was shortly to contribute to the common cause an army of two millions—the greatest volunteer army in the world—and to achieve brilliant feats of arms against both Germans and Japanese. The British Government in India never had to employ its arms against great Indian armies, as Generalissimo Chiang Kai-shek has had to employ his arms to fight great Chinese armies. And India did not suffer the extent of invasion from the Japanese which China has suffered during so many unhappy years.

The sense of proportion just indicated might have been explained by adolescent exuberance. But it was also the scale of values of much of the intelligentsia of the left, the isolationism of the right, of many Congressmen and, if Elliott Roosevelt is to be believed, even of the President—though one may doubt whether very many accept the former as a very accurate reporter.

However all that may be, the fact remains that neither world war was caused by the revolt of colonial peoples. Whatever the offenses of Britain in India or in Africa, the unrest of the peoples there played no part in precipitating either war, except in so far—and the qualification is important—as Germany argued, which she did on both occasions, that the British Empire was in process of disintegration, moribund, therefore a relatively easy prey. Japan may have argued similarly in regard to China, since, though internal unrest did not result in wars in colonial India, it did in Free China, a fact which, as we know, encouraged Japanese aggression. There is no evidence that the withdrawal of Britain from India or Africa would have saved them from invasions such as those which China actually did suffer; and if Germany or Japan or both had replaced Britain—as they probably would have done if the British Empire had been liquidated —there is little evidence to show that the Indian or African peoples would have gained in freedom or welfare by the change.

Indeed, in the light of what has been happening in India since her liberation, one may go further: the abolition of the empire will not bring to the millions of India either greater freedom or greater welfare. At the moment of writing, millions of Hindus go in greater fear of Moslem fellow countrymen, and Moslems of Hindus, than either of the two groups went in fear of the British.

A condition of a public opinion, therefore, which becomes violently excited over the slowness of India's march to independence, but not at all excited over a country's isolationism and its failure to co-operate with the rest of the world in creating some sort of international order; becomes excited about the continuation a year or two longer of a government in India that had lasted two centuries, but not at all excited about the position of German or Japanese power during the next two months; whose feelings are deeply moved by what Britain was doing in Hong Kong but not at all moved by what Germany was doing in Europe—all this represents an emotional barking up the wrong tree which has in fact been disastrous for the safety and peace of the world.

This is not intended to reflect in any way upon the sincerity and depth of the feelings which were stirred. For about the hundredth time, it must be insisted that it is precisely the sincerity of these misdirected emotions which is one of the most disturbing things in the whole situation. Here, too, we have another example of a deviation in that compass of the mind which should point the right direction for the emotions, but points in fact in the wrong direction. It was right that the American public should have some feeling about misgovernment in India; it was wrong that they should have none or very little about the failure of nations to fulfill those obligations which alone can render them secure from criminal or fanatical violence.

Some similar misdirection of our emotion occurs when our moralists insist that war is due to the wickedness of men, their narrow selfishness. For in war men are prepared to give not only money but life. If every nazi had refused to fight until he got a clear assurance of what he personally would gain economically by it, if the Japanese suicide dive-bombers had made similar demands and stood by them, neither Germany nor Japan could have gone to war at all. The passion which animated the youngsters—German and Japanese as well as British, American, French, Polish, Greek—was no passion for money or profit. War was possible for Germany and Japan because so many Germans and Japanese were ready to give their lives for their cause, men capable of merging their individual lives into that of their country. This is not a fact unknown to those who make the generalization that war is due to the selfishness of men. It is there in their morning newspaper, staring them in the face.

Similarly with the assumption that wars are the result of "unredressed grievances." Before the war of 1914, which is the most important of the modern wars because the next was in a sense its continuation, all the specific grievances of Britain against Germany, or Germany against Britain, of the kind which arose over the Bagdad railway and the Morocco questions, had been settled. As Edward Grey avowed somewhat plaintively at the time, he could not "settle" with Germany because there was nothing to settle. Britain had no grievance save the supreme grievance that German domination of the Continent by the conquest of France would render Britain defenseless. Nor was Britain attacked either in 1918 or 1939: on both occasions Germany desired Britain to remain neutral. These two greatest wars of history arose not out of unredressed grievances, except in so far as absence of security is a grievance, but out of the competition for relative power which in a world of anarchy is the one means of national survival. They were wars of power politics in the sense (the justifiable sense, perhaps, since one cannot justly ask a people to commit national suicide) that power politics are the politics of not being overpowered. Such motives may be good, bad, or indifferent, but if we are to understand the nature of the forces which, ill understood, may annihilate us, we must not continue to assume that they are of one kind when in fact they are something entirely different.

As to poverty and the revolt of men against it being one of the major causes of the wars, Germany, particularly the Germany of 1914, whose action was the beginning of a whole generation of crises, was not a poverty-stricken nation. The standard of living of her people was, as European standards go, a high one. Her foreign trade was expanding by leaps and bounds, entering into new markets the world over. If it be argued, as indeed it is argued so ardently by many socialists, that such wars as those of 1914 and 1939 arose out of the conflicts not of peoples but of capitalists fighting for new markets and larger profits (profits presumably like those the British capitalists are now enjoying under a socialist government and the existing taxation), then the cause is not poverty but wealth; for the capitalists who are presumed to be at the root of the causes of war are rich—or were. And if the people, as distinct from the capitalists, had no part in the causation of these wars, then their poverty did not enter into the matter.

Our thinking is so often twisted on this subject, and our emotions take a wrong turning, because of a whole series of presuppositions commonly accepted as so self-evident as hardly to be worth discussion. Some have been dealt with. But we shall see more clearly their significance if we group them together into a summarized catalogue thus:

We commonly assume that:

Since the people want peace, the failure to get it must be due to the conscious wickedness of governments, rulers, diplomats, capitalists, imperialists, who for selfish reasons of their own bring war about, indifferent to its human costs.

In so far as war has a more general cause it lies in the selfishness of men refusing to do justice. Or,

It is due to the poverty of the common man resulting from the selfishness of privileged classes, the revolt of the Have-nots against the Haves. Or,

It is due to the struggle of oppressed peoples, particularly of colonials against imperialist powers. Or,

It is due to the refusal of the right of independence to subject peoples.

Only by making a just and permanent "people's peace" in which the "common man" shall at last get his rights, heretofore denied him by the avarice of the powerful, the privileged, shall we eliminate war and the risks of atomic destruction.

This set of propositions creates at first sight such an impression of high-minded idealism as to silence not merely criticism, but any real analysis or examination. Yet acceptance of them will not produce peace. It will lead to disillusionment and cynicism, owing to the coming to power of those who accept these assumptions and then discover that they do not indicate the road to peace. The resulting failure furnishes stimulant for a more intense "agin the government" drift, by which the revolutionary of the communist type of mind profits. To avoid such disillusion and to get onto the right road we must realistically face the facts.

It is not true in the Western world that war comes because the peaceful purposes of the people are defeated by governments which want war. The policy of the government in America in 1918-19, the administration, that is, of Woodrow Wilson, the "ruling class" of his time, would have been more likely to give peace than the policy of the electorate, the people, who repudiated Wilson and who for nearly twenty years showed themselves hostile to the internationalism which might have preserved peace. When we insist that "the people are peaceful" we perhaps overlook what we have been saying of the German people, the Japanese, the Italian. Their governments would have been powerless to carry out aggression if the people had been resolutely opposed to it or had known how to put their resolution into effect. They were either acquiescent or helpless.

It is not true, however, that war arises from the conscious wickedness of either peoples or governments. It arises more frequently from good intentions expressed in bad policies due to faulty political judgment.

It is not true that men fight mainly for selfish reasons. When they fight, they are willing to give their lives. They cannot do this from selfishness.

It is not true that the wars which have concerned the modern world most, the two world wars of this generation, have been due to the fact that the poverty of those who precipitated them was greater than the poverty of their victims: Germany notably (especially in 1914) was not poorer than her victims who would have remained at peace. She was much less poor than some of them.

It is not true that these wars arose from refusal to redress just grievances, using that term in any ordinary sense. There were no specific unresolved "just grievances" of Germany against the Allies or of Japan against China; rather was the case the other way about.

It is not true that these wars arose from the revolt of colonial peoples against imperialist oppressors: Japan, Germany, Italy were not colonial peoples living under imperialist masters; neither war arose from revolts in India or other parts of the British Empire.

It is not true that experience justifies the notion that to make all nations completely independent, free, sovereign, would make peace easier. Experience is to the contrary. When Europe was united under the authority of the Roman Empire it had the longest period of peace it—or the world—had ever known. Since the breakdown of that empire into separate and sovereign nations, war has been constant. The dissolution of the Spanish Empire of Latin America did not bring freedom from civil wars, revolutions, or wars beween the twenty republics which succeeded the empire. The dissolution of the Hapsburg Empire making Austria, Czechoslovakia, Yugoslavia, Hungary, Poland independent states did not make the maintenance of peace easier or end the forces which make for war.

It is not true that wars usually arise out of the machinations of capitalists, or out of "the contradictions of the capitalist system," or the need for sources of raw material, or fields of trade or investment. The two world wars have subjected capitalism in Britain and in Europe generally, and to a lesser degree in the United States, to enormous costs and burdens, and have very greatly impoverished capitalists. In Britain, yesterday the greatest capitalist nation in the world, the burden on the capitalist is such that large incomes have virtually been wiped out; a whole class has been dispossessed.

It is not true that the causes of war are basically economic; they are basically political and psychological. Peace has been secured between the states of the American Union not by the economic policy of abolishing capitalism but by the political policy of federation. States not subject to that political (as distinct from economic) condition, such as the states of Europe or Latin America, go to war for what are fundamentally noneconomic reasons: the security of national rights, the possession of power as the means of that security.

It is not true that nations need to control politically the areas from which they draw raw materials, to "own" (i.e. govern) their sources. Britain built her foreign trade mainly on raw material of territories she did not govern (e.g. the southern United States in the case of cotton). "Loss" of the thirteen colonies did not end Britain's capitalist profit therein: trade, investment, was greater after the "loss" than before. Britain, of recent years, has greater economic concern in South America, which she does not politically control, than in India which she did. The smaller states of Europe—Sweden, Switzerland, Denmark, Norway, and others—maintain a high standard of life for their people without needing or desiring the colonies about which Germany, Italy, Japan have talked so much.

It is not true that either of the world wars arose simply from German wickedness nor that any repetition will be prevented by simple "extermination of fascism." The willingness to commit aggression was shared by the Japanese and the Italians. Aggression and dictatorship had been a commonplace of the history of every people who had the power to be guilty thereof: the Spaniards in the New World, the British in many unnecessary wars, the French under the Bourbons and again under Napoleon. The second World War arose not mainly by reason of Germany's power but by reason of the inability of her potential victims to unite to form a society, an inability due to nationalisms, isolationisms, the failure to reconcile notions of national right with the need of an international society.

In a United Europe, still more in One World, the criminal elements in Germany would have been impotent to cause the torments they have done. The foundation of any organized society is the capacity to combine its collective power to defend its constituent members against the violence of criminals or fanatics.

This list by no means exhausts our defiance of the self-evident.

One looks back on some of the demagogic rampages of the peace making that followed the first World War: some three hundred members of the House of Commons supplying Mr. Lloyd George with a memorandum to the effect that Germany must be made to pay enormous indemnities, but not permitted to increase her exports. She had to pay "in money, not goods." As the gold available in Germany would not have satisfied 1 per cent of the claims made upon her, "money" must have meant paper money which could only be converted into goods in Germany. But the goods must not leave Germany: no increase of exports. This writer suggested, therefore, that, in the terms of the demand, the only way of getting reparations was for a favored section of the British population to be given the German money and with it emigrate to Germany and there drink German beer until the reparations were exhausted.

It took the British public ten years to see that point—which could certainly be explained to an intelligent adolescent in ten minutes. The French never saw it. The Americans in the matter of the British war debts valiantly refused even to consider it. "They hired the money." Some nine hundred American economists who, not having congressional seats to hold, were willing to face the facts notified Congress to the general effect that if the United States were to have any hopes of collecting the British war debts, the tariff must be lowered, not raised. If the tariff were raised, hopes of recovering the debts must be relinquished. Congress thereupon raised the tariff and went on demanding the debts. "We don't want their goods," explained a Senator, "we don't want their gold." (He had heard of the hoards in Fort Knox.) "We want their money."

Not very dissimilar is the general hostility in Britain to the employment of foreigners at a time when the country faces utter catastrophe from lack of manpower.

More than a generation since it became evident that if the British

Commonwealth, including as it does great empty territories in Canada, Australia, New Zealand and elsewhere, was to duplicate the history of the United States and become a series of powerful and rich nations, it would be by adopting what was, in the years of American expansion, the American policy of fairly free immigration. All Dominion governments have until yesterday refused even to consider putting down the barriers. While now at last there is some slight modification of this attitude alike on the part of British workers and Dominion governments, the modification may have come too late to remedy what has become in Britain at least a desperate and paralyzing difficulty that may kill any real prospect for the prosperity of her people and the freedom of their lives.[6]

Again we are confronted, not with any lack of knowledge of the relevant facts, but with a refusal to face them because to do so would compel us to shed phobias we prefer to indulge. To assume that this is inevitable, that we can do nothing about it, is to accept the all but inevitable disintegration of the kind of civilization we have built up in the West.

Our refusal to face undeniable facts applies not merely to political and economic phenomena of the world about us; it applies also to our own innate desires—as in the determination, already noted, to put national security and survival before peace when we continued to protest that we put peace before everything.

This last point is not a piece of hairsplitting verbal distinction. It is a distinction concerning what we really want, want most and put first, which is quite indispensable to the rational guidance of policy. For wars have arisen, mainly out of an aspect of the confusion between peace and defense; arisen because of the faulty steps we have taken to ensure defense, steps by which usually the security of one means the insecurity of some other, producing the very rivalries we would avoid. The confusion certainly contributed to bringing about the second World War. If we had seen more clearly and earlier that we—British, French, Americans—did not in fact put peace first in our purposes (we could all have had peace by supine surrender to Germany) but that we put first of all national security, the defense

[6] For a fuller discussion of the subject of migration, see the author's *You and the Refugee*, Penguin Books.

of certain rights, the preservation of our own modes of life in our own lands, freedom from foreign challenge to those things—if we had faced this, the evidence of which lies in our own natures, not in learning and erudition, the story of British appeasement and American neutrality would have been so different that the second World War almost certainly would not have occurred.

About the good intention of those who evade the truth there can be no doubt. But we know with what the road to hell is paved. Surely if there is one thing which stands out starkly in man's long history of cruelty and error it is his propensity to put intense moral indignation behind the wrong methods of remedying evil. We cannot organize men into good societies if we misunderstand the nature of the motives we obey, the reasons why our good intentions have miscarried, our purposes been defeated. If we ignore fact, event, experience, we shall end by finding that we have put moral passion behind evil, as even Professor Laski has now discovered that the communist movement has ended by doing.

CHAPTER VI

The Loaded Dice of the Emotions

W E OF the Western world have set before ourselves certain ideals which we desire to see realized in our society. They include freedom, democracy, justice, national right, welfare, economic security, not alone for the few but for all. Behind these purposes there may grow up deep emotion. Particularly on behalf of such ends as freedom and national right are flaming passions easily aroused. The independence movements of the East, causes like that of Zionism in Palestine, are but examples of similar movements the world over.

There are certain very plain conditions indispensable for the attainment of those purposes, conditions with which men have been familiar ever since they have discussed the nature of man and of his society. But they are conditions which we are always forgetting, and because we forget them our emotions constantly miscarry and defeat our ends.

When we become passionate about freedom, we so readily forget that it is not and cannot be something complete, absolute. Freedom cannot exist unless we are willing to surrender some. If anybody's life (and so any freedom of anybody) is to be really secure on the motor highway, then each must give up the freedom to drive as he sees fit in disregard of traffic rules: if all had complete freedom none would be sure even of the freedom from sudden death. Not only must each observe the rules, he must paradoxically pay taxes in order that the traffic policeman may stop him for speeding; as we all pay taxes for police, detectives, courts, to defend others whom we do not know and may not like. If we did not do so those others would not pay taxes for our defense, and there could be no security for anyone; no security for the first of all rights, that to go on living.

Without the organization of government, not even that freedom is secure.

But just as freedom cannot be defended and survive without government, and government means the limitation of freedom, government itself can and frequently does exercise its power in such a way as to destroy the thing it was created to defend. It does this, too, because of forces inherent in the nature of men; and governments must be composed of men. Power corrupts. It is futile, however, to proceed from that premise to the conclusion: "Because power corrupts, men must not hold power." For the absence of power in governments would not put an end to its presence among men; there would be more power than ever, the power of the most ruthless and the most cunning. Absence of power in governments would merely transfer force from law to lawlessness. (It is a strange thing, incidentally, that the leftist, who can be so eloquent concerning the dangers inherent in the possession of property, has so little to say, as a rule, of the evils inherent in the possession of power. And men lust for power more than for property.) The quantities of the equation must be kept in balance: freedom must be limited sufficiently to create government; the powers of government so limited as to prevent its destruction of freedom. But, as we shall see, the feeling behind each quantity is not in balance.

So with democracy. Democracy is government by consent of the governed. Its principle—the assumption seems to be—is violated if a people are asked to live under a government they believe wrong and oppressive. Yet there can be no democracy at all unless a big proportion of the people, all the time, consent to live under governments they believe to be wrong, oppressive, unjust: unless democrats consent to live under republican governments, republicans under democrats, conservatives under labor governments, laborites under conservatives. Even the majority principle cannot be invariably accepted: more electors in Britain, in the 1945 election, voted against the labor government than for it. In democracy, as in freedom, we see the same impossibility of applying one simple and narrow principle, the same need of adjustment of opposing principles: the right to be represented at all must be paid for by the obligation to live under governments that do not represent us.

All this is familiar enough. Yet the world rings with passionate demands for "absolute and complete justice," the implication being that justice consists in the assertion of clear RIGHT over clear WRONG.

One would have supposed that a glance at the report of any case at law would have convinced the most ardent absolutist that even in the simple matters of daily personal quarrels concerning property, or injuries, or libel, the doing of justice is an infinitely complicated problem. How much more must it be the case in the multitudinous claims and counterclaims of passion-ridden nationalities.

If we look for a moment at that world about us which we hope to save from the atomic and bacterial wars, or from chaos that will invite dictatorship, we see at once that the conflicts we must settle arise far more from the struggle of two rights (which can never be adjusted unless two parties accept something less than what they regard as absolute right) than from the struggle of right v. wrong. Chaim Weizmann, the greatest of all the Zionist statesmen, had the courage to state the real nature of the problem when he declared that of course the attainment of Zionist ends would do some injustice to the Palestinian Arabs. But he went on to add the obvious truth that we live in a world in which complete and absolute justice is in any case impossible, and to imply that if everybody continued to demand it, it would drench the world in blood.

What is true of Palestine is true in different circumstances of the nationalist struggles everywhere. Every national group in the world (supported usually by the leftist idealists everywhere) makes demands for a "right" which can only be granted if it is denied to some other—the right to complete national "freedom and independence." The followers of Gandhi are prepared to die in order that India shall be free of Britain; but the Moslems are prepared to die in order that Moslems shall be free of Hindu domination. The southern Irish are as passionate for a form of freedom and justice which the Protestant North would regard as a form of slavery and injustice. The Chinese communists are convinced that "free" China means a communist China. Chiang Kai-shek is convinced that a communist China means an enslaved one. To the Arab, Jewish freedom means Arab subjugation; to the Jew, Arab freedom means Jewish subjugation. This leaves out of account the conflicts of the phantoms, as when Hitler managed to stir deep passion among his people concerning Germany's "enslavement to international Jewry"; or when Colonel McCormick of the Chicago *Tribune* makes the flesh of his readers creep with his daily proof that King George, operating through a fifth column in the shape of Rhodes scholars, is about to reconquer the United States; or British leftists reveal the plots of "the bandits of Wall Street" to enslave the British worker. The fights of Moslem and Hindu, Jew and Arab, communist and Kuomintang, are at least fights between physical realities. The protagonists exist. "International Jewry," in the form in which Hitler painted it, was a figment. But it was a figment which has precipitated some of the most appalling horrors which the sordid history of man reveals. The other figments in the end may do as much.

The facts about us shout the truths we will not face: freedom cannot be defended and preserved unless we surrender some of it; democracy, the system of government by which the governed are represented, cannot exist unless men are willing to live under those who do not represent them and whom they dislike; free speech is nearly valueless if there is no willingness to listen, if the spirit of faction is such that it is considered something resembling treason to give the other side credit for sincerity with views worth careful study; justice cannot be done unless we know what justice is, a difficult intellectual task that mere feeling will not accomplish; an impossible task if we assume it to be so easy to determine that a lynching party or a Palestinian terrorist or a Russian director of purges can easily do it.

It is an ancient and hackneyed discovery that such ideals as freedom do truly consist in the working together of two opposing principles. Yet in the establishment of the necessary synthesis, our emotions are loaded and are put behind one of the principles only.

Thus in the matter of free speech, we are passionate over our right to state our case; we are not passionate about our obligation to listen to the other fellow. We may do so from a sense of duty, but the listening to the other man's view has behind it a very different type of feeling from that which animates the statement of our own.

This emotional unbalance prompts us to reject quite simple social truths. Thus:

Our first task is not to do justice, whatever happens. It is to find out what justice is. Unless we find out what justice is we cannot do it.

Independence is not the inalienable right of every nation. It is an anti-social claim which if maintained can only end in jeopardizing that maximum degree of independence possible in an organized international society.

Right and might are not mutually exclusive opposites. Right cannot be maintained unless it is defended against those who would defy it; and defense at times demands the use of might.

Power is not in itself evil. It may corrupt, as prosperity often does. The cure for the dangers of power is not to be weak, any more than the cure for the dangers of prosperity is poverty. For weakness and poverty, too, may corrupt. The cure for the dangers of power is to know its proper function.

Acts of injustice by a government do not necessarily give the right to rebel, since every government, being human, is at times guilty of injustice. There has never been and never will be a perfectly just government. Sound decision as to the wisdom of a given rebellion or revolution depends upon the capacity to weigh obligations against rights. Behind the latter is usually passion; behind the former little but a heavy sense of duty.

We have linked our international relationships to the repudiation of these simple truths, with the result that deeply moving words have become traps in which human understanding is so often caught and imprisoned.

CHAPTER VII

Passion in the Wrong Place

WITHOUT emotion men would not act effectively in society either against evil or for good. Our problem is not to eliminate emotion but to see that it is put behind the right purpose. A flaming passion of justice (of the eye for an eye variety) may prompt a mob to burn a Negro whose guilt they have not proved. An equal passion can be aroused to protest against the act. In our day not only of possible atomic bombs in the future but of contagious strikes and political violences bringing misery upon millions in the unhappy present, the need is not the elimination of emotion but its guidance by reason; a feeling for the moral obligation to use reason. Yet reason is so feeble a thing, of small power in men's lives.

The compass of a ship is an instrument of very small power. But it determines the direction in which the engines, which have great power, shall drive the ship: onto the rocks, or away from them. If the compass goes wrong, the power of the engines becomes just so much added force for the ship's destruction.

Because there is so much confusion about the relation of emotion to thought, a simple illustration or two may not be amiss.

Suddenly I encounter my old enemy. Anger surges up in me; I strike out at him murderously; he raises his right hand—and then I see that it has all its fingers. My enemy had two missing. Because my mind can go through a process of thought, logic, I realize that here is a case of mistaken identity. My desire to kill drops from me and becomes instead a desire to make amends, to help. The change in the direction of emotion has been brought about by thought, logic.

Let an incident, not altogether fictitious, illustrate an extension

111

of the same process, an extension which illustrates certain events of our time and may help to illuminate policy in relation to them.

Evidence seems to point to the fact that a junior partner is at the bottom of a swindle by which A has been ruined and his family plunged in misery. The evidence is difficult to disentangle. If gross injustice is not to be done to the young partner, A must bring to the preliminary examination of the evidence patience, suspension of judgment, disciplined reason. It is not easy. A never much liked the junior partner, who was vain, opinionated, uppish, and, in certain social relationships, unscrupulous. Furthermore, the two partners differed sharply on political and other questions. It is pretty clear, therefore, that the judgment won't be impartial, the evidence alone determining it, unless behind A's effort there is deep regard, emotional in character, for the obligation to be guided by the facts alone. That resolve must have feeling behind it, in order to counterbalance the feeling of personal dislike for the partner. Without this sense of obligation, a feeling for intellectual integrity in the interpretation of facts, he will almost certainly forget that appearances are often deceptive, human testimony often misleading, truth difficult to disentangle. One feeling must counterbalance the other. The situation needs not less feeling but more; two emotions instead of one.

It will not suffice, of course, just to have the will to see the evidence aright. The will must be enlightened by certain commonplace knowledge, which ought to be the possession of every citizen, knowledge, that is, of the deceptive nature of evidence and the tendencies of our own minds in judging it; how easily we may go wrong, jumping to false conclusions, and why. That there can be such feeling for intellectual integrity we all know, for we all know men, sometimes very simple men—the Lincolnesque people—of no great erudition who have that quality. They seemed to have derived from the lessons of the lives about them and of their own natures what the erudite sometimes have not managed to derive from their libraries. And we have all known the other type, the cocksure and hasty, the man who has no faintest feeling that he may be wrong, rapidly acquiring a passion for his judgments and his theories. In politics his cocksureness is often demonstrated by demands that the heretic who does not share his theory shall be excommunicated or liquidated. We know the type, in every sphere of life; so quick, so instant with their verdicts, so positive; the religious bigot damning eternally most of mankind, the demagogue so ready to exploit irrelevant passions of the multitude; the fanatic of the past who fed the guillotine with his hundreds of victims, the fanatic of the present feeding the labor camps with his millions. Such men were and are often very learned, sophisticated, bookish.

It is difficult to discern just what enters into the making of such different types of mind; just as it is difficult to know why the general trend of policy in one nation differs from that in others; why German trends have differed from those of the Western democracies. But certain things we do know. We know that men desire to conform to the code of their social environment: the gangster usually will not squeal and betray the members of his mob, even under the torture of the third degree; the gambler pays his debts, though there be no legal compulsion; a man tips, though the tip may be his last coin and there be no law about it at all; a man does not kiss and tell. Such things are "not done" and there is strong feeling behind the not doing of them.

But one of the strange things of our modern world is that no corresponding moral sanction seems to be applied to the observance of an effective code of intellectual behavior in the discussion of public policy, in the press or by commentators generally. When men take sides in some matter on a basis of obviously incomplete evidence, and violently attack those who do not agree with them, it is not regarded as morally reprehensible. For months, previous to the election of 1944 in America, a round dozen commentators were daily representing Franklin Roosevelt as a crook; when British troops remained in Greece in a situation of terrific complexity, other dozens of commentators were sure it was just another piece of grabbing British imperialism. No evidence was needed. After Roosevelt's death, Churchill, who heretofore had been on the whole the hero, began to be the crook. One commentator knew all about Churchill's motives, alleging that his policy was dictated by bankers who had once saved him from bankruptcy. Mr. Louis Adamic, writing a book largely about Churchill as the embodiment of evil, swallowed the story whole (as of course much of the public did), later having to admit (at some cost to his publishers) that he had no evidence for the statement. But such commentators are not regarded as having violated any recognized code of behavior and their immunity is mainly, of course, due to the fact that their public has no code of evidence, no test such as would be applied in any court of law.

All this is pretty generally admitted, and encounters commonly two attitudes. One runs about like this:

Irrational judgments with passions behind them are part of human nature and there is nothing we can do about it. To go on proclaiming how nice it would be if we all agreed is mere evangelistic utopianism, naïve, unrealistic.

This attitude leads, of course, to fatalism, confusion, drift, living in political matters from hand to mouth at the mercy of tides of feeling.

The other attitude might be described thus:

Men won't be moved to action unless they are passionately convinced that they are the victims of wrong and oppression. It is futile to inveigh against the fact. Let's use it to get rid of the system which creates the wrongs that provoke the passion. This can be done only if we get mass unity. A disciplined and ruthless minority, employing dictatorship alone, can get that unity. Everlasting talk and discussion can only produce stalemate. Let the minority dictatorship, therefore, use the feelings of the multitude—including their sadistic cruelties and intolerances—to establish the new order which will give them the maximum of welfare possible in a society which, whatever its form, is going to be imperfect.

If it is to be a choice only between these two attitudes, obviously the second, which is the attitude of communism and its ideological allies, is going to win. Put a small, dynamic, disciplined minority against an indifferent, lazy, inert, easygoing or divided majority, and there can be little doubt as to which will triumph. Ten communists or fellow travelers in a trade union or political organization who make a point of sitting through every committee (and tiring it out with objections) will have more influence than a thousand moderates who don't attend the meetings and who, for the sake of peace, give way in the committees. It helps to explain why revolutions tend to drift out of the hands of moderates into the hands of extremists, who, once in the saddle, liquidate the moderates by terrors and purges. The process is little affected by the fact that the new order established by the extremists is almost invariably as oppressive as the one it destroyed. (A Russian author living in New York has just calculated that for every political prisoner under the czar, there are a hundred under the Soviets.)

But these two alternatives really do not exhaust the possibilities.

In one important function of society in the West—that of a court of law—we recognize all the human tendencies to which reference has just been made. Because we recognize them we make attempts to subject them to discipline. We do not accept the assumption that a lynching is the only alternative to letting all criminals go free; nor that the emotional tendencies of men must necessarily render all human testimony valueless.

Note some of the process.

A man is accused of crime, theft, or murder. Justice demands that he shall have full opportunity to "state his side of the case." A jury takes oath to hear the evidence, impartially, without prejudgment or passion. In England, at least, the members of the jury are isolated as far as possible from outside influence; the press is not allowed to stir up feeling on one side or the other, newspaper discussion of a case *sub judice* being a serious offense. In order that the accused should have every opportunity of explanation, of submitting his evidence effectively, he is allowed counsel. The presentation of evidence is itself no simple matter: "What the soldier said is not evidence." We know that the fallibility of the human mind is such that hearsay gossip, tittle-tattle, can bring innocent men to death, and make justice impossible. And when both sides have been presented by experts, another expert, the judge, sums up, warning the jury against the traps of misinterpretation, showing the relation of the evidence to the law, and so on. When all these precautions have been taken, miscarriages of justice are innumerable. But we know that justice could never be done at all, except by accident, if judge and jury believed it to be a mark of moral elevation to show passionate partiality from the outset, either to jump to conclusions on the ground that theft and murder must be put to an end once for all; or, contrariwise, that governments and their bullying police are always oppressive; or if the spectators—as in certain People's Courts and Revolutionary Tribunals—having none of the responsibility of judge and jury, shouted angrily their preferences in the name of The People Whose Voice is the Voice of God. (A lynching party, too, is an expression of the people's will. We do not necessarily regard it as God's.)

Hitler, it will be recalled, repudiated "dehumanized" legalisms, and insisted that justice would be better served if the healthy instinct of the people disregarded them. The German judiciary under him was instructed to take "the feelings of the people" into account as well as dry-as-dust documentary law. He did so on the ground that it was a nazi principle to "think with your blood"; and that the feelings of the mass about, say, Jews, were more in accord with the new rule.

Now any ordinary criminal case of theft or violence is usually simplicity itself, compared with the infinite complexities of domestic and foreign policy in which the average voter is called to act as judge and jury. Yet in the grand assize of an election we do not commonly apply any large part of the moral and intellectual code which we know to be necessary, in the simpler case of a citizen accused, say, of having picked a pocket or pilfered a till. We have instead usually floods of emotion, passionate invective, undisguised partisanship, and sweeping judgments hastily made amidst the din and noise of irrelevant clamor.

As one who has fought four parliamentary elections and rather enjoyed them, I have a feeling of being a kill-joy in suggesting that elections should become anything as funereal as a court of law. And I am not suggesting it; or indeed that in any institutional form the methods of a court could be applied to the discussion of politics, whether at election or at other times. I am suggesting that if public judgment is to become sufficiently sound to make democracy, which, again, is government by discussion, compatible with the safe possession of the atomic bomb or with the maintenance of a free and humane society in a world where so much of it drifts to chaos, then the sense of responsibility and the principles of judgment we apply as a matter of course in law must be applied, at least, as a code of intellectual behavior, in arriving at our daily decisions of public policy.

In fact we do apply them in rudimentary and imperfect form. Both sides in the electoral debate have access to the evidence, to the facts about which decision has to be made—access, that is, to the degree to which they have learned to put value on facts and evidence. A relatively free press and platform are means of open discussion, if real discussion is what the public wants. The existence of a political opposition ensures some statement of the case against the government on the basis of those facts and discussion of them. The whole should put the public in the position of a jury giving its verdict, if the public wants to occupy that position. The method does something more than give the public a chance of deciding wisely in specific cases: it helps to form a certain type of mind, to develop the capacity for considering contrary views, to maintain a certain public temper of tolerance (since it keeps alive some awareness of the fact that there is usually more than one side to a question) to render the people hesitant to accept doctrines and theories for which infallibility is claimed. These are habits and qualities that help to keep passion and fanaticism at bay.

The working of parliamentary institutions—more successful in Britain than in some other countries—although it has not eliminated irrationalism of public judgment, heaven knows, has nonetheless helped toward health of the public mind, particularly in making possible a national unity such as that displayed during the war.

The leftist tendency to disparage the value of these bourgeois institutions of Parliament and public discussion as merely instruments of capitalist interests, and to insist that the achievement of vital economic ends demands the unhampered action which only dictatorship and single-party government can secure, misses the point. For the soundness of the decisions—which must in practice be daily decisions, since the situation changes—as to how much freedom must be surrendered for how much economic good, at what point the "direction" of labor, for instance, becomes simple chattel slavery, as much chattel slavery as that of ancient Rome or Egypt—all this will depend upon the quality of the public judgment; whether or not tiredness or cynicism prompts it to accept submissively abominable things, as the Germans got in the habit of doing; or irritation prompts it to rebel against reasonable things, as parties in so many nations in Europe and in Asia have of late been doing. The "Anglo-Saxon character" is no guarantee against errors of that kind, because national character is not a fixed thing; it changes in response to all kinds of subjective and objective factors. There can never be much hope of applying the scientific method to society unless the habit of discussion and the preservation of the balance and toleration it calls for are preserved by practice.

This of course applies as much to the ruler as the ruled. A dictator, surrounded by frightened men who dare not question his judgment, who is never obliged to consider a contrary view, never compelled to go through the unpleasant process of considering whether or not he may not be making a grave mistake—any human being who never subjects himself to that discipline, in the end loses his capacity for it, and his mind becomes in the true, if not in the technical, sense unbalanced. Nearly all biographers of the great dictators of history have especially noted this tendency. The behavior in the sphere of international negotiation of the Soviet Government and representatives already reveals tendencies in this direction. What is most disturbing is not the fact of obdurate obstruction but the temper displayed; the constant accusations of bad faith directed at all with whom the Soviet Government may not happen to agree; the personal abuse, leveled even by Stalin at respected leaders in countries with which he is in alliance; the possibility of such things as the publication of stories such as that coming from Cairo in the midst of war accusing Britain of negotiating secretly with the enemy and being about to betray her allies; the accusations of gross cowardice leveled at British sailors convoying cargoes to Russia; the incredible features which marked the "story of our efforts at wartime co-operation with Russia," as related by Major

General John R. Deane (who was General Marshall's representative in Moscow) in his book *The Strange Alliance*; the abusiveness of the language habitually employed by Russian diplomats in normal matters of negotiation; the absence of the most ordinary courtesies of debate—all this is indicative of a state of mind which quite easily can end in making further discussion of differences useless or impossible. It will not do to dismiss it as just "bad manners" and with the plea that we are not going to fight because the other fellow's language is a bit rude. For it is all a symptom of an underlying social disease, the disease which comes of despotic and irresponsible power, irresponsible in the sense that it has never in Russia to be rationally defended, despotic because it cannot be resisted. The little clique of Soviet rulers are not obliged to defend their conduct in their own country, and they naturally find it exasperating, "unfair," that they should have to do so to mere foreigners. This underlying feeling emerges all too visibly.

It is not true to say that there is nothing we can do about it. We can refuse to adopt the system or the methods which produce that result, cease from disparaging the institutions which so far have prevented us from being quite as bad. For if we, too, come to take the view that social change is a war to be fought with the temper of war, and that discussion with its code of tolerance is out of date; that dictatorship is indispensable; that "liberal democracy which received its letters of credit in the last quarter of the eighteenth century has broken down" (in the words of a leading professor of British leftism); that the model and pattern of the New Order is to be found in Russia—then we, too, will find ourselves adopting, not necessarily by deliberate intention, much of the violent invective, the intellectual arrogance, the angry intolerance, the constant imputation of evil motive, which seem to go with class war. And that way lies the throwing of the bomb; or the dictatorship of the most ruthless minority.

CHAPTER VIII

The Scientific Method in Social Problems

MUCH of the preceding discussion comes down to this question: is it possible to apply to the field of politics and social science generally the method of interpreting fact which we have applied so successfully to matter? We apply that method to some extent, as we have seen, in such spheres as the administration of law. Is it possible to extend it more widely in our attempts to solve the social problems of our time?

It was noted in an earlier chapter that we could have avoided some of our most tragic disasters, such as the second World War, if we had recognized early, truths which we did in some measure recognize late. The fact that the American public was willing to accept under Truman a degree of internationalism which they rejected under Wilson was cited as a case in illustration. This gives proof of the possibility of change in attitude and is one reason why this book is no sweeping indictment of the human race, no assumption of overwhelming and incorrigible human folly.

Cynical, or hopeless, or panic pessimism concerning the possible improvement of public wisdom can be as fatal as complacent optimism. If the ship caught in the current is in danger of being carried on to the reef and the navigator insists that all is well, it is likely to be destroyed. But equally will destruction come if, recognizing the drift somewhat late, the navigator decides that the current is too strong to stem, or panic prompts a premature rush for the boats. Salvation will depend, not necessarily upon the external facts of current and rocks, but upon the navigator's opinion of the action which those external things should dictate—upon, that is, the nature of his mind, upon that mind's capacity to balance hopes which, ill balanced, may be dupes, or fears which may be liars.

This analogy gathers force when applied to the guidance of public policy. For in that case the vital facts are not those of the external physical world of oceans, soils, and climates. We ourselves are the rocks and the currents. The obstacles to good navigation toward a happier world lie not in matter but almost wholly in the minds and hearts of men, which, too, are part of nature.

It is not flattering to our modern social understanding that Aristotle's Politics still has a modern sound; and that the professor of political science in the twentieth century can still tell his students that if they want enlightening clarity of thought on politics and social problems, they can find it in the works of men who did not possess a printed book or a newspaper or the radio or telegraphy or any of the marvels by which two men on the opposite sides of the earth can hear each other's voice. Obviously, it is easier to make advances in technology, the science of matter, than it is in the science of society. The same truth is revealed by the way in which today peoples who have not so far been able to operate the political methods of the Western democracies have shown themselves entirely capable of adopting the West's technology. As was Japan, with tragic results for the West. In China, India, Russia (which three, incidentally, contain between them many times the population of the Western democracies), we find railways, telegraphy, radio, all the gadgets; but not democracy. Furthermore, dictatorship governments can use their powers to hasten industrialization and employ it for political and military purposes—witness Russian achievements in this respect.

We know the method of interpretation and of reasoning which has given to the scientist, the physicist, this mastery over the physical world: open enquiry, trial and error, inductive as well as deductive reasoning, any theory or hypothesis to be subject always to the test of experiment and experience; the rejection of authority as the final basis of truth, no claims to finality of judgment or to infallibility. We know also that this method can be lost or swept away after it has been used. Europe lost it. The Ages of Faith rejected it as impious and immoral. "The fact, written plain and large on the page of history," says H. A. L. Fisher in his *History of Europe*, is that "progress is not a law of nature. The ground gained by one generation may be lost by the next. The thoughts of men may flow into the channels which lead to disaster and barbarism." Greece was but "a brief gleam."

As Lecky and other historians have shown, the particular way of thought, the method of interpreting fact, which has given us that modern world of science, which began somewhere about the time of the Renaissance, involved turning upside down the intellectual and moral assumptions which had guided men during long centuries and even millennia. Intellectual vices had to become virtues, and virtues vices. An attitude of doubt and criticism, which had been regarded as criminal in the Ages of Faith, became the first virtue. Unquestioning acceptance of authority, whether expressed—as in earlier times—in taboos, the pronouncements of the gods, the traditions of the tribe, or in later times in the edicts of popes or priests, which had been accepted as the necessary basis of all orderly society, became, with the coming of the scientific method, an offense against truth.

In our attempts to grasp the nature of the forces which explain the human story, we probably underestimate very seriously the power of the emotional urge to defy reason in favor of the instinctive or the familiar and the traditional. It was—is—no easy task for men to think inductively, "objectively," to accept conclusions which seem to demand renunciation of cherished and familiar belief, threatening to cut us adrift from secure anchorages. The triumph of the scientific attitude and method, even in the field of physical science, was no easy conquest, and has never been complete. The physicist, even in our day, has been compelled again and again to suffer something of the old pains and penalties meted out to the heretic: witness the early attitude of medical authority to the use of anesthetics, to the microbial theory, to the work of the Pasteurs.

It is commonly argued, indeed, that it is impossible to apply the method of the scientist dealing with nonsentient material, where changing and obscure passions, prides, tempers are absent, to the problems of society, where those emotions are all too obvious. If we are asking for a 100 per cent application, this may well be true. (As just noted, 100 per cent application is impossible even in the physicist's laboratory, and for long ages it could hardly be applied at all.) The urgent question now is, not whether we can get theoretical perfection in the application of reason to society, but whether we can get enough to enable us, without sacrificing the freedoms which give life value, to become secure from dangers such as atomic warfare. It is true that men have never been guided much by reason; which is why it is so important to develop reason and keep its feeble flame alight. It may be that we cannot "change human nature." But we know that we can change human behavior: the things which once excited fears or hates—goblins, devils, witches, evil eye, heretics to our religion—and prompted a certain behavior about them, no longer excite such fears or hates and prompt a very different behavior. This is one instance the more of the way in which we have brought about the change of behavior by changes in the methods of interpreting phenomena. We do not see in the external fact quite the social lesson that our forefathers saw. To that extent the way of thought which we call the scientific method has triumphed, not only in the fields of invention and technical power, increasing the physical comfort of man, and not only in lifting from our society (in the West at least) terrors as bad as those of war, the horrors of leprosy, the Black Deaths, the Plagues of London, but also in lifting from man's mind the spiritual terrors of witchcraft, sorcery, the cruelties of the inquisitors, the evil hatreds of the wars which arose from rival interpretations of the religion of mercy and compassion, when both sides were so fatally certain that they were right and that they fought for the right. The new way of thought brought about, in these fields at least, a new way of feeling, too.

Again, those changes in the product of men's minds were the result of no biological changes. Blood and glands, sinews and gray matter, remained as before. The physical tool of the brain was unaltered, but man acquired new ways of using it.

The advance toward the better way of thought has been marked by no steadily rising line: the modern democracies are much nearer to the political and legal concepts of Rome and Greece two thousand years ago than to those which prevailed in some countries now democratic two hundred years ago or less, or prevail today in many countries boastful of their democracy. The light so easily goes out and the dark can last so very long.

PART III

The Place of Power in a Free Society

CHAPTER IX

The A-Bomb in an Urban World

A NY discussion of the place of power in the organization of society must raise the question of whether the coming of the A-bomb has not eliminated the use of physical force in international relations altogether.

Take the case of Britain, which from the point of view of American security in the light of two wars, is a possibly indispensable advance post. It is a smallish island lying just off the coast of the European continent, within easy range of self-propelled bombs even as they now exist, and equally, of course, within easy range when those bombs carry an atomic war head. It is populated by nearly fifty million people tightly packed into a small area. Its people cannot hide in jungles as in Africa, nor disperse into vast spaces as in China or in Russia. Nor is its population so vast that the extermination of any considerable proportion of it is impracticable, as would be the case of an Indian population of four hundred million or a Chinese one of five or six hundred million. The whole apparatus of daily life in the island—railroads, power stations, water reservoirs, factories, sewage systems—could be wiped out in forty-eight hours after an atomic Pearl Harbor, especially if the attack were leveled, not from a base thousands of miles away, but from a base only a few hundred. Britain as a people, a greater European state, a power, would be wiped out; finished. *Kaput.*

In warfare today the idea of solemnly telling your enemy that you are going to hit him has gone completely out of fashion. It belongs to the day of the despised diplomat with his striped pants, wearing his old school tie; if, indeed, it does not belong to the code of chivalry of the now out-of-date gentleman. Pearl Harbor,

The Hague, Amsterdam, Rotterdam, Belgrade, mark much more the fashion of our time.

It is not surprising, therefore, that many now take the view that the time has passed when Britain can effectively defend her type of civilization—which is that of the Western world—by power. Her situation, it is argued, is just simply too vulnerable. Even after the Napoleonic Wars there were statesmen like Canning and Castlereagh who felt this mood that Britain had done her bit in defense of the principle of national freedom, that she could make no more sacrifices on its behalf. Subsequent events were to prove that, exhausted as Britain was in the struggle against the Napoleonic dictatorship, she could and did recover, to play a very great part in saving the West from two major assaults of authoritarian dictatorship. She was to build a new empire and to play a role in world politics which was marked by a very great expansion of the principle of national freedom and democracy.

A widespread feeling in Britain now is that if she is caught in a conflict between the Russian and the American giants, she may be ground between them, or used as an instrument by one or both. She would be the natural base for American operations against a Russian-dominated continent (as she was when the United States operated against a German-dominated one) and Russia might deem it a necessary part of her defense to see that Britain did not so become. The British base from which America would operate would be a cinder heap, a mere tool to be used for no purpose really relevant to the safety and welfare of the British people.

Quite apart, therefore, from any question of the superiority of communism or socialism over capitalism, it is, runs the argument, to the final British interest to adopt henceforth a policy of benevolent neutrality toward Russia. In the past, American anti-imperialist idealism has insisted that Britain's proper place is that of a small island bereft of empire, a sort of larger Ireland. In that case, again, say those critics, if Britain is to be just an Ireland, let her adopt an Irish policy: neutrality in America's wars. Mr. De Valera's government consistently resisted all pressure by the United States to allow its ports to be used in the second World War, as they were used in the first, as bases for the American navy. From the point of view of the peace and security of the Irish people, the policy of neutrality has paid rich dividends. Although Ireland made no contribution to victory over Germany, she has derived more profit from that victory than Britain or the United States or France, without the dreadful cost. Nor is Ireland the only state that has so profited. There are Sweden, Switzerland, Portugal.

It is an exceedingly attractive policy, not lightly to be dismissed.

Simple, but disturbing considerations, however, arise:

1. Britain may say her choice is neutrality. But the choice won't be left with her but with the belligerents. Norway, Denmark, Holland, Belgium, chose neutrality, but they did not get it.

2. The second World War came because nearly all the nations of the world, the smaller states of Europe, the United States, and even Russia, decided they would be neutral. The war ended their neutrality. If, well beforehand, they had realized that they could not, or would not, be neutral, that when the crisis came their policy would be resistance, the war almost certainly could have been averted. The war arose because their decision on this matter was too long delayed; the nations were not sufficiently conscious of how they would act when the danger of alien domination starkly faced them.

3. Hitler's power for evil, and the temptation to use his power for aggression, arose from the popularity of the neutrality idea among his potential victims in the interwar years.

4. In the military power which is now being used as the instrument of dangerous political expansion and domination, the A-bomb plays no direct part: those who have the bomb recede before those who have not.

5. The final question is whether a policy of resistance to further expansion or aggression formulated now would involve greater risk than a policy of indefinite and indeterminate retreat or non-resistance—with probable resistance, as before, at the last moment.

6. The issue would be more likely to arise if, in a struggle between Russia and the United States, Russia were to follow, in the case of the western states of Europe (including France and Britain), the policy she has followed in the case of the eastern states of

Europe, and demand the right to occupy the territory or to establish "friendly" governments in Britain in order that the country should not become a base for enemy action. In two world wars Britain has been the base of American action against the European continent. It is doubtful if Russia could from a military point of view afford to take the risk of a noncommunist government in Britain. The more that Britain becomes economically dependent on the United States, the greater, from the Russian point of view, would this risk become.

7. Russian military power is ensuring the spread of totalitarian forms of government throughout the whole of Eastern Europe—in Poland, Rumania, Hungary, Bulgaria, Yugoslavia, Albania, while the prospects of such in eastern Germany and in Czechoslovakia increase, to say nothing of China, Korea, and other regions of Asia. If the Russians fear the bomb may be used against them, the fear is not manifest in any hesitation about pushing their point of view and extending the sway of their authority.

8. The A-bomb, despite our fears, may never be used. No man can tell. If the territorial and political expansion goes on beyond a certain degree Russia would not have to take the risk of using the A-bomb, since her main task may have been accomplished without it.

To the above points, others already considered should be added: in territories actually incorporated into the Union, that part of the former population likely to prove troublesome is simply deported; the remainder kept under control by the secret police; the children and younger generation so indoctrinated as to become ardently communist.

The more indirect method employed in territories not actually incorporated in the Union has also had a great measure of success. Assume that the communist-dominated governments in Poland, Hungary, Rumania, Yugoslavia, Bulgaria, Albania, are spontaneous expressions of the popular will, and that the communist movements in France, China, Latin America, receive little help or inspiration from Moscow, it is none the less certain that all alike are extremely valuable instruments of Russian foreign policy and of the spread of Russian influence. It is obvious, for instance, that what France does in the future will in some degree be influenced by Russian interests.

No great power in the world, facing a period of possible international anarchy, would reject or throw away the opportunity thus offered to consolidate her position, a consolidation which would mean still further extension of the same general process or method.

For the West to be weak and divided is almost to compel a policy of expanding power on the part of Russia. We must judge nations by what they do. Wherever Russia finds weakness on her borders she expands in order to forestall expansion on the part of others. In the atomic world all nations are on her borders.

We have to judge the possibility of a policy of neutrality for Britain in a Russo-American war, in the light of experience. If ever there was a strong case for a policy of neutrality, detachment, isolation, independence of outside quarrels, what you will, it was the case of the United States in the two world wars into which finally she was dragged.

Here was the whole new world, which for a century had been dominated by an immensely powerful nation: twenty lesser nations led by one. This predominant power was in a position to give the lead to the twenty without too much difficulty. The new world was insulated from the old by two great oceans. The United States had proved twice in its history that it could defeat the greatest empire then existing. At the outbreak of the first World War air power, annihilating distance, making the new world a near neighbor of the old, had not yet proved itself; not a single plane had crossed the Atlantic. As to the guided missile which has still further broken isolation, that had not yet appeared by the time that the United States had virtually though not formally entered even the second war. In the view of public opinion as a whole America was impregnable, with no valid defensive reason whatever why she should enter the war. All her traditions—the counsels of the Founding Fathers, old grudges and hostilities, suspicions of Europe, especially of Britain—were against it. So deep were these feelings and convictions that even after the experience of the first World War public opinion as a whole believed that isolationism could be made to work. Indeed, the country came out of that first war determined never to repeat the experience. It was no momentary mood. It grew steadily for a decade after the defeat of Wilson's policy, until the framing and passing, by overwhelming majorities, of the intricate Neutrality Acts which were designed to make it impossible for the country ever again to take part in a European war.

Well, we know what happened. Five years after the passing of that elaborate legislation, prompted by deep and intense isolationism, the United States had dropped it all and was in the midst of her second world war. It was the more noteworthy—when we consider the case in relation to the possibility of Western Europe's detachment from a Russo-American conflict—that in the politics of the America which became on two occasions Britain's ally, there was no such thing as a pro-British party, or a British vote in America. There was an Irish vote, a German vote, an Italian vote of which Congressmen seemed frightened; and these votes were all anti-British. Congressmen who would not dare (apart from Senator Bilbo) to say a word against the Irish or the Italians or the Jews found it politically profitable to be continually abusive of the British, and particularly of the British Empire. Yet American isolationism, buttressed by a traditional Anglophobia, a detestation of British imperialism, could not stand up against the forces pushing America into the conflict, contrary to popular feeling and on the side of the "traditional enemy." America was to find herself sending her sons to defend in every part of the world that British Empire which Americans are in the habit of abusing so roundly.

In the light of such an experience what chances are there that Britain would be able, in a battle to the death between such giants as Russia and the United States, to remain outside that conflict, and "above the battle"?

It has been noted that some of the neutrals in the second World War have reaped the benefits of the defeat of totalitarianism without having to share its costs: Ireland, Sweden, Switzerland, Portugal. But these were not the only smaller states which had pursued a policy of neutrality before the war: Norway, Denmark, Holland, Belgium, Finland, Esthonia, Latvia, Lithuania, to say nothing of certain other states of Eastern Europe. Prewar neutrality did not pay them the dividends it did the more lucky ones. Their strategic position mainly explains their bad luck.

If we in the West are to adopt a policy of indefinite retreat before Russian power, we must face now just what that involves and not see it through rose-colored spectacles. Otherwise there will happen what happened before the second World War: we acquiesce in the advance of a hostile system because we insist that it is not so bad. Then when it is on top of us, we conclude that it is very bad indeed and decide to resist. But by that time the policy of aggression has attained a momentum too great to stop. The aggressor might have been deterred if he had realized earlier that he would be certain to meet the resistance he did finally meet. A policy which adopted early could have prevented war, failed of prevention when adopted late. World War II was caused by the desire of nations to cling to neutrality, their refusal to co-operate in resistance to prospective aggression. The fact does not give much hope that neutrality will prevent, or prevent involvement in, World War III.

Meanwhile, nonatomic military power is still an instrument of politics, still a major factor in determining the kind of life that men will live upon the earth and the kind of men that will live it.

It behooves us to take note of the nature and present functions of that power.

CHAPTER X

Power as the Guarantor of Reason

WATCHING the misery and suffering inflicted by men who possess power, it is not surprising that we should regard power as itself something evil. The terms of our common speech have prompted us to oppose RIGHT to MIGHT as mutually exclusive alternatives; to speak of force *or* reason; to put "power politics" in the category of criminal rackets and those who take part in them as on the moral plane of Chicago gangsters.

Yet the truth is, as we saw in a previous chapter, that RIGHT cannot be defended from criminal violence, or reason from the violence of the fanatic, without the use of MIGHT; aggression in the international field can at times only be prevented by the use of power, which can only be assembled by agreement between those who possess it, the operation immediately becoming one of power politics. In innumerable circumstances of everyday life, reason and law can only operate to settle disputes and differences, if force is used to restrain those who would oppose both law and reason as the means of such settlement, if power is used to defend the victim of violence.

Let us clarify what to many seems to be sheer paradox.

To my neighbor with whom I have (say) a right-of-way dispute, I offer third-party judgment, the court, or an arbitrator, so that the matter can be decided by third-party, impartial examination: reason. But so passionate is my neighbor's conviction of the justice of his case that he will not tolerate the interference of indifferent persons (as he puts it), with their dry-as-dust legalisms. He will cross my land, and if I interfere he will liquidate me in one way or another —the sort of situation with which the frontier was so familiar. Now, if I submit to my neighbor's threats, *or if I have no power where-*

with to resist, whether my own or that of the community in the shape of the police, the settlement of this dispute does not reach the sphere of reason at all, the sphere, that is, of sober discussion, the hearing of both sides, the impartial weighing of evidence. In the absence of my resistance it is settled by force, my neighbor's force. If reason, impartial decision, law, is to settle it, it is indispensable that I should resist. But resistance means force. I propose to use it, not to settle the dispute, but to ensure that the court or arbitrator, reason, so far as human beings can apply it, shall settle it. If I call in the policeman, representing the power of the community, he does not settle the dispute. He knows nothing about it. His job is to restrain my neighbor from settling it so that the court can. I use force to make reason possible; my neighbor to make it impossible. I use force to eliminate violence as the determining factor; my neighbor to ensure that violence shall determine it. How can we describe the issue here involved as one of "force *v.* reason," or "force *v.* law"? Without force there can be neither reason nor law. The instrument of power is used not merely for different but for opposite purposes.

We are not in this contingency confronted with mere verbal acrobatics but with a vital distinction commonly and dangerously confused, a confusion which arises largely from the power of words over men's minds, particularly, perhaps, when the words are an inadequate description of the thing they are supposed to describe.

The fact that there can be no dependable rule of law based on reason in a human community without the exercise of force, the collective force of society, to defend the individual, does not arise merely from the presence of criminal elements within a society, from the need of "repressing" the criminal. It arises even more from the need of defending the rights of the citizen against the violence of groups or parties so honestly and passionately convinced they are right that they are ready to impose their view by violence. The armed party, whether of the right or of the left, prepared to challenge constitutional processes and assert its doctrine by the armed seizure of government, became, after the first World War, one of the commonest phenomena of European politics, as it had been for a century a commonplace of Latin American and for many centuries of Asiatic politics. This is inevitable if the national community has neither the unity nor the political judgment to use its power aright. There is probably no country in the world where fascist or communist groups have so little appeal to the people as in England. Yet if in the late thirties a government of absolute pacifists, pledged to use no force at all, one that had disbanded the army and would offer no military resistance to an armed party marching on Parliament or Whitehall—if such a government had been in office, it is altogether probable that Mosley's fanatics would have attempted the coup, unless they had been anticipated by the communists. Either party, a tiny fraction only of the people, once in possession of power, would of course have suppressed political opposition, free speech, free press. Government by reason, where the people have free access to the facts and the habit of interpreting them by the kind of restrained discussion in which alone reason can operate, would have come to an end.

Far from such an occurrence being fantastically remote from experience, it is commonplace. The seizure of power by minorities has happened again and again, all over the world. Where violent minorities have prevailed, it has been, not because the majority has been pacifist, but because it has been confused, divided, subject to the appeals of emotional irrelevancies, to fits of irrationalism which the minority usually exploits.

It is true that in those years of the thirties when the policy of collective defense against aggression in the international field failed us, pacifist thinking played its part in the failure. But pacifism was adopted, curiously enough, only toward foreign aggression, not toward aggression from British parties. As this present writer had occasion to point out at the time, the first thing that would happen to a nation which had elected a government pledged to nonresistance, the refusal to use force, would be, not foreign invasion, but seizure, or attempted seizure, of the government by fascists or communists at home. What, he asked, would be the government's attitude? Would it bring the army, the apparatus of killing, into play? If it did, the position would then be that it was prepared to kill in resistance to (say) British fascism or communism, but not in resistance to foreign fascism or communism. It would be ready to take arms to resist a British fascist or communist government, but not a foreign fascist or communist government.

If the arming of political parties within the state were met by a policy of pacifism, the nation would then have to stand by and (if the arming were by fascists) see Jews expelled or segregated or maltreated, men of liberal or socialist views imprisoned, bullied, bludgeoned, bumped off, and—most importantly of all as bearing upon the success of the pacifist endeavor—children dragged into camps and schools, there to be indoctrinated with evil theories designed to make them willing tools of a totalitarian state. The prime fact we should have to face would be that that process of education would usually, almost invariably, succeed. The totalitarian state would educate a generation willing to imprison or execute its parents for the "fatherland" or the "cause"; believe it right so to do. Again, that thing has happened this last few years before our eyes; is happening now in many parts of the world. An unarmed government would be at the mercy of even a small body of patriots honestly convinced (and the honesty of fanatics is usually unquestionable) that force to "save the country," first by seizing the government and then by waging war against the enemies of the new government, at home, was not only justifiable but a bounden duty encumbent upon them. (Particularly would this be the case if they could count upon foreign help.) Having seized the schools, the churches, the press, the radio, they would make their will the people's will.

So nonresistance, or even Mr. Gandhi's nonviolent non-co-operation, would not dispose of the problem of force within the state; nor of war with other states. It would merely accentuate the truth embodied in the paradox that if brute force is not to rule our society, national or international, then force must be employed to prevent the employment of force as the instrument of decision, so that reason, open discussion, can become the instrument.

In the illustration used earlier, the means of achieving settlement by reason was assumed to be by such forms of third party, impartial judgment as are provided by an arbitrator or a court of law. But the means of reason can also operate in the form of open discussion between rival political parties, the electorate filling roughly the function of a jury in a court of law. For a government which accepts the right of peaceful political opposition to resist by force the revolutionary overriding of the constitution by armed rebellion is, despite easy derision of the paradox, to use power in order that force may not prevail and destroy reason. It defends the instruments of reason, in the form of free public criticism of government. Similarly, to use the pooled power of nations, in the international field for resistance to the state which, rejecting arbitration or peaceful settlement, wages war in order to enforce its own partial judgment, is to use power as the means of making an unforced settlement possible.

Although there has not, heretofore, been organized means in the field of international relations for ensuring the objective at which constitutional government within the nation has aimed, some similar objective has lain behind the foreign policy of certain states.

In 1914 Britain saw that, in the event of German conquest of Europe, she would be at Germany's mercy. German power would be so preponderant that no negotiation or dispute between the two countries could be conducted on equal terms. One of the disputants, the preponderantly powerful litigant, would be in a position at any moment to make himself the judge because he had the force so to do. Britain's "right to national life," her own modes of life, would be at the mercy of German preponderance. Later the United States was to feel the same menace to American national independence, alike in 1917, when it seemed probable that France would be overcome by Germany, and again in 1940, when France had been, and it looked as though Britain might be. On both occasions the purpose of the intervention was to ensure such equilibrium of power that the dictatorship of one state should not become possible. Both wars represented an effort by threatened states to ensure by their own power what in a properly organized international society would be ensured by the collective power of society. "Balance of power" has an ugly name, almost as ugly as that of "power politics." But the balance of power and some "playing of power politics" were the only available substitute in international society for the defense of that right of free discussion which is the basis of Western democracy.

Balance of power is not the inevitable accompaniment of the relations between nations everywhere, nor everywhere necessary. When in 1823 Britain proposed, and later supported, the Monroe Doctrine, she was aware that the policy would make the United States preponderant in the Western Hemisphere. The decision not to seek balance of power with the United States had indeed been reflected in an earlier Anglo-American political operation—the agreement in 1815 to leave the longest land frontier in the world, that between the British Empire in North America and the United States, unfortified; an operation to be followed a century and a quarter later when Britain invited the United States to establish American bases and strong points actually on British soil. Similarly, the Latin-American republics, though at times resenting United States preponderance (and the Monroe Doctrine), have not done so to the extent of combining to resist United States domination, as in 1914 half a world and in 1939-41 nearly the whole non-German and non-Japanese world combined to resist Germany. For a hundred years after Waterloo, Britain had all but unquestioned domination in Europe: it did not provoke a European combination against her corresponding to that which Germany twice in a single generation had provoked. And while the United States has lived, ever since she became an independent state, cheek by jowl with the British Empire on the American continent, it is quite certain that the United States would fight to the death to resist the creation of a German or Japanese state in Canada or the West Indies. Indeed, on the very eve of the American revolution against Britain, Americans fought side by side with the British to prevent the permanent establishment of France in Canada; and less than two decades after the American Revolution Jefferson was prepared to ally the United States to Britain in order to prevent France from establishing herself permanently in Louisiana. Public opinion in the United States shows more dislike of Britain than of any other nation in the world, with the single exception of Russia, which is a very recent development. And the much disliked Britain is the one nation with whom the United States has maintained close and intimate political co-operation, a co-operation marked by a fundamental identity of aim which does not exist between any other two nations.

Where there is this identity of fundamental aim, nations seek—if they are wise—not mainly a balance of power so that they can talk on equal terms, but mainly a combination of their power to promote and defend common aims. Where that identity of ultimate aim does not exist, the balance of power is a very rough and ready method of maintaining that situation of equal-term discussion. It represents resistance to a preponderance of power which might silence discussion.

Freedom has always, both within the state and as between states, rested upon the possibility of resistance to dominant power, which does not in the first instance necessarily mean physical resistance. Within the democratic nations the possibility of a check upon authority is provided for by the right of political opposition. In the international field, where there is no international government, no "superstate" developed along democratic lines, the only possibility of freedom lies in the existence of some power of resistance or a possibility of resistance to absolute power. There can be no real partnership where one partner possesses preponderant, unquestioned, and unquestionable power: that stronger member will end by dictating to the weaker, by being judge of disputes between them and insisting upon his own decision. This does not imply that the stronger is necessarily wicked or tyrannical; he may act in honest and sincere conviction that the view he is imposing is right. One of the functions which resistance to dictated decisions performs is to compel discussion and consideration of the other's point of view. Spain was no more wicked than England when the former claimed divine sanction for exclusive possession of the New World. Any real debate of the question would have been impossible if the Spanish Armada had not been defeated; the English colonies which that defeat made possible had become convinced by the end of the eighteenth century that they would never secure justice without resistance to British power; the British in their turn a quarter of a century later felt that the preponderance of Napoleon over the whole of Europe would deprive them of all means of defending British rights; the French themselves a hundred years later felt the same thing when threatened

by the preponderance of Germany; the Americans themselves a year
or two later, in 1917, were to feel the same misgiving concerning
the danger of unchecked and uncheckable power possessed by
Germany; a quarter of a century later the same thing in respect to
Japan. In all these cases, stretching back over centuries, all these
nations have felt that the possession of overwhelming power by
others with whom they may have to negotiate differences involves
a threat to rights which may be involved in those negotiations: their
security, their freedom.

The defense of the right to national autonomy was, in all the circumstances of 1914 and 1939, equivalent then to defending the
right to discussion on equal terms, and constituted resistance to tendencies which by their nature would put free government in jeop-
ardy. If we could have imagined Germany either in 1914 or as a
result of the second World War extending her authority over all the
nations of Europe, including Britain, such a German Empire could
never have maintained itself if it had permitted the right to organize
political opposition, the right of free discussion of political grievances. A centralized government of the nations of Europe would, in
order to avoid risk of disintegration, separatism, secession, have been
compelled to become totalitarian, as totalitarian, probably, as the
government of Russia, either czarist or Soviet, has always been.

It is in this sense that the war just ended was a war for the defense
of freedom.

CHAPTER XI

Methods of Power: Western and Russian

THERE have arisen of late both in the United States and Britain curious confusions concerning the facts just outlined. The confusion seems to have extended even to such able critics as Mr. Walter Lippmann. In a series of articles which appeared in the spring of 1946[1] he elaborated the thesis that a struggle had begun between Russia and Britain for the control of Germany as a means of controlling the Continent, and that the contest—six of one and half a dozen of the other, with little to choose between the parties— was one in which the United States should have no part. Mr. Lippmann indicated further that the effort of both protagonists would fail because the nations of Europe are reviving and "cannot for long be regarded as clients, wards, or prisoners of war"; and that they "will resist in all its forms the idea that they are the stakes of the diplomacy of the non-European powers." As the nations of Europe recover, they will, he implies, seek more and more the means of their old independence. America, he adds, should aid this effort toward the national independence of the continental nations, instead of lining up with either Britain or Russia in their contest for the "control of Europe," which, it is implied, represents the continuity of British policy.

Here, surely, are strange confusions.[2] For centuries it has been the main element of British policy to preserve the independence of the nations of Europe, so that its Continent shall not be dominated by any single power. If the independence of the European nations is the proper policy of the United States, it finds itself at one with

---

[1] In the New York *Herald Tribune*.

[2] This chapter is in part a reproduction of the article which appeared in the *Herald Tribune* (May 23, 1946) in reply to Mr. Lippmann.

the traditional policy of Britain. This independence was the motive of Britain's resistance to the continental hegemony attempted in turn by Spain, the French monarchs, Napoleon, the Germany of the Kaiser and of Hitler. The defensive principle involved, whatever may be urged against it, was clear enough. So long as the nations of the Continent were independent, it would not become one great power, so preponderant that Britain would be defenseless.

It was a policy of self-interest for which Britain has often in the past been bitterly criticized, on the ground that it represented the exploitation of nationalist rivalries, preventing the unity of the Continent—so the charges have run—which, say, a Napoleon might have given it, or which a Stalin might give it today.

But this selfsame principle, which has so often guided British policy, must guide the United Nations or any other international authority which hopes to survive. If we could imagine a dictatorship able to apply to the greater part of Europe and Asia the policy now applied to Poland and other nations of Eastern Europe, that would be the end of the United Nations, or world government of any kind which Western nations would accept. For one nation would then be so preponderant that it would have no need to seek its security by troublesome co-operation with others, sometimes being obliged to subordinate its opinion to theirs. It would have the power to impose its will upon any nascent international society and would constantly be tempted so to do. Britain is hardly exposed to that temptation just now; being perhaps the most vulnerable of all the nations, a superb target for atomic bombardment; while the steppes of Russia and the wastes of Siberia could take the bomb as urbanized Britain could not do.

What Western society has actually done in two world wars in resisting Germany proves that its ultimate purpose is not merely peace or one world; it could have had that by humble submission to Hitler. The purpose of any international organization which is to have the real support of its members must be to ensure to those members the maximum of independence compatible with an organized society, the right of each to its own mode of life in its own land under the social, political, and economic system it prefers.

This will mean (as the Iran case among several reminds us) sometimes supporting nations of doubtful political quality, as when Britain declared war (for the second time in a generation) upon Germany in order to vindicate Poland's right to exist as a nation, whatever the defects of Polish domestic policies. Again the British motive was obvious. If the piecemeal absorption of Europe by Germany were not stopped at the point of Poland, it would probably have become impossible to stop it at all. A Hitler, able to draw upon the resources of the whole Continent, unimpeded by British resistance, would have been able to face Russia with immeasurably greater chances of success than in fact he had in June, 1941, when Britain, though herself sorely battered, was able to offer aid and alliance to Russia. Britain was able to do this because she had rejected the repeated proposals of Germany that she should stand aside while the latter dealt with communism and the Soviets.

The discussion concerning Western and Russian policy is bedeviled by the constant use of the same words for two things often not merely different but sometimes opposite. Thus we are told that the Anglo-Americans compete with Russia for the "domination" or "control" of Europe, as though the domination which Russia exercises over the nations of Eastern Europe meant about the same kind of thing that United States domination has meant in the Western Hemisphere. Indeed, it is often argued that Russia's relationship to the governments of Poland, Rumania, Bulgaria, Yugoslavia, Hungary, is merely the application of a Russian Monroe Doctrine.

Examine it. The essence of the American doctrine is that any American republic attacked from Europe would be defended by the United States. But that has not involved normally any interference in the internal affairs or form of government of American countries. They have been entirely free, with only very occasional and temporary exceptions, to choose their own governments, their own social or economic systems, their own modes of life. To apply something like the policy of Russia in Eastern Europe to, say, Mexico, the United States would bring together in Washington a number of Mexicans of one particular political party, set up these as the Mexican Government, occupy Mexico militarily to ensure that this government was sustained, help it enforce the purge of elements likely to oppose it, deporting large numbers to, say, Alaska, extend this process to a dozen other Latin-American republics, encourage throughout every Latin-American country minority political parties favorable to the United States, its policies, and social doctrines.

This is not precisely what the United States has done under the Monroe Doctrine. There is no American-directed Comintern, pledged to promote among its neighbors American religious, social, economic, and political doctrine. The United States has never liked monarchism, colonialism, imperialism, and, in the case of some of its people, Catholicism. Yet it has left Catholicism undisturbed in Latin America, monarchism undisturbed in Canada, its near neighbor (as well as in Brazil until ended by the Brazilians), and has agreed upon undefended frontiers with Canada. During Canada's colonial days it made no demand that its governments should conform to the American conception of democracy. It recognized the right of its neighbors to be different, to have their own political, social, and economic doctrines, working out their destiny in their own way.

So with British "domination" of Europe in that "British century" during which, after the defeat of Napoleon, Britain's sea power gave her an almost unchallenged world influence. It was at the pinnacle of British power that the nations of Europe and of the world made their greatest advance toward national independence. True, at the close of the Napoleonic Wars, monarchies were restored, as in the case of France, since that seemed the shortest cut to a generally accepted legitimacy of government. But in the French overturns and revolutions of the nineteenth century neither the British Government nor British organized parties took any part whatever. This general tendency toward national freedom extended even to empire territories. Canada, Australia, New Zealand, South Africa, Ireland, became independent nations. India has followed suit. Ireland has immense strategic importance in the defense of Britain—certainly as great as that of Poland in the defense of Russia. But Britain did not make the granting of dominion independence to Ireland conditional upon "friendly governments" in Dublin, or Mr. De Valera's would not have remained all these years.

These distinctions are important, not in order to prove any mythical or mystical superiority of Anglo-Saxon modes of life or government, but in order to establish the real differences between

Russia and the West as a necessary prelude to agreement. The differences are real and deep, but not, in the view of this writer, insurmountable, if only we realize what they are. Fundamentally, they are differences concerning the proper function of power in national or international society.

The Russian view, tied up with its long indoctrinated conception of Russia as the spearhead of a new system of society destined to liberate mankind from poverty and oppression, is that the power of a government should be used to repress heretical objections to the true doctrine, to forbid political oppositions, even in its satellite states.

The Western view is rather that the function of power in a free society is the precise opposite: to ensure the right of political opposition, the right of access to the facts upon which governments base their policy, the right to discuss those facts and to oppose the conclusions drawn by government. If we could get agreement on that point and on the reciprocal freedoms of information, movement, inspection, reportage implied in it, we should have taken the first step to understandings and adjustments, which, without it, are likely to fail completely.

CHAPTER XII

The Changed Purpose of Victory

WHEN Britain and France declared war upon Germany in fulfillment of the pledge to defend Poland, the guiding purpose of the Western allies was clear enough. It was to ensure the right of nations (first, of course, each his own right) to live as national units, under the political, social, or economic system each preferred, or which its circumstances necessitated, free from external aggression or domination; free, that is, from the external imposition of alien systems.

This did not mean that nations should or could have absolute independence free of all obligation to one another. No such condition is possible in the modern world. But France and Britain fought to resist government by a dominant alien nation, the struggle gaining intensity by reason of the character of Germany, the nation then menacing the principle of national right. By 1939 Germany had become a state which virtually repudiated the right of the individual to discuss or even know the fate which authority might impose upon him.

So clearly did the political aim of security, national survival, the preservation of each nation's right to its own mode of life, take precedence over ideologies that when communist Russia became a belligerent as the result of the German attack, her aid in the war purpose was warmly welcomed by a British Prime Minister who happened also to be the head of the British Conservative Party and to have been all his life an opponent of communism. The United States was shortly to add her aid to that accorded by Britain. The two capitalist states united to help defend Russia's right to be communist, as Russia's power was to help in defending America's right to remain capitalist. Britain, in order to defend her own right to national life, had to defend France's and Poland's and Russia's.

But this conception of the war's purpose as the defense of national right, the right of each freely to choose his own way of life, gave place, under pressure from forces of the left, to a conception not merely different but opposed. The war, argued a large part of the left, was a revolution against an old and outworn economic society and should be used as the instrument of its final destruction. Arguments in that sense became prevalent on the left—as some of the following pages indicate. "The purpose of the war," declared Mr. Henry Wallace, then Vice-President of the United States, "is to see that every child in the world gets a pint of milk a day." As a statement of the motives which led to a war which began with the defense of Poland, whose social-security system and measures of child welfare were certainly less effective and thoroughgoing than those of the German state we were fighting, this is just not so. The fact that Britain gave guarantees, involving war, to the somewhat reactionary Polish state in order to uphold an international principle (which she had to defend in Poland's case in order to be able to defend it in her own) does not mean, of course, that Britain was indifferent to child welfare or other social-security measures, as her history before and since the war has proved. Her social-security system is as developed and thoroughgoing as any in the world. But her challenge to Hitler was in fact an assertion of the right of each nation to work out its social problems in its own way; and particularly in the case of Britain was the feeling strong that the challenge to Hitler constituted a defense of the right to work out social problems by the method of political freedom—by open discussion, by the criticism of an organized political opposition, free speech, free press, all the organs of free enquiry; trial and error.

The conception of the war as an instrument of world revolution, of a new social and economic order, very soon encountered this difficulty: there was no agreement among the progressives as to what the system should be. The only clear and coherent policy on that point came from Russia, who left no doubt that she regarded the Russian as the only workable form of socialism, and believed that the only dependable way of bringing it about was by the Russian totalitarian dictatorship method.

In which view much of the left in Western Europe and in the United States concurred. The relations of Moscow with the new British regime of social democracy were no better than with the preceding coalition or Conservative Government—if indeed they were not worse. Obviously if the West was to meet Moscow's views, much more than an economic change was involved. Moscow did not seem to relish the prospect that the nations of the West might demonstrate for the benefit of the Russian public that socialism could work successfully while permitting of free political opposition and criticism. If power was to be put behind the Russian conception of things it would be put against the right of an organized political opposition. The new order must deny the right of the people to know the facts upon which their government acts, the right to examine those facts, to discuss them, to criticize the conclusions their government may draw and freely present those criticisms. This is not merely a political method, the basis of free government and popular right since the very earliest times; it is also the method of establishing the truth which in the West has prevailed ever since the Renaissance. The issue is completely distorted if it is presented as one merely of socialism *v.* capitalism. The issue is really whether political and intellectual freedom shall be the instrument of social change or whether the state—the international dictatorship of the proletariat—is to use its power to impose the orthodox doctrine and penalize enquiry and discussion, whether power shall be used to defend the right of political opposition or to forbid it. This is no minor issue.

Proposals to put the power of the Grand Alliance behind some particular political or economic doctrine, instead of behind the right of each nation to choose its own doctrine, are rooted in a dangerous fallacy, fatal to peaceful social development.

Some of the confusion has arisen from the form that slogans have taken. For Wilson, the first World War was a war to make the world safe for democracy—to give nations the right to be democratic if they wanted to be and could be, secure from outside coercion. That was correct enough. But to make it a war for democracy is to change that purpose: it implies that democracy is to be imposed as Mohammed imposed his religion. As in the case of socialism, the question arises, what is the true faith? What is the "true" democracy? Moscow insists that it exists only in Russia. We in the West are disposed to insist that that is precisely where it does not exist.

Does it mean that the people as a whole shall have the right through press and assembly to criticize their government, to replace it by another springing from organized political opposition? Every child, almost, knows that these conditions of democracy do not exist in Russia or in China, and are not likely to in any calculable period. This does not necessarily mean that the majority of the Russians or Chinese greatly resent the powers which their governments exercise.

It may be that in the conditions which the rulers of Russia and China face no other method of stable government would be possible. Doubtless, the two dictators, our war allies are honestly convinced of this. But in that case it makes it vastly dangerous for us to insist that our purpose is to inaugurate democracy throughout the world. For our dictator allies would not tolerate for a moment dictation from us as to what is and is not "democratic" in their countries.

One American commentator recently, in search for some sure criterion of democracy, did indicate a test. Since a monarchy was essentially antidemocratic, any party opposing monarchy was on the face of it a better reflection of the will of the people than a party which supported monarchy. This test unhappily would make Germany, Turkey, Portugal, and Argentina, which are all republics in form, more truly democratic than, say, Norway, Denmark, Sweden, Holland, Britain, Canada, Australia, and New Zealand, which all accept a monarchy as the symbol of national or imperial unity.

It is just possible that Allied unity in the postwar period would not be greatly promoted by telling Norwegians, Danes, Swedes, Hollanders, British, Canadians, Australians, New Zealanders (to say nothing of some 250,000,000 Arab and Moslem peoples, where the monarchical tradition is even more deeply rooted than in the Western world) that before they can really qualify for partnership in the idealistic purposes of the United Nations they must destroy those symbols and traditions which have come down to them through countless generations.

If there is to be a common uniting ideology for our fifty-odd United Nations—Asiatic and European, African and American, dictatorship and parliamentary, socialist and capitalist, republican and monarchical—then it must be an ideology of tolerance and of freedom, with limits to the distrust and criticism of each other and of the governments in charge. Such restraints and disciplines, which alone can give us an ideology of unity, are not easy. They are extremely difficult. But they are the price of permanent victory and peace.

If the United Nations is to survive at all, it must recognize the limits of its powers. The last few years have revealed something of the difficulty which an experienced federal government working in the midst of its own countrymen has had to encounter in carrying out even such limited plans as those of the United States New Deal. What would have been the fate of a world government attempting anything similar on a world scale? Or if even the United States Government, with all its predominance in the Americas, had attempted it for the Western Hemisphere? If the Washington administration as the central government of the Western Hemisphere had to carry through a New Deal in all the twenty-two republics of that hemisphere, including Negro and Indian countries where the device of the vote has seldom worked, where for generations nearly every election was a civil war, and where the habit of revolution is very deeply rooted—in those conditions it is reasonably certain that a hemisphere administration would encounter insuperable difficulty. In attempting to execute the will of twenty-two such different countries and apply the new order to all, it would face the alternative, either of reducing the electoral process to a sham (as in the Russian constitution and in the Chinese practice), and of applying methods which have been common enough in Germany, Russia, and China, or of witnessing the hemispheric New Deal become a dead letter.

The real problem, moreover, of a world revolution against the old order, and the setting up of a new one would be far more complicated than imposing the New Deal on twenty-two American Republics. No one power occupies in the world as a whole the position the United States occupies in the Western Hemisphere. Europe alone includes four hundred million people, China over five hundred

millions, India four hundred millions; Africa uncounted millions—
to say nothing of the place which Russia would occupy in it all.

The situation presents us with two alternatives, one possible,
compatible with the democratic freedoms, and indeed indispensable
thereto, which in fact the neoliberals reject, though they may give
it lip service; the other which, if it succeeds, will be at the cost of
the democratic freedoms and the human decencies, and if it fails
will confront us with unutterable chaos.

A world union for peace, using collective power for the prevention of aggression, the defense of national rights, and by that fact the
defense of democracy, where it exists and may grow—all this we
know, on the basis of experience, we can have. That nations which
differ widely in economic and social structure can co-operate for
those purposes we know, because they did it during the war. But
this common action by capitalist, communist, republican, mon-
archist, by which the national freedom of each has been defended
against aggression, was possible only because the combined power
of the nations was not put behind a particular ideology or doctrine,
and was put behind the right of each to have his own ideology,
which might differ from that of his allies.

This does not mean that socialism, say, is unattainable. It does
mean that the instrument of socialism must be the independent
nation-state, and the instrument of international socialism the free
co-operation of those states, not the power of some world center.
It means, further, that the purpose of our victory should not be to
give power to the fifty-odd United Nations to bring about a world
revolution and build some brand new society on its ruins, but, as
far as is humanly possible, to make sure first of all of peace, the
prevention of aggression, by defending in common the victims of
aggression.

That surely will be task enough, and we shall be extremely lucky
if we accomplish that much.

PART IV

Ignored History

CHAPTER XIII

After Empire—What?

NOW that the British Empire is in process if not of liquidation then of profound transformation, it is well to remind ourselves of a fact which even Englishmen are apt to forget, and the significance of which is seldom faced, even by those who should be most concerned.[1]

If the British Empire had not existed in 1939 Hitler's Germany would have won the war—a fact not quite so apparent in 1939 as in July, 1940, after the surrender of France, when most of the world was persuaded that Hitler *had* won the war. The fact that he did not win does not concern merely Great Britain. It concerns everything we embrace in the term "Western civilization," the preservation of certain freedoms and social values, the survival of a certain type of free and humane society. But for the existence of the British Empire, which has so much stirred the animosity of liberals, any chance of maintaining a liberal world would have been defeated. Had there been no such empire, the antiliberal forces, represented by the power of Germany, would almost certainly have triumphed.

It is true that Britain's role in the year when she "stood alone" and mankind's debt to "the few" are often referred to. But these terms themselves are misleading and distort the significance of what

[1] A personal note here may be excused. For forty years the author of this book has been a critic of imperialism. His first book was an attack as severe as he could make it upon Britain's role in the Boer War and its jingoism. He has labored to expose the economic fallacies of imperialism. This in the interest of peace and internationalism. But the danger to those causes does not lie today in British imperialism, but rather in a failure to appreciate how the motives and forces which led to imperialism can now be rallied to the cause of internationalism; and to realize how easily in dissolving empires in the wrong way we may jump out of the frying pan into the fire.

actually happened. Britain did not stand alone. The Commonwealth and the Empire stood with her, and the United States was already beginning to furnish help (in defiance, incidentally, of the spirit of the then existing neutrality legislation of America). But for those two facts—the existence of the Empire–Commonwealth and American resources—Britain could not have stood at all. The fact that Britain stood is commonly attributed to some special doggedness or stubbornness on the part of the British, a special courage. But the British have no monopoly on courage. The French who surrendered and set up a collaborationist government were as brave as the British. But they did not show the capacity for national unity which the British displayed in that emergency; and it is the national unity which made British courage effective.

The proposition that but for the existence of the British Empire Hitler would have won the war is never seriously challenged. It is sometimes, however, pointed out that as much could be said for the indispensability of Russia in the defeat of Germany, and that the fact does not justify Russian imperialism or power politics. The objection misses the point of what we should learn from the fact that the existence of the British Empire in 1939 made the continuance of a free and liberal world possible. If Russia had not been an empire, which had expanded from a small duchy; if the sixteen republics now embraced in the USSR had all been completely independent nation-states like Norway, Denmark, or the nations of the Balkans, refusing to build up any system of co-operation even for the most elementary purposes of common survival, then of course Hitler would have been able to do to those sixteen states what he had already done to about the same number in Europe: he could have picked them off, one by one. The case against Russian imperialism is not that it has unified a great many different peoples, but that the authority thus set up is an authority of dictatorship, repression, secret police; founded upon terror and the denial of what in the West we call democracy. Government frequently becomes autocratic and oppressive (dictatorships under the forms of democracy are common in the New World). We do not argue from this, "all government is bad; let us have no government." As little can we argue that the British Empire was condemned for the simple fact of being an empire and being imperfect.

A further argument is sometimes used in an attempt to deny the quite undeniable proposition that but for the existence of the empire the antiliberal forces represented by the power of Germany would have triumphed. It is argued that had the imperially governed peoples in Africa and Asia been entirely independent, Egypt left to resist the Germans and defend the Suez Canal without the aid of British forces, that all these separated fragments would have come together to form a world federation, capable of dealing with an assault like that of Germany. The state of Europe in 1939 is itself an answer to the argument. The nations which Hitler overran so easily, applying "the simple and deadly plan of one by one," were all free and independent. Most of them had been for centuries. They were quite incapable of sufficient unity to make common resistance to Hitler. The longest period of peace and security Europe has ever known was the imperial peace of Rome[2] and the next longest that between Waterloo and 1914, when British power was predominant throughout the world.

The British Empire at the time that Hitler began his thrust embraced a population considerably greater than that of Europe, but scattered all over the world, in Europe, Asia, Africa, America. The empire was able to do for all these elements what Europe as a whole was not able to do for itself. When all criticism is spent the fact remains that India was not subject to the degree of invasion which free China suffered; the viceroy was never obliged to employ great Indian armies to fight other Indian armies, as Chiang Kai-shek was obliged and is still obliged to employ Chinese armies to fight other Chinese armies. The empire held. Its existence made possible the immediate deployment of American power as soon as the United States began to play a belligerent role. It provided not only Britain itself as the "unsinkable aircraft carrier" and as the base for opera-

[2] Friedlander writes (*Roman Life and Manners*): "Rome had stayed the endless confusions of incessant warring states; she had united peoples and dynasties into one organization of peace. . . . Hill and dale were cultivated; the mercantile marine increased, and trade between all countries. Nowhere were there wars or battles or bandits or pirates. This was the majesty of the Pax Romana. . . . All peoples prayed for the eternity of this gift."

tions against Hitler's European fortress, but bases, beachheads, springboards all over the world. Without these, the incalculable power of American industrial production could not have been brought into play.

Without the British Empire that process of fragmentation into small units of power which made it possible for Germany in so short a time to overrun or dominate the whole of the European continent would have been extended to the whole world, to the advantage of Japan as well as of Germany.

The difficulties which Britain and France encountered at the beginning of the war in wrestling with national independence will be recalled. The smaller states, such as Norway, Denmark, Holland, Belgium, knew themselves to be menaced. But having previously built up a policy of neutrality so that no plan of common action could be devised in advance, each of these states had to wait upon actual hostile action by Germany before calling upon Britain or France for aid. But to wait for the moment of actual invasion was to wait until aid could no longer be effective. The United States as well as Britain encountered the same character of difficulty in the matter of the naval bases of the Irish Free State: they would be available when German invasion had actually taken place, not before. Fortunately, although the lack of bases in southern Ireland was costly in British ships and lives, the bases of northern Ireland were available alike for the United States and Britain.

On the larger strategic field, however, fragmentation of empire had not developed so far as to make the rallying of power in opposition to the totalitarian thrust impossible. Britain possessed strong points in the Mediterranean, Gibraltar, Malta, bases for the defense of the Suez Canal, arrangements with Egypt for the garrisoning of troops. These were sufficient to prevent the Italian alliance with Germany from becoming a means of opening the road through North Africa to the Indian Ocean to the Germans. Later Malta, Gibraltar, and the Egyptian bases became available for American forces, military and naval, to defeat the German effort of the same kind.

An isolationist American critic of the early years of the war wrote that not until Britain had restored Gibraltar to Spain, Malta to Italy, evacuated her troops from Egypt, restored the Sudan to that country, given up the strong points on the Red Sea, withdrawn from Palestine, handed India over to the Congress Party—not until these steps had been completed and others which for the moment escape the writer's memory, would anyone in America believe that Britain's repentance of the sin of imperialism was sincere.

Well, some of those steps have been taken, as in the case of India. Risks are certainly involved. However that may be we may rejoice that they were delayed until the passing of Hitler.

Had dissolution taken place, shall we say, at the close of the first World War, it is quite evident that there would have been no means of preventing the European conquests of Hitler from extending to all the countries of the Near East (including Palestine) and Africa, and of preventing a junction of his forces with those of Japan in the Indian Ocean, thus exposing India to the same degree of invasion which China has actually suffered.

If Australia and New Zealand had been left to their own resources in resistance to Japanese power, if India had been as much the victim of internal strain as China has been and unable to call upon British seapower for its defense, if the lifeline through the Mediterranean had been cut in pieces, if northern Africa and Africa as a whole, including the bulge of Dakar, had been opened to German forces, then not only would Britain herself have fallen but the bases from which the enemy was reached by American power, the routes by which aid was given to Russia and to China, would not have been available. The position in that respect is plain enough, and in fact no serious strategist questions the proposition as a whole.

But a word or two should be said as to the political results which spring from the existence of the Commonwealth and the Empire.

The British community, unlike the American or the Russian, is not gathered into one contiguous territory, but is scattered over the earth at the antipodes, at Australia and New Zealand, at Canada, South Africa, and in other parts of Africa. The mere separation by sea often causes Britain to be regarded as an empire when that label would not be applied to it if it were gathered into one mass.

There is one detail of the political results of the existence of the Commonwealth which bears on the matter under discussion and which is commonly overlooked. Because Canada had accepted the vague and unwritten implications of Commonwealth membership, she became a belligerent and entered the war against Germany within a day or two of Britain's declaration of war. If she had not done this, if she had exercised her statutory right to remain neutral (as the Irish Free State did), the amazing political achievement of Roosevelt in an "administrative repeal" of the Neutrality Act and in extending as quickly as he did the aid of lend-lease to Britain; the virtual abandonment of neutrality long before formal belligerency in December, 1941—all this might have become impossible. Roosevelt's fight for intervention was often very nearly defeated: the carrying of the Selective Service Act by one vote illustrates how very near a thing it sometimes was. If the isolationists had been able to cite the fact that a "British community" like that of Canada, a part of the Commonwealth, had itself refused to join in Britain's war, it is extremely doubtful whether the degree of aid which the United States did extend to Britain long before formal belligerency would have been given. But apart from that, the aid which Canada gave in three important respects was itself indispensable to the success of the stand made by Britain after the fall of France.

After France fell, not merely the very able German General Staff, but nearly all professional soldiers everywhere, believed that Britain's surrender following that of France was only a question of time, and a very short time at that—at that moment of time, the aid of Canada was sufficient to have made the difference in favor of a decision to stand instead of one in favor of surrender. Canadian assistance was prospective as well as actual. Britain knew that if the worst came to the worst, the fleet and the government could be moved to Canada. Meantime, the training of pilots, which was difficult in Britain because of the blitz, could go on in Canada. And there was the factor already mentioned, that Canada, as a belligerent, acted as a link between American policy and Britain, notably in such details as the delivery of planes across the United States–Canadian border by the simple process of pushing them over. There were many such ways in which the actual presence of one of the belligerents opposed to Germany on the soil of North America made possible actual and prospective aid which may well have been quite indispensable to the continued resistance of Britain.

The fact that Britain could and did stand up multiplied many times the later effectiveness of American power when it was brought to bear on Germany. Britain was to become a vital American base. A certain comparison may be recalled. At a certain stage in Anglo-American relations, some Congressmen and Senators became insistent on the need for the United States to acquire a number of islands in the Carribbean as well as in the Pacific, in order to ensure the future security of America. There are two islands, however, which the events of the war show to be unmistakably indispensable to American security; one of them is Britain, which became the headquarters of Eisenhower and the base of his operations against the Continent; the other is Australia, which became the headquarters of MacArthur and the base of his operations against Japan when the latter had completed her conquest of the Philippines.

The significance of all this can be better appreciated if we could have imagined the surrender of Britain to Germany following that of France in June, 1940, and the resources—seaports, shipping, factories—of that country therefore as much within the grasp of Hitler as those of France actually became. With these added resources and his flank secured, with German power closing all the roads by which American help could reach Russian forces, the attack which Hitler made in July, 1941, upon Russia would have had a very different outcome. If Moscow had fallen, as it very nearly did, the junction of German and Japanese forces would not merely have closed India as a future base for American operations; it would have brought German and Japanese air power to the shores of the Bering Sea, and the American cities thereby within relatively easy bombing range.

If it be said that much of this is speculative, it is precisely the possibility of such contingencies arising which on two occasions in a generation have made the United States an ally of the British Empire. For, be it noted once more, when America finally did challenge the power of the totalitarians both in Germany and in Japan, she found the means of reaching those enemies in the British Empire itself. There was hardly a corner of that empire, in North

Africa, in the Near East, on the Red Sea, in India, in Australia, where American forces were not to be found. Why were they there? We know that Americans as a whole feel a deep and strong moral disapproval of the very existence of the empire. Why, therefore, did they defend it? They defended it because so to do was necessary for the defeat of forces which challenged liberal civilization, the American way of life.

The United States defended Russia, too. And now fears her. When, after Hiroshima, it was understood that Canada and Britain had or might have the secret of the A-bomb, not a soul in America was in the least disturbed. The possibility that Russia might acquire this secret has poisoned Russo-American relations ever since. Why the difference? Socialism? But Britain has a socialist government, and the success of her kind of socialism would be far more of a threat to American capitalism than the thirty years of experimentation in Russia has proved to be. The nature of the difference here displayed is worth a little examination.

After the fall of Napoleon, when British sea power enabled her to exercise a strong world influence, the result in the century which followed was the greatest extension of national freedom, of the right of each nation to choose its own way of life, that the world has ever known. There was freedom of movement and migration. Men were free to emigrate. They could travel around the world without pass-ports—except in Russia. Britain did in a sense dominate the Con-tinent of the Old World, just as the United States, aided by Britain after the promulgation of the Monroe Doctrine, began to dominate the New World. But neither Britain nor the United States used their power as Russia has already used hers. After the defeat of France in 1815, Britain did not continue the military occupation of France or the other seaboard states, did not exact that their governments should be "friendly"; did not establish a vast and omnipresent secret police, eliminate by deportation or other means the political parties hostile to her. Although the influence of Britain was used to restore the Bourbons, there was no active intervention by Britain when the Bourbons were once more deposed, or when France and other coun-tries went through the various revolutions of the nineteenth century. Similarly with the United States in its promulgation and enforcement of the Monroe Doctrine, as already noted. If Russia had confined herself to asserting over the states upon her periphery a form of suzerainty similar to that which the United States has exercised over Latin America, the freedom of the world would in no sense be menaced.

We are beginning to realize that the liquidation of an empire is no simple thing, and that done clumsily it may bring disaster on the world. It is not going to help that difficult process to be content with sweeping moral condemnations without any attempt to understand the nature of the choice which at times led to empire. The government of one country by another is at best a very imperfect method of government; but like so many things in politics, it has, time and again, been the only alternative to something worse. When the Roman Empire went to pieces it was not followed by something better but by the Dark Ages. We don't want something equivalent to happen when the British Empire dissolves. It will help us to avoid that to examine some of the forces which went into the building of that empire.

When the Spanish Armada sailed up the Channel, what were the English to do? Submit? Allow the totalitarian power of that day to establish its Gestapo, the Inquisition, in England, and accept the principle that only Spaniards were to have access to the New World? When the Armada was defeated, the Atlantic opened to English ships (like the *Mayflower*) and the eastern coasts of North America to English settlement, the struggle against Spain had to go on or Spanish power would have been reasserted and the English defeated. And Spain was succeeded by France. Britain had to defeat the French power of the eighteenth century or be defeated by it, a fact which Benjamin Franklin, among others, insisted upon to his countrymen. If Britain had suffered defeat at the hands of the French in India, she would almost certainly have been defeated in Canada, and so in the Ohio country. And a French empire would have stretched from the mouth of the St. Lawrence to the mouth of the Mississippi, blocking the expansion of the English-speaking colonies of the eastern seaboard westward, toward the Pacific.

Now all this imperialism, this struggle of England, first against the power of Spain, then against that of France, may have been utterly wrong. It may be that a finer civilization would have blossomed in the Western Hemisphere if England had been defeated by Spain and France and that hemisphere had been entirely Spanish and French. None can ever know. And most certainly, when the Elizabethan sea dogs defeated the Armada, or when Clive fought in India, or Wolfe defeated Montcalm, none of them was speculating on these things. They fought, even when their thoughts were of booty, because England had to defeat rivals or be defeated by them.

It is futile to blame Britain for acting upon an instinct of survival, not merely common to all nations, but common to all living things. What we should blame her for is, not for defeating those who, undefeated, would have overcome her, but for the misuse, to the extent that there has been misuse, of her preponderant power once it had been achieved, for bad government, for refusing to associate the governed sufficiently with the government that ruled them, or being too slow in doing it. But to lay down as an absolute principle that in no circumstances whatever must one people govern another, or self-determination be denied, would be to condemn Lincoln's denial of secession (for the purposes of self-determination) to the South, to condemn the arrangements the United States is now making for long-period controls in Germany and Japan. Such a principle would condemn the moral beginnings and foundations of the United States, which were the outcome of English imperialism.

Often the only means by which law emerges out of anarchy is for the parties or groups who have preponderant power to exercise that power for the purpose of imposing order and government, and then to allow the preponderance to develop into partnership with those over whom the power has been exercised. The historians of law have a name for the process: the development from status to contract. And such development has on the whole undoubtedly been the most constant tendency of the British Empire; so much so that today it has for the most part ceased to be an empire in the sense of a central authority governing subject provinces.

To surrender power to others before there is any assurance how it will be used, to dissolve an empire into a number of independencies, regardless of what the independencies will do, is usually to exchange the evils of empire for the sometimes very much worse evils of anarchy and chaos. The theory that as soon as nations are released from "imperialism" they will necessarily come together for co-operation is denied by all experience. The European nations which refused after 1918 to combine to meet the danger of aggression, and have consequently become its victims, were all free and independent; none of them was under imperial domination. Yet they could not learn co-operation, could not end the international anarchy. Not in the thousand years that succeeded the fall of Rome have they managed as a group of independent states to achieve the unity which they possessed under the empire. The nations which once formed the Hapsburg Empire, and whatever the oppression they suffered at the hands of Vienna, at least managed to avoid war with each other, have not today a peace which is more dependable than that which they had under the Hapsburgs.

While experience shows clearly enough that dissolution of all the ties of empire gives no assurance that, after dissolution, the component parts will come together in some form of nonimperial co-operation, experience gives a great deal of justification for the belief that imperial ties can be much more easily transformed into voluntary co-operation if there is no complete rupture. This indeed is the story of the British Commonwealth, a story which the British people and government have shown great capacity in not telling to the world—or to themselves.

Of course there have been grave faults in the government of the colonies. There have been grave faults in the government of Britain and France and the United States. If we can demand abdication, irrespective of what may follow, simply on the ground that the administration has revealed defects, then we are indicting not imperialism or colonialism but the whole principle of human government. Furthermore, merely to withdraw from colonies not at present ready for self-government would not lessen financial exploitation by the whites. It would in most cases very greatly increase it, and we should return to earlier conditions under which white traders and concessionaires, by means of bargains with local chiefs and sultans, obtained native approval for a degree of exploitation which modern imperial control, with all its faults, does a great deal to restrain.

The UN would do it better? Which brings us back to the original question whether the consequences of the dissolution of existing political organizations, some of which have lasted centuries, would promote or retard the foundation of the world authority. And, as we have seen, on that point experience is not altogether favorable to the answer which critics of empire seem to expect.

Part of the reason why the process of deimperialization within the empire has been so little realized by the world at large is that on the whole, since the American Revolution, it has taken place without large-scale war. It has been mainly a peaceful evolution. The freedom for which the thirteen colonies had to fight has been achieved by the Dominions of Australia, New Zealand, and Canada, at least, without fighting. If there had been wars and Declarations of Independence, or even the agitations and troubles which today mark India, the world would have heard a great deal about it and would understand better that these nations are independent, far more independent than they would be under any scheme of world federation. To the seven existing Dominions the British Government is doing its best now to see that India will add two new Dominions, although it will not oppose the decision of complete dissociation from the Commonwealth.

Britain has never set herself to maintain an unchanging imperial status quo. Ever since the beginnings of the empire, it has undergone constant change. The problem is to ensure that the change and the development take a form which will maintain the unity and co-operations so direly needed for the preservation of those freedoms for which two world wars have been fought, will ensure that the ending of the empire, which has been going on for about three hundred years, does not leave the world with any result similar to that which followed the ending of the Roman Empire, and mark the beginning of a new Dark Age.

A final note seems indicated. Any discussion along the above lines in America is apt to be closed by the question: "Do you then regard the American Revolution as a mistake? Yes or no?"

The question is of the order of the old forensic catch: "Have you left off beating your wife? Yes or no?"

Whether, abstractly considered, the American Revolution was a mistake or not, it was inevitable, for the reason that independence was immeasurably to be preferred to the only other available alternative: continued subservience in many matters to a distant government (distant with eighteenth-century distances), falling more and more into incompetence and corruption. For a long time many Americans (including Franklin and Washington) wanted to avoid complete rupture (Franklin suggested a solution somewhat along the lines of present-day Dominion status) but London's unwisdom made agreement impossible.

Let the above question be put in another form: "Would it have been better if Britain had been ready in the eighteenth century to accord to colonies the degree of independence accorded in the nineteenth century, and had made of the whole English-speaking world a federation somewhat on the lines of the present-day United States, with all having the same rights as the mother state?" Put in that form the answer to the question is yes. For the event would have brought immeasurably nearer that system of world federation toward which we are now so painfully and so belatedly struggling.

CHAPTER XIV

What Makes a Nation Fascist?

W HY is not Britain fascist? Or, if you will, why did she not remain neutral in 1939 like other great states, Russia, the United States, or like all the smaller states, Sweden, Switzerland, Ireland, Portugal, and, until they were attacked, Norway, Denmark, Belgium, Holland; or why did she not make a bargain with Hitler as did Russia; or become a satellite of Germany like Spain; or why, when she saw that the game was probably up in 1940, did she not follow France into surrender and set up a government of collaboration (as did France) based on the emergence of the famous Cliveden Set, of which we heard so much at the time, and which was supposed by so many Americans and some English to rule Britain?

Why, in other words, was Britain the only great state in the world that did not follow any of those policies, one or another of which became the policy of other states? Why did she neither remain neutral nor wait to be attacked before challenging Hitler, nor make a bargain with him when things looked black?

If these questions seem a bit far-fetched, the reader would do well to remember that they are concerned with forces we must take into account in guiding future policy. Unless we can answer them, we do not know where we are strong, where we are weak; how we may best avoid the kind of situation which might have arisen in the world if Britain in 1939 and later in 1940 had adopted any of the policies just indicated—neutrality, bargain with Hitler against Russia, surrender, collaboration, or, owing to an earlier and accelerated deimperialization, had found herself in the position, say, of a Spain or an Ireland.

After the fall of France in 1940 a certain eminent American was heard to declare: "How thankful will our children and the children of all free men be that the Atlantic today is still held by the friendly hands of Britain." But what made the hands friendly hands? Why were they not the hands of a very weak state—a sort of larger Ireland—or hands which were friendly to Germany, like those of Spain, a country which is also the motherland of many republics on the American side of the Atlantic, occupying an area very much greater than that occupied by the United States? It was no law of nature, of gravity or atmospheric pressure, which had prevented Britain from going the reactionary and totalitarian ways of past or passing empires like Portugal, Spain, Turkey; or indeed of new and expanding empires like that of Russia, which at the time that the American spoke was in partial alliance with Germany.

The commonly accepted dogma among so much of the interwar left was that capitalist Britain's enemy in the next war would inevitably be Russia. The nature of capitalism dictated it. The reader will recall the arguments.

Ruled as Britain had been in the interwar years by governments that were capitalist, conservative, imperialist, the center of a great empire from which the capitalists were supposed to be drawing their main profits, she found herself faced by a great socialist state, "The Fatherland of Socialism," to whom socialists in every quarter of the earth did homage, and in whom they found inspiration. It is true that, in the second decade of the interwar years, the Labor Party did not accept the view that Britain's coming enemy was Russia because that party was by no means a Marxian party nor even altogether a socialist one. But nonetheless the John Stracheys and others were writing books to prove that fascism was the last throw of capitalism, that fascism found its economic resources often in international finance, and much more to the same effect. Indeed, there is no reason to write in the past tense in this matter. Not merely up to the day of Churchill's offer of alliance to Russia was the thesis maintained, among a great deal of the left, that the war would be switched and we should find Britain making a deal with Hitler to attack Russia, but at this writing, in 1947, commentators and authors galore accept the general assumption that it was

Churchill's purpose then as it is now to crush Russia. Not a few of the same commentators—including, of course, many commentators in Russia itself—assert that the Labor Government is about as imperialist as its predecessor. British imperialism is still, in 1947 America, the target of the right, represented by Colonel McCormick, of the left by Mr. Henry Wallace, and of the center by a variety of Anglophobe Congressmen. A new feature of this general charge of aggressive movements by the capitalist states against Russia is the "rebellion" of the members of Parliament, who, bitterly critical of Mr. Bevin, insist that he is allowing himself to be dragged at the heels of Wall Street and American capitalism generally bent upon war with Russia.

By all the leftist criteria Britain ought to have been fascist. Her constitution still retained its feudal form; many privileges had remained undisturbed. She was not even republican. She retained not merely her monarchy but a hereditary House of Lords. When she made the choice to oppose Germany she was under a Conservative Government, and one in which capitalist influence was supposed to be very strong. Its head was a businessman, a Midlands industrialist. The make-up of the country was normally described as capitalistic. The conditions were under constant fire from socialists and more revolutionary-minded critics, prepared to prove that the privileged classes of the old order were all-powerful, that the beneficiaries of that order permeated the church, the administration of law, education, setting up, as a result of the "public" schools, the domination of the old school tie. The press was similarly dominated, and supposed to be drifting toward a series of capitalist monopolies. The charge sheet of crime was indeed a crowded one, the record positively shocking.

And then, of course, there was the empire, and nearly all the evils that were presumed to go therewith: the creed of the white man's burden, inequality of racial rights, sahibism . . . The very existence of the empire appalled the progressives, especially in America. Such things as the guidance of four hundred million people in Asia by a small island thousands of miles away were regarded as a shocking and intolerable anomaly.

Compare all this with far more "progressive" constitutions elsewhere in the world. Germany had got rid of not merely one monarchy but a round score, and had introduced a constitution which won the encomiums of the progressives of the world. Spain had not merely got rid of her monarchy, she had got rid of her empire. Russia, of course, had not merely liquidated the monarchy but also the bourgeoisie, the professional classes, and the whole economic system over which the czarist order had presided, the achievement representing perhaps the most complete, radical, thoroughgoing revolution in the history of the world. France, of course, had a long tradition of revolution, of democratic revolt. The republic of 1939 was the third republic, there having previously been many other forms of government succeeding one another in quick succession, while the life of governments set up under the constitution of the Third Republic was usually only a few months. On the other side of the Atlantic were twenty Latin nations that had overthrown a previous regime by revolutionary action of one kind or another and were all established as republics with correctly democratic constitutions, devised by experienced constitution-makers, by men of progressive and usually revolutionary thought.

If the ironic note has crept into this, it has not been intentional. There are many and serious evils not only in the institution of empire but in Britain itself, where conditions have often fallen very far short of the ideal toward which men should constantly strive. Life in England is at numberless points cursed with all the defects that go with a sheer mulish refusal to change old habits, adopt new, or to disturb the smooth surface of life (underneath the changes are often deep and significant). As to the evils of imperialism, this present writer has spent much of his life indicting them with all the severity of which he was capable.

But the purpose of this analysis is to establish the order of vital need in the matter of social values, canons of behavior in a world where our only final security against extinction in conditions of unimaginable horror is a capacity to agree on what comes first, what is of first importance, that is, and what second; on our ability to put first things first and to act together in so doing.

Now in 1939 most of the nations of the world—despite the communists, some socialists, the isolationists of the right and of the left—had no doubt whatever as to what came first. This was true not merely of the world of Western Europe and of the European society of the Americas; it was true of much of Asia. For China knew invasion much as did France, and knew bombardment much as did Britain. Most of the world wanted to resist its possible subjugation to what might become a universal power which, once fairly established by the overthrow of those who were resisting it, would impose on mankind a certain type of society and life, a complete subjugation to totalitarian dictatorship.

This dictatorship came very near indeed to accomplishing its purpose (it is necessary to keep reminding ourselves of that fact). The debate as to who defeated it could go on to the end of time because many defeated it. It is like arguing which leg of a three-legged stool really holds it up. If any leg is missing, the stool falls down. The fact which concerns us at the moment is this: (a) if the indispensable leg which Britain represented in the early summer of 1940 had collapsed, the stool of Western civilization would have fallen; and (b) it held up largely for the very reasons which the progressives, the leftists, the revolutionists, the fanatical anti-imperialists so violently condemn and find so unquestionably and so completely evil.

Again, it was not courage which saved Britain; of that quality the French had as much. Nevertheless, the French surrendered, and not merely surrendered. Though continued resistance on the soil of France had become physically impossible owing to the German military advance, there was an alternative open to France which was not impossible at all: to move the French Government to North Africa, the French fleet to British and Mediterranean ports, and to continue the war in that form as so many of the smaller states did. What the Free French under De Gaulle did as a separate group could have been done by France as a nation. If it had been done the long tale of bloodshed, destruction, hate, chaos would almost certainly have been immeasurably shorter.

As we now know, this decision was very nearly made by the French Cabinet and was lost by only a very few votes therein. It would not have been lost, and the Pétain government of collaboration would not have been established, if the political situation of France had been somewhat different. But there were, as we know, deep internal divisions and stresses in France. French historians of all parties are agreed on this; they differ only as to what the divisions were. The *haute bourgeoisie*—those two hundred families of whom we heard so much before and during the war—presumably preferred Hitler to the communists. The communists themselves were even then, at the outbreak of the war, very powerful. They have since become more so. But even in 1939 they had seventy-two members in the Chamber of Deputies, and up to the time of the surrender in June, 1940, were as a party strenuously opposed to going on with the war, which they declared to be a mere imperialist adventure of the capitalists, in which the proletariat had no interest. (The somersault in which this doctrine was completely reversed did not take place until a year later, after Russia was attacked.)[1]

In other words, what enabled Britain to stand up, after France had not merely fallen but had refused to go on with the war from North Africa in the conditions just indicated, was not that the British had more courage than the French but that Britain had more political unity. Without that unity the existence of the Channel as a tank trap could not have saved her. If in Britain there had been four or five major parties contending for power; if there had been seventy communists in the House instead of one; if communist intransigent opposition to the war had infiltrated into all the unions and into the Labor Party itself, and had induced that party, when Churchill took power, to refuse co-operation with him;

[1] It is no part of the purpose of this analysis to enter into a discussion of such facts of French life and journalism as those revealed by Henry Torres in his book, *Campaign of Treachery*, the story of the strange ease with which the press of France was corrupted before and even during the war by both Germany and Italy. Two comments, however, by Percival Knauth who reviewed this book are worth noting. Mr. Knauth (New York *Times*, August 30, 1942) suggests that an additional chapter might have made it clear how "Germany, in the traditional and frequently admired French characteristic of always being 'anti' somebody or something, found the crevice into which she could drive the wedge that split the nation wide." This, with the multitudes of competing papers, made it possible for Abetz, so Mr. Torres says, "to prepare the 'miracle of Munich' by spending, between May and October of 1938, the greater part of a budget estimated at nearly 350,000,000 francs allocated by the Fuehrer for 'work' in the field of international opinion."

if the Cliveden Set (whatever that was) had played in Britain the role the "two hundred families" (whoever they were) had played in France; if the wearers of the old school tie had really been concerned only to defend their special privileges[2] (as so many leftist critics had for years contended and some critics contended even during the war); if, perhaps most important of all, there had been no Commonwealth and no Empire (as noted already), then quite certainly Britain would have followed the example of France. Instead, the socialists and the labor men for five years worked as a team side by side with tories, under the premiership of a capitalist-imperialist-conservative, and the capitalists and the old-school-tie men showed no tendency whatever to prefer Hitler to the possible future victory of a Socialist Labor Party.

But this decision to reject any sort of deal with Hitler was not fated in the material order of things. It depended upon the decisions, the judgment, the wills of certain men at certain definite moments. Had judgment been twisted a little the other way, even perhaps momentarily—for there were crises after crises when wrong judgment would have been so fatally easy—then the example of France might have been followed.

As already noted, the decision of France not to go on with the war from North Africa was itself an example of the near thing, of how a little more or a little less might so greatly have changed the outcome. The shift-over of two or three votes from one side to the other in that fatal cabinet meeting that resulted in the coming to power of Pétain, Laval, and Darlan would have changed the whole course, not merely of the war, but of the postwar world.

No generalizations are more elusive nor commonly more misleading than those concerned with national character. That such a thing does exist seems probable; just as we know that a particular

[2] At the 1946 conference of the Labor Party a group had criticized the presence of so many public-school men, the product of Eton and Harrow, in the public services. They should, insisted the critics, be eliminated, liquidated, in favor of those of proletarian background, unimpeachable political orthodoxy. In reply Bevin reminded his critics that when the Battle of Britain was being fought, "we did not object to the presence of boys from Eton and Harrow in the RAF; nor did the Labor men want to throw them out," and added reflectively, "By God we did not." Bevin, who at times has a little habit of repeating a phrase, remarked again slowly, "By—God—we—did—not."

province or neighborhood acquires an accent of speech quite peculiar to itself. The differences are sometimes most marked. How do they arise? No one knows. But they are a fact.

Certainly standards of national behavior, what we regard as good, and what as bad, what "isn't done," are deeply affected by the influence of certain men, an influence wielded through leadership of one kind or another. The most determined of economic determinists would probably agree that if Lenin and his colleagues had never been able to reach Russia by means of that famous sealed railway carriage provided by the Germans, the story of the Russian Revolution would probably have been very different. The influence of such men as Lenin, Stalin, of Marx of whom they made a prophet (as much a prophet for most Marxists as Mohammed is for Mohammedans), has, despite all doctrines of the economic interpretation of history,[3] been obviously very great. To say as much does not condemn one as "accepting the great-man theory of history." Labels of that kind are usually quite misleading.

If in justice one must recognize the influence of Marx, Lenin, Stalin on the course of history, no less must one recognize that of Churchill. It was Major George Fielding Eliot who once, speaking of Churchill, said something to this general effect: "If the courage and faith of that man had wavered and faltered just for one hour of all the critical hours through which he had to live in the war years, the whole course of Western civilization would have been altered, and altered disastrously." Yet it is necessary to concede this much to the opponent of the great-man theory of history: if Churchill's influence was what it was, it was because he reflected in his person so many of the qualities of his countrymen. Leadership implies a willingness to be led on the part of those who follow, a capacity to recognize the leader when he appears, and to reject the mis-leader.

The election of 1945 is sometimes accepted in America and elsewhere as a "repudiation of Churchill and all he stood for," as one American commentator put it. The facts even of the election do

---

[3] A certain cynical French statesman once remarked of a Marxist friend: "He is now engaged in writing a book on the economic interpretation of the Immaculate Conception."

not justify such a verdict as already noted. The simple electoral fact is this: the Labor Party did not poll a majority of the votes. They polled 48 per cent. Had the voting been by proportional representation, nearly a hundred liberals, holding the balance of power between the two parties, would have been returned, for the Labor Party majority would have been small. There are curious anomalies. While fourteen "national" liberals were elected by three-quarters of a million votes, it took two and a quarter million to elect eleven straight liberals. The motto of the Churchill family is *fiel pero desdichado*—faithful but unfortunate. Those curious electoral anomalies might have worked for Churchill. They worked against him.[4]

We have to take these things into account if we are to estimate not merely Churchill's place in the history of England and the world but the nature of that revolution which the election does in a sense represent. If revolution is the word, it is revolution in the English manner. It has come about, one of the chief labor spokesmen declares, because the middle class has come over to labor—the technicians, lawyers, doctors, schoolteachers, university professors, businessmen, journalists, army officers, members of the House of Lords. The class war has become a class co-operation in a sense and in a degree which Marx not merely did not foresee but which he insisted was impossible. History for him was class conflict. The very classes which in the Russian Revolution were so largely and so ruthlessly liquidated are precisely the classes to which the British Labor Party owes much of its power. The Labor Prime Minister is a product of the English public school and of Oxford; the Labor Chancellor of the Exchequer, public school and Cambridge; the Labor President of the Board of Trade, public school and Oxford; the Labor Lord Chancellor, *idem*; the Labor Privy Seal, Cambridge. (These, it is true, are not newcomers to the party. The class co-operation as opposed to class conflict goes very deep indeed into English history.) It is no new thing, of course, for revolution to be made from the top by intellectuals and men

[4] The estimate of Churchill which follows is from a review of Churchill's collected speeches, *The Dawn of Liberation*, which appeared in the *Saturday Review of Literature*, August 4, 1945.

of wealth, aristocrats. (Revolutions are usually so made.) It is a new thing, and a very English thing, for the rank and file of the revolutionary party to include great sections of those classes, to absorb and amalgamate them into itself. This has meant not merely "revolution by consent"—consent, that is, of those against whom the revolution was presumably directed; it means that socialism may be made compatible with those political freedoms and civil liberties which Britain, more than any country in the world, has known how to preserve. Clement Attlee, too, is an Englishman in that tradition. He installs no guillotine; nor does he want to put his colleagues of yesterday into concentration camps. When it is said, as it is often said, that Attlee is no moving orator, we may take it as evidence that he is not moved—as some of his colleagues may be—by doctrinal passion, but is conscious, by long years of contact both with poverty and with politics, that the price of welfare is work and patience. The task before him is not the task which faced Churchill. The Prime Minister of yesterday had so to move his countrymen that they would be ready to die and see their children die in order to preserve freedom at all. It is Attlee's task to use freedom for the purposes of welfare; to work out changes by humdrum, dull details; to reconstruct, reorganize.

Commonly, those who try to do justice to Churchill speak of him as a great "war" leader, a man of bull-dog courage, helping his people to show the same courage, but beyond that no friend of democracy. For a year or two now, "progressives" both here in America and in England have at times referred to him as one might refer to Colonel Blimp in the flesh (also a man of courage and patriotism) fighting the war just to preserve the empire and the privileges of his aristocratic caste, romantically captivated by monarchies, "a sort of glorified boy scout," as one eminent progressive phrased it.

If that were true it would be a severe reflection, not merely upon the political instinct and judgment of the British people and Parliament who put him in power and gave him for five years such loyalty, admiration, and affection, but also a severe reflection upon the labor leaders who for five years sat in his cabinet under his leadership and shared responsibility for his policies. Was the best

that Britain and all its parties, including the Labor Party, could do
in the way of leadership in its darkest hour facing all the fury of
the enemy, a "glorified boy scout"? In fact, despite the exigencies
of an electoral contest, no labor leader who has had any opportunity
of judgment at all denies the quality of authentic greatness in this
man. Harold Laski—no tender critic, with no reasons to be—
declared on the morrow of the election returns: "Churchill, even
in my socialist view, has been a very great statesman." No one
whose opinion is worth a straw thinks otherwise.

Let one fact illustrate. When Churchill took office the survival of
a virtually disarmed England depended upon ample help from the
United States. It was Churchill's business to get that help from a
country still isolationist, still in so many of its sections bitterly anti-
British, extremely suspicious of tories, suspicious of aristocrats,
suspicious of imperialists. Churchill happened to be British, Tory,
aristocrat, imperialist.

When the *Saturday Evening Post* was still in its isolationist phase
it had a leading article running to a page and a half, entitled "The
Saving of England" and sketching, by quotations from Churchill's
own speeches, the development of his relations with Roosevelt and
the United States. The article ended with this paragraph:

There, in Mr. Churchill's grand words, is the story of the evolution of
American foreign policy as if you were reading it in a mirror; the story
of how the United States became involved the second time in a war that
was Europe's business—and a record of the most amazing single-handed
feat in the whole brilliant history of British diplomacy.

We shall not get to the heart of Churchill's service to his country
and mankind unless we give some rational answer to a question
which is fundamental in this context and yet which is not answered
because it is virtually never asked, this question: "Why did Britain,
under the leadership of the most brilliant Tory and imperialist of
modern times, deeply hating communism (and never disguising it),
reject alike fascism, all deals with nazism to destroy Russia, all
offers for collaborationism, all appeals for surrender?" Such a
question is usually brushed aside with impatience. "Of course,
Britain could never make a deal with Hitler." But why? France,

France of the republics and the revolutions, of a powerful Communist Party, not only could but did. Parliament, the press, nearly all the institutions of Britain, are dominated, we have been told, a thousand times this last twenty years, by the old school tie; by Blimpery; by capitalism, aristocracy, wealth, imperialism; by a Tory influence embodying all those evils. Surely a "natural" for fascism. And then to cap it all, a conservative imperialist who happened also to be the greatest political orator of his generation, who manages somehow to make his words as immortal as those of Shakespeare, a glamorous and popular national figure, takes charge. Surely now would be the chance of the ruling class, the Cliveden Set, the City, all of whom (so we had for so long been told) hated the prospect of reform at home so much more than they hated Hitler, and who indeed (again we had been assured) were desirous of encouraging Germany to destroy Russia. It would not have been difficult for an astute politician and a great orator to make Pétain's case for England, to urge that if republican and revolutionary France could accept collaboration in the Hitlerite new order, if communist Russia could undertake a nonaggression pact with Hitler, and if communists the world over, and many socialists (including many in the United States), were condemning the war as ruthless and unjustifiable capitalist imperialism—then surely Britain could join Russia in coming to terms with the new order, the wave of the future.

But that is not precisely what this Tory imperialist did. It is not true to say that it was just this one man who kept Britain in the war after France had surrendered and while yet Russia was still keeping her pact with Hitler. No man could have done it, but for certain qualities in the British people, a certain code and scale of values to which they hold. But it is probably true to say that he alone of living men could have rallied those qualities in time, held his people to them during long years of torment, and made of them, finally, that instrument of human freedom which they have proved to be. Again, it was not merely courage, in Churchill or the people, though nothing could have been done without courage. It was courage expressed in a national unity which rose above divisions of party or of doctrine. Thrust by destiny into a key position at a crucial moment, he filled that position as almost certainly no other living man could have done, because the values which make England were incarnate in his mind and character; and to that fact all Britons of every creed and party reacted.

When Churchill asked the labor leaders to take office under him, they instantly agreed. Bevin the former truck driver, Morrison the former errand boy, did not boggle because they were to work for years side by side with the Tory grandson of a duke. England was saved because Churchill was able to show such men that Tories are not necessarily at all times the enemies of the people, that there are motives which can rise above class interest and party doctrine. Englishmen have always recognized this truth—it explains why, without civil war for three hundred years, England has made greater advances in freedom and in welfare than other countries, not less fortunately placed, where revolution can be said to be almost endemic. A readiness to recognize that the other fellow may be partly right, that because he is different he is not necessarily an enemy, that in human society there must be give and take and toleration—these are English qualities. If they had not been present in the common people of England, Churchill would have been powerless to save his country—and theirs. But he had just the gifts which enabled him to make those qualities come alive at the time they were most needed.

Foremost among those gifts was the gift of expression, which is literature. His words are as simple as those of the Bible, or of Lincoln, and as moving. They have the force of great poetry, which they are. There have been poets who have written of men of action. Churchill is a man of action who is his own poet. Listen:

And now it has come to us to stand alone in the breach . . .
Bearing ourselves humbly before God, but conscious that we serve
  an unfolding purpose,
we are ready to defend our native land.
Here in this strong City of Refuge,
Which enshrines the title deeds of human progress
and is of deep consequence to Christian Civilization,
we await undismayed the impending assault.
The whole fury and might of the enemy must very soon be turned
  on us.

We are fighting by ourselves alone;
but we are not fighting for ourselves alone.
Hitler knows that he will have to break us
in this little island or lose the war.
If we can stand up to him, all Europe may be free,
and the life of the world may move forward
into broad, sunlit uplands.
But if we fail, then the whole world,
including the United States,
and all that we have known and cared for,
will sink into the abyss of a New Dark Age
made more sinister, and perhaps more prolonged,
by the lights of a perverted science.
Let us therefore brace ourselves to our duty,
and so bear ourselves,
that men will say, . . .
"This was their finest hour."

Because in the strange oscillations of mass opinion there are some, both in Britain and in America, today writing books to prove that Churchill's influence has been evil throughout, it may be well to recall what was the general and accepted view in all quarters in America when he stood in the breach. An account of the *Lives of Winston Churchill,* written by Charles J. Murphy and John Davenport, begins thus:

The German war, for which Winston Churchill rallied civilization, is over, and now this Englishman stands forth as the last truly great man of the Western world. Among his contemporaries no one else has understood so well or expounded so eloquently or defended so fiercely the conception of a "decent, tolerant, compassionate, flexible, and infinitely varied society" which is the free state. He was among the first to see the holocaust making up and the only statesman with the courage to tell the unpopular truth that the "stakes . . . are mortal." With all Europe lost he held on until Russia was adventitiously drawn into the struggle and until the New World slowly swung "to the rescue and the liberation of the Old."

Mark Sullivan wrote:

Know, reader, that you have seen greatness in our time. When on your radio you heard Winston Churchill in his hour of victory you were listening to one of the authentic great of history.

It would be a pity to lack awareness of this, to suppose you must turn to Gibbon and Plutarch to find heroic characters and exalted drama, to fail to realize that before our living eyes is the grandeur of action and stature of personality as great as any that history provides. It would be tenable, indeed, to use the superlative and say that Churchill's greatness is unexcelled. If only by the immensity of the arena in which he spoke and fought, Churchill's part in this world war reduces the classic figures of Rome and Greece to the relatively inconsequent stature of actors in drama of minor scope.

Greatness was within him. What brought out its finest form was the stark descent upon him of the tragic moment when England had to stand alone. The fall of France in 1940 created the occasion at once for Churchill's greatness to emerge and for the momentous effect it was destined to have on civilization.

Read those words of Churchill as of the dark days of 1940 and early 1941. Then realize that in the slow unfolding of time Churchill was destined to announce on May 8, 1945:

"Yesterday morning at 2.41 A.M., General Jodl, the representative of the German High Command, signed the act of unconditional surrender. The German war is therefore at an end. . . . God Save the King!"

Observe the contrast between Churchill's moving eloquence when desperate danger was upon him, his matter-of-factness when victory came. That—to be unmoved by triumph, but to be moved magnificently by struggle and danger—that was part of Churchill's greatness. Both were spontaneous reactions of his personality. When disaster threatened, he did not need to summon up courage; courage was as much a part of him as his arteries. Churchill will be quoted as long as Shakespeare. Within the scope of the subjects upon which both wrote, the man of action was not inferior to the poet. . . . But what Churchill said was actual. It was taken down in shorthand. Churchill was the fighting leader, and was his own poet. Shakespeare's battle cry was generated in the heat of imagination, Churchill's in the heat of action and responsibility. As between the two—what Shakespeare imagined in his remote and sheltered study and what actually poured out of Churchill as he breasted the enemy— Churchill's words have the greater reality and the truer eloquence that goes with reality.

What we have seen, not merely in the war but as a characteristic of English political development through the centuries, is the capacity to put a limit to rivalries based on differences of political opinion. The Englishman, in political practice, at least, does not give the immense importance to social theories and the distinctions between them given by Latin peoples, who find it necessary to create so very many parties to express the various differences. Doctrine is not in England so all-important.

This tolerance of contrary opinion is distinctively a British characteristic. A year or two since, Mr. Herbert Morrison published a collection of his more recent speeches.[5] In an introduction he deals with the effect upon international relations of the policies which would be introduced after the war. He foresees that the British would accept an extent of economic planning which Americans would not, but utters a caution against the idea that because of this difference the two countries are therefore destined to drift apart. He insists that the very first lesson which we must learn is how countries of very different economic and political structure may continue to co-operate for purposes which are common despite the differences. "It is quite certain," he writes, "that the nations of the world will present an extraordinarily varied picture of many different forms of economic society. If this is to prove an obstacle to rational world order, we may indeed despair." The future will demand "an atmosphere of tolerance and of understanding—a readiness to accept the fact of difference between nations and to comprehend what those differences really are—so that there is no risk that methods unlike one's own will appear as perversions of the one and only truth, or as stubborn forms of original sin to which foreigners are especially subject."

It is significant that Morrison should put this point in the very forefront of what he has to say. The need for its emphasis is all too evident.

In an "Introduction for American Readers" for this same book Morrison writes:

Genius is a big word, but what I think is meant is that the whole of British political history, since the country was a unity at all, has been a strenuous and persistent struggle to reconcile the principle of liberty with the principle of order—to solve the fundamental problem of political life and growth . . . otherwise there is no explanation of nearly nine

[5] *Prospects and Policies*, by the Rt. Hon. Herbert Morrison, New York, A. Knopf, 1944.

hundred years of continuing and developing national solidarity, marred by an exceptionally small amount of civil conflict, of which indeed there has been none worth mentioning for three hundred years.

Herbert Morrison, son of a policeman, wearing no school tie, beginning his career as errand boy to become Secretary of State for Home Affairs, member of the War Cabinet, instrument of that national unity without which England could never have stood up against the nazi hordes, and subsequently Lord President of the Council, is in his own person and career no bad example of embodiment of that political genius upon which the maintenance of freedom depends.

The realities of English conditions are somehow subject to strange distortions, particularly, perhaps, in America.

Not long since in a talk at the faculty club of a Middle Western university, a certain professor was showing more than a little anti-British feeling, though professors—especially those of the social sciences—are as a rule friendly to Britain. I asked him why he felt that the power and influence of Britain were not on the whole good.

"It ought to be plain why an American feels as I do," he replied. "In this country we stand for the common man against all forms of privilege; for equality, republicanism, the independence of peoples. And what do we see in Britain? Monarchism, feudalism, a hereditary House of Lords, an established church, empire, colonialism, caste, so that a man born in a lower class remains there his life through. Frankly, it sometimes turns the stomach of a free American."

Of course, views such as these are still expressed by a certain type of American politician, still current in newspapers. They were common among the farm hands and cowboys of the West when I worked as one of them many years since. But it was unusual to hear them expressed by a professor in the year 1946. I said:

"In passing judgment on a nation or political system, don't you take into account at all the fruits, the results, especially the results which have been so enormously to the advantage of the United States?"

He looked genuinely surprised. "I did deal with results, bad results."

I went on:

"You dealt with outward forms, and in so far as you touched results you turned the plain facts upside down. At a moment when a labor government is in power with a great parliamentary majority, drawn so largely from the workers, the outcome of their political power, the third labor government in the last quarter of a century, you suggest that the common man has less weight in politics and public affairs in Britain than he has in the United States. I suggest that this is simply not so. As to what you call the 'class system,' have you examined the social origins of the men who make up about half the British Government—the Bevins, Morrisons, Bevans, Halls? One of them not long since made this remark: 'My father was a policeman. At eighteen I began to busy myself with politics and the trade unions—and have been a member of the ruling class ever since.' In fact it is much easier in Britain to rise out of 'the servant class,' as you call it, than it is in America. You express astonishment? But the explanation is simple: the 'servant class' in America is predominantly Negro, and Negroes have not been precisely common in your governments. Nor, for that matter, have trade unionists. When you speak of the passion in America for equality, the absence of class, perhaps you forget the colored class, possibly others. It is getting on for a century now since we made a Jew Prime Minister of Britain. Could a Jew even today very easily become President of the United States? It is true that in our constitutions we have no grandiloquent phrases about liberty and equality. But slavery in the British colonies was abolished a whole generation before it was in the United States. And though Jamaica, for example, is commonly described here as an oppressed colony, it happens to possess a colored government, a country in which white men can be and are tried by a Negro judge and a Negro jury. Does it happen in the United States?[6]

"You imply that democracy and freedom demand the abolition of monarchy and the House of Lords and all titles. Well, titles have

[6] Since the above was written a Negro has been added to the United States bench.

become in Britain a medal that you hang onto a man's name instead of onto his coat. The whole principle of medals may be wrong. But medals are not quite unknown in the United States—or in Russia. The average Soviet general is commonly as much plastered with medals as Goering used to be. If a communist state has adopted so lavishly the principle of visible recognition of service, it is likely that that state has discovered that the practice has social utility. The title as it exists in Britain is a medal, moreover, given to civilians as well as to soldiers, for recognition of peace as well as of war service. The House of Lords has now quite a number of what you would call working-class members, men who began life as agricultural workers or miners and have now a seat where, in an advisory capacity, they may proffer opinion without one eye on whether it would be pleasing to an electorate. Who was it said that any sanely organized state would arrange for an assembly whose members could say what they damn pleased, whether pleasing to the public or not? The House of Lords has little power. But its members can say what they damn please without fear of expulsion.

"As to abolishing the monarchy. Well, Germany abolished a dozen royalties and instituted the most correct of republics. The republic did not prevent the coming of Hitler. Russia liquidated all royalties. She remains a dictatorship. Spain has got rid of both monarchy and empire, as you desire Britain should do. Does this result please you? Turkey is a republic; Portugal, like the daughter nation Brazil; and also Argentina. Does anyone argue that since Argentina is a republic it is a more democratic or better neighbor than Canada, whose stamps still carry a king's head? There are twenty Latin-American republics. Do their histories really compare favorably in stability and social progress with that, say, of Australia, where the king's brother represents the king?

"The monarchy is retained because, though theoretically an absurd institution, it has in practice proved of great political utility and value. Any meeting where contention between different parties is rife needs a chairman who shall be above parties, whose office shall be to obey the parliamentary rules without regard to any opinion of his own. His job is to say: 'It is your turn to speak, Mr. Jones'—or form a government. This chairman is the head of the state, but not the party head of the government. And because he is not a party creation the party in opposition has no need to represent him as crook and thief and scoundrel, as I have heard so many Americans describing the head of the American nation. I am not sure it makes for good citizenship to call the representative of your nation, its head and symbol, a crook and a gangster. If you are to detach such an office completely from party wrangles you cannot elect the man who holds it: considerations of party would prevail in the election. It is deemed logical enough to select juries by lot. The monarch, the chairman of the national meeting, is selected by lot—the lottery of birth, a lottery, however, in which to some extent he is trained for his job, and by a life's practice taught to regard himself as above party. How otherwise would you propose to get these results? What might well be utterly absurd for other nations to adopt might be equally foolish for us to abolish. If it is not necessary to change an institution; it is sometimes necessary not to change it.

"The king serves also as a symbol, as a flag is a symbol, uniting those independent nations of the Commonwealth we call Dominions. An American historian has expressed the view that without the symbol of the Crown the Commonwealth could hardly hold together. The fact that it did hold together when we had to deal with Hitler has been of some value, not alone to Britain, but to the world.

"I agree that if Britain is the only great nation of Europe which did not drift to fascism or dictatorship or national disintegration or collaborationism, it is not due to the fact of keeping certain relics of feudalism. But it is in some measure due to qualities which that fact indicates: to a preference for reality over form; to the habit of asking that a political system shall work and give the desired results irrespective of theoretical constitutional perfection; to the recognition that class co-operation may be at times preferable to class conflict, even as a means of abolishing class and privilege; that traditional loyalties are sometimes better than none; that an imperfect system rendered workable by habit and tradition is to be preferred to a perfect one which does not work because these things do not lubricate it. First things first."

CHAPTER XV

The Tragedy of Anglo-American Failure

IT IS a strange fact that the most cogent statement of the case for Anglo-American co-operation, as the quite indispensable foundation of the power which alone could prevent another war, and so preserve Western civilization, has come not from an Englishman or an American or an Anglo-Saxon of any brand, but from a famous Frenchman, the leader of his nation in one of its darkest hours. From Georges Clemenceau.

Anyone who happened to be in Paris in the winter of 1918-19 (as this writer happened to be), seeing anything of the French negotiators of the peace, knew that Clemenceau and those around him were trying to present to Lloyd George and to Woodrow Wilson a certain argument which in its simplest terms ran something like this:

"If," said the Frenchman in effect, "you Anglo-Saxons, now in this year 1919, make it plain you will defend France if she is again attacked, you won't have to do it. For if Germany knows for certain that she will have to meet both of you, she won't attack, and you won't be dragged into a second world war. If you *don't* make this plain now, in 1919, she *will* attack, and you will once more find yourselves in a second world war and have to leave the bones of your sons upon the soil of France. You will discover once more, and once more too late, that the defense of France is indispensable to your own safety. Only America and Britain can give that guarantee. Who else is there in this year of 1919 who could give a guarantee to France that would deter Germany? Russia—in the midst of revolution? Russia who made a separate peace with the enemy, and who was prepared to accept a Brest-Litovsk in order to try the revolutionary experiment at home? Italy? Japan? Guatemala? In all the wide world today there are two powers and two powers alone who can give to France the guarantees that will prevent a second war. And those two powers must act together. We want the guarantee from both of you. If Britain gives it alone, she will hesitate to use her fleet from fear that Americans will make trouble over the freedom of the seas; America cannot give it alone because the Germans know that a neutral Britain in any action against them would paralyze that action. A co-operating Britain is indispensable to any American action against a European enemy. The first step toward that warless world of which Mr. Wilson speaks is for his country and Britain to guarantee the defense of France."

We know that that argument was carried on not merely from what the historians have said but from what the chief actors in the drama did. For what they did proved that President Wilson, so hostile on general principle to partial alliances, and Mr. Lloyd George, so suspicious of the French—and also of alliances—were both convinced by Clemenceau's arguments. They agreed to urge the ratification of the tripartite guarantees. That ratification was never completed. Congress failed to give it, and though Parliament ratified, the English version had a saving clause to the effect that if the treaty failed of ratification by the United States, Britain would be relieved of its obligations.

The historical details need be only very briefly recalled. Foch and his followers had demanded that Germany's western frontier be fixed at the Rhine and that the ten thousand square miles of territory between the Rhine on the east and the Netherlands, Belgium, and France on the west be erected into an autonomous, neutral state, more or less under French protection. Wilson and Lloyd George opposed this.

After prolonged bargaining Clemenceau agreed to a compromise. Wilson and Lloyd George promised to sign special treaties which should guarantee that the United States and Great Britain would come to the aid of France in case of "invasion" by Germany. Upon Clemenceau's insistence, the word "invasion" was changed to "aggression." On June 28, 1919, therefore, when the Versailles

Treaty was signed, two supplementary Guarantee Treaties, one Franco-British and the other Franco-American, were also signed. These documents specifically guaranteed the eastern boundary of France against aggression (and this despite Wilson's statement, in a speech of September 27, 1918, that "there can be no leagues or alliances or special covenants and understandings within the general and common family of the League of Nations") and provided that Great Britain and the United States, respectively, should "come immediately to [France's] assistance in the event of any unprovoked movement of aggression against her being made by Germany."

Well, we know what happened. The United States Senate would have nothing to do with the American treaty and thereupon the one with Great Britain, although already ratified, automatically became void, since its acceptance had been made "contingent upon the United States Government undertaking the same obligation."

It cannot be said that the American public rejected this treaty: speaking broadly, they never heard of it. Public discussion raged around the League, busied itself with domestic issues (shortly to include prohibition and all that it implied), indulged in recrimination, while academic circles devoted vast energies to assigning responsibility for the war, by no means agreeing that the bulk of the blame was Germany's. For the big public of the popular press, the net conclusion was that America had once more been "played for a sucker," particularly by the British, who refused to pay their debts. The drift to "normalcy," to isolationism, expressed finally in the Neutrality and Johnson Acts, continued for two decades.

In Europe the French by no means gave up the hope of specific guarantees of security. When it became evident that America would turn her back for the time being upon Europe, friends of collective security in both Britain and France attempted a European substitute. Lord Robert Cecil and his friends managed to draft and secure provisional acceptance by the British Government of the Treaty of Mutual Assistance. MacDonald's first government refused ratification, but found that it was obliged, in order to meet the French view, to devise something of its own along the same lines. The Geneva Protocol was the result. With the fall of Mac-

Donald's government, this also, in its turn, lapsed, rejected by the conservatives. The conservative government which followed Mac-Donald's did manage to secure ratification of the Locarno groups of treaties. But by this time the European situation had set so definitely in the old anarchic mold that the Locarno treaties failed to reshape it.

The point for us today is to understand the nature of the forces which defeated the leaders of the nations, such as Clemenceau, Wilson, Lloyd George, and others who saw the need of policies which, after the event, we recognize as those most likely to have kept the peace. If we forget this past, we are, as the phrase runs, in danger of repeating it.

It is impossible, of course, to say with certainty that even if both American and British opinion had been more alert and had ratified those treaties, war would have been prevented. What we can, however, say with certainty is this: if the forces of public opinion which defeated provisions as elementary as these against recurrence of aggression are to continue, no provision, no treaty, no arrangement can be depended upon. We must know why this failed if future policies or arrangements are to succeed.

Let us note the outstanding features of this episode:

1. To secure domination of the Continent, Germany must conquer France. The prevention, therefore, of further German aggression, and so of a second world war, depended upon a guarantee of French security so dependable that Germany would be deterred, would not gamble, that is, upon assistance to France being too little or too late.

2. Only Britain and America together could give that guarantee; there were no other nations in the condition of the world at that time who were in a position to furnish such security, neither Russia nor Poland nor Italy nor Japan nor China nor Latin America.

3. Far from the Anglo-American "bloc" being resented in those circumstances by France, as something threatening an Anglo-Saxon domination of the world, it was precisely France which demanded its creation as the one sure safeguard of her future peace and security.

4. Such a bloc would not have stood in the way of a larger internationalism. It was still open to the United States, having given the guarantees, to have joined the League. The fact that she did not do so cannot be ascribed to her having given a limited guarantee; for it was not given. The League's success would have been more probable if the guarantees had existed. They would probably have formed the nucleus of a larger system of collective security, which could have developed in the direction of a federal rather than a League form of constitution.

5. The event would seem to indicate quite clearly that in so far as the three-nation arrangement was opposed on the ground that partial alliances were inimical to the universal alliance of world security, that opposition was wrong-headed. It not only made the best the enemy of the better; insistence on the best resulted in the worst.

6. The French guarantees would have constituted an application to international politics of "the principle of predictability of power." No amount of power, however great, can deter aggression and be made an instrument for avoiding war unless the potential aggressor knows with reasonable certainty that it will be used against him if he offends. America might, then, in 1919 have possessed the greatest army and the greatest navy in the world, but that fact would not have deterred Germany unless she regarded it as reasonably certain she would have to meet it in the case of aggression. In the neutrality legislation, the United States proclaimed to the world that she would in future be neutral, take no part in "Europe's unending quarrels." We may assume that Hitler took due note.

We read the history of the interwar years to little purpose if we cannot recall how the mood of the time met Clemenceau's argument that power could only be used as a deterrent of aggression by making its purpose plain beforehand. The prevailing argument was to the effect that any "threat" of the future use of force would merely rally the people of the nations against whom it was directed, and bring the war nearer. An eminent theological leader in Britain wrote a book in the early thirties, entitled *Conciliation versus Coercion.* Collective action—like that now once more suggested under the

UN constitution—against aggression was condemned as coercion, ruled out as a resort to war camouflaged under the term of police action. A very distinguished Dominion statesman termed resort to collective defense an attempt to turn the League from its real purpose of conciliation and peace into "a sort of international War Office." Some progressives opposed common action against the aggressors on the ground that the basic principle of the Covenant was wrong: states never could or should be coerced; the proper constitutional form of any international organization should be federal; coercion, when called for, should be only of individuals. In the unhappy event, however, states had to be coerced, and that event proved they could be.[1]

The gravamen of Clemenceau's argument was: if you desire that your power shall prevent others committing what you regard as aggression, let them know beforehand that you will use it for that purpose. Then you won't have to. Yet example after example could of course be given of the way in which failure to make the purpose of power predictable prevented power from being a deterrent of war. Had Germany known for certain in 1914 that Britain would come in, known at all that America would, the German General Staff might have been deterred. Had the tripartite Guarantee to France in 1919 been ratified, Germany warned, that is, that in the event of another attack she would without any sort of doubt have to face the whole power of the Anglo-Saxon world on French soil, the German General Staff would have been less disposed to gamble on continued American neutrality. If, in 1931, which was before the coming of Hitler and the rearmament of Germany, the British Government had made the very utmost of Mr. Stimson's proposal about warning Japan concerning aggression in Manchuria and possibly applying sanctions; and Mr. Stimson himself had been able to assure Sir John Simon that if sanctions resulted in war the United States could be

[1] Great play was made in the argument with the fact that the United States Constitution made no provision for the "punishment" or "coercion" of states. The whole argument confuses coercion with defense. The United States Constitution makes ample provision for the collective defense of its member states, and Section 3 of Article IV of the Constitution, defining the obligations of the Union to its member states, reads: "The United States shall protect each of them against invasion." That provision was binding as much against invasion by fellow members as by states outside the Union.

counted on to stand with Britain; if it had been made plain to Mussolini that whatever the other members of the League might do, Britain would defend Ethiopia as energetically as though it were British territory, the tidal wave of aggression would have been checked before it gained the terrifying momentum which it did— and which finally engulfed both Britain and the United States.

In all these cases there occurred the same strange psychological phenomenon. There were some who did urge that if the growing aggressions were not to develop into an armed conflict, the potential aggressor should be plainly warned that there was a line he must not cross if he desired to avoid war. But the very suggestion was regarded as saber-rattling and war-mongering. Only after the event did the expression "appeasement" take on the quality we now give it in describing the period immediately preceding the war. Before the war "appeasement" was regarded as the alternative to war, a synonym for peace-making, peace-keeping.

In the early postwar years progressives, particularly in America, insisted that the severity of the Versailles Treaty was destroying peace and would provoke a second world war unless revised in the direction of restoration of colonies and so forth. Yet we see today that it was not mainly the nature of the Versailles Treaty which produced the second World War. (If the treaty was the cause of the second, what was the cause of the first? Europe was not living under a Versailles Treaty in 1914. And as to absence of colonies, Germany, when she went to war in 1914, possessed her colonies.) The second war came because the anti-Axis nations had lost their power to act collectively in resistance to aggression when aggression might have been prevented. It is a mistake to ascribe this impotence to disarmament. For at least fifteen years after the signature of the peace treaties the Grand Alliance still possessed overwhelming preponderance of armament over the enemy of 1918. Hitler did not come to power until fifteen years after the Armistice; he had not yet built up German armament, nor occupied the Rhineland, nor annexed Austria, nor formed his alliance with Japan and Italy, nor tried out blitzkrieg methods in Spain. It was not lack of armament in those early years which prevented action against aggression but lack of a common will, a common policy, political unity.

To ignore this fact is to make the question of whether the peace of 1919 was too soft or too hard irrelevant. Suppose the "hard" policy had been adopted at Versailles. To carry it out the Allies would have had to remain united, which they did not. A "harder" treaty would have failed as completely as did the treaty actually written. And for the same reasons.

Power for the control of Germany became impossible from the moment the Allies began to turn their forces against each other. That canceled out their power, especially when much Allied power (beginning with that of Japan and Italy) was actually transferred to the enemy side.

Disintegration of the alliance began, of course, before the war was over. Russia withdrew and made a separate peace with the enemy. British and French policy began to diverge before the peace was signed, and that divergence grew in the immediate postwar years. America soon withdrew from all formal association with the alliance. This disintegration would not have been prevented either by making the treaty more severe or by making it more lenient. Greater severity would still further have alienated liberal (particularly American) support; greater mildness would have still further alienated realist opinion (especially French) and would have made it easier in some respects for the enemy to stage a comeback.

We failed, not mainly because our estimate of the enemy and the treatment applicable to his case was necessarily wrong, but mainly because our estimate of ourselves, of the policy we should apply to each other, was wrong. We are still making that mistake, and are in danger of failing once more, from precisely the reasons which caused us to fail before.

In 1918—the violent anti-German period so quickly to be followed in both Britain and America by important outcroppings of pro-Germanism—we were persuaded that the kind of wickedness which had launched the war was quite peculiar to the German race or nation. They had been infected with a kind of political rabies from which other peoples were immune. As one British statesman of the time put it: the cause of war is Germans. The peoples on the Allied side could never by any possibility, we were convinced, be guilty of that sort of crime, be bitten by the German madness.

As a matter of historical record, however, the serious aggressions following the peace of 1918 did not begin with the Bad Man of the world; they began with members of the Grand Alliance which had caged him and who were to prove that the German disease was catching, and German wickedness more than German. Italy was the first home of fascism; Japan threatened world peace before the arrival of Hitler, who was, no doubt, impressed by the fact that Japan and Italy both enjoyed complete immunity when they challenged the peace and took the law into their own hands.

The second World War was not conceived in 1939. Its seeds were sown in the failure of France to secure the Anglo-American guarantee for which she had asked. This failure was only the first of a whole series of notifications to potential aggressors everywhere that no law would be enforced against them, and—which is even more important perhaps—that they could look to no law with power of enforcement to defend them. Defense, their survival in the struggle for national existence, would depend upon their grabbing sources of national power before others could grab them. And the grabbing went on from the Baltic to the Aegean and Mediterranean; as it is going on again a quarter of a century later, after another world war.

In the interwar years one of the commonest explanations of the slide to war (as previous chapters reveal) was Britain's imperialism and her hostility to Russia. It is a strange interpretation. If British imperialists had been more concerned than they were to protect Britain's imperial position against the encroachments of Japan and Germany, they would have been more willing to offer an earlier resistance. To ascribe Britain's long-continued diplomatic retreat before the constant encroachment which went on, capturing one vital strategic position after another—in the Far East, in Africa, in Austria, Spain, Czechoslovakia—to describe this, as it has been described so often in leftist circles, as due to Britain's determination to play power politics, to her "ruthless and ceaseless imperialism," is to play havoc with all the facts; to make nonsense of them. Incidentally, the more far-sighted British imperialists, notably Churchill, saw clearly the danger from the imperialists' point of view of the policy of appeasement, opposed it tooth and nail, but were defeated, until too late, by the weight of conservative and imperialist inertia.[2]

As to appeasement being explained by the determination of capitalist powers to "gang up against Russia," one is prompted to ask how, for instance, the continued American refusal to combine with Britain and France and the common refusal of all three to come to agreement on any common policy can be described as "ganging up" against Russia or anyone else. Certainly there was some fear of Russian communism and Russian expansion—expressed in the early policy of the *cordon sanitaire*. But if in the later period of the interwar years it had been the determining factor in international grouping, then capitalist America would have shown a much greater readiness than it did to join the capitalist states of Western Europe either through the League or by other means. We can hardly ascribe America's refusal to join the League or ratify the guarantee treaties to "fear of Russia." As to British fear of Russian territorial expansion, that is an old, old story which was a force in British foreign policy long before Bolshevism was heard of.

The political right during those years was as little discerning as the extreme left. Deeply concerned about national defense, the conservatives insisted it should be each nation for itself; no internationalization of defense. Which, of course, created an international situation in which the aggressor could conveniently swallow his victims one by one.

What concerns us most now about this recent past is that it has today a disturbing parallel in the development of Anglo-American relations.

Britain today occupies in many respects a position similar to that occupied by France in 1918. Like France in 1918, she emerges from a war largely drained of power. The weakness of France constituted a great danger to Great Britain, as the events of 1940 were to show so tragically. Yet in the decade following the first war very few in Britain were concerned with France's weakness. Liberals were much more disturbed with France's militarism, her invasion of the Ruhr, her alliance-making, failing to realize that the militarism and "power politics" in which France engaged were a helter-skelter search for

[2] See the author's *Defence of the Empire*.

security, some assurance of national survival against the pressure from the East, and that the way to get better political behavior from France would be to associate Britain with French security, as statesmen like Churchill have always wanted to do, even, in his case, to the extent in a dark hour of offering France a Solemn Act of Union with Britain. If such an offer had come in the interwar years, or indeed something very far short of it, but constituting constant political co-operation for purposes of defense, there might well have been no second World War. What was not realized in the moral reprobation of those interwar years was that whatever the causes of French weakness in defense, Britain would be embroiled in any trouble that might result from it, and, as a measure of her own security, should remedy it as far as lay within her power to do so.

Today the United States can as little be indifferent to the security of Britain as Britain could be indifferent to that of France.

CHAPTER XVI

Freedom in the Stream of History: An Untold Story

THE fact that twice in so short a time, in a young man's lifetime, the two branches of the English-speaking world, despite bickerings and deliberately exploited grudges, and in spite of what they would wish to do, have nevertheless been compelled to combine their power for ends which both agreed were deep and vital and similar, this fact is not, of course, an accident; nor is it something peculiar to our generation. It belongs to a real historical process which has been going on for centuries, which, intelligently interpreted, might help us to use our common power aright. By seeing why we have been led to use it as we have done in the past we might help to avoid its misuse in the dangerous and confused future ahead of us. But unhappily the impulses of nationalism, the human tendency to blame our troubles on others, to find at all cost scapegoats, all this has caused us to twist some of the plainest facts of our common history, get them out of perspective, and see them in distorted form. In discussing the role played by the empire in the shaping of Western civilization, I have sometimes had occasion to remind American audiences—and sometimes university students—that in their sweeping condemnation of British imperialism, they would do well to keep in mind that if there had been no British Empire, there could have been no United States of America. The statement of this very elementary historical fact has sometimes been received a little boisterously. To a New Englander who retorted somewhat truculently that the Pilgrim Fathers had fled to escape English power and tyranny and that the final destruction of that power would serve the cause of freedom, it was pointed out that the Pilgrim Fathers could never have reached the shores of America, and that New England could never have established itself on the eastern seaboard, had it not been for English power. British "imperialism" began with the defeat of the Armada. If that particular expeditionary force had been successful, England ("Britain" had not yet come into being as a political entity) subjugated and the English power destroyed, Spain would never have allowed the Puritan heretics to settle in America and found there a Protestant theocracy. The defeat of the Armada represented the beginnings of a struggle against totalitarianism which has been carried on by Anglo-American power for over three hundred years: against Spain mainly in the seventeenth century and early eighteenth century, against prerevolutionary France in the eighteenth century (established in the St. Lawrence, Ohio, and Mississippi valleys), against Napoleon (who threatened to occupy New Orleans) and the Holy Alliance headed by Russia in the nineteenth century, and Germany and Japan in the twentieth.

The purpose of Spain in dispatching the Armada was to make good the claim that Spaniards and Portuguese alone had the right of access to the Western Hemisphere, a claim for which they believed they had divine sanction. The Inquisition, which had already been firmly established in Mexico (then covering much of what is now the United States) and in South America, would have extended its power to North America; and though the principle of religious freedom might ultimately have been developed out of a universal Spanish Catholic empire, its development would have been much slower than was the case when the power of Spain became checked; and the type of society which now exists in the United States would have been a very different one. Spain was then what we should now call totalitarian (as, indeed, so many insist she is today, although she is not, like England, an empire). The Gestapo or OGPU or NKVD of that time was the Inquisition. Queen Elizabeth represented what was still an almost absolute monarchy, but the forces which sprang from the principles asserted in the Magna Carta three centuries before were gaining in power. It may well be that the English Elizabethans were no more civilized—in some respects certainly much less civilized—than the Spaniards of their day. Indeed, those who resisted the Armada were in large part shameless pirates who had little notion of extending the area of free government as against authoritarianism. No suggestion to the contrary is here made. They fought because the Spaniard had become an enemy with whom they had collided on the seas and in the New World, which the Elizabethan veterans had been asserting their right to share; because Protestantism as an expression of intellectual freedom had already taken deep root in England; and because of the nascent nationalism which already was beginning to emerge as the dominant force in European politics. (It is worth note in that connection that the English admiral who commanded the fleet which defeated the Armada of Catholic Spain was himself a Roman Catholic, Lord Howard of Effingham.) But above all they fought because to do anything else would have involved what they feared would be enslavement. Few would urge that it was the duty of the Elizabethan to submit when the Armada sailed up the Channel, and none with any knowledge of the nature of man would suppose for one moment that an island nation like the English would do it.

We are not, however, concerned with motive so much as with results, and one of the results was a great extension of free government in the New World and ultimately the creation of the United States.

The English, having decided to fight, and having defeated the Spanish fleet, the matter could not end there. The settlements in North America which began to multiply as British power asserted itself had to be defended, and this brought Britain into continued conflict not merely with Spain in America but with prerevolutionary France. That feudal and, as we should now say, totalitarian power was established at the mouth of the St. Lawrence, in the Ohio valley, and at the mouth of the Mississippi. If it had maintained its position there, its empire would have extended from the St. Lawrence to the Mississippi, and the expansion of the seaboard English-speaking colonies to the Pacific coast would have been shut off. Among the soldiers who fought to resist the French pressure in the Ohio country was a British officer named George Washington. The American settlers had developed a society already for the most part self-governing and democratic.

No serious historian today disputes this fact, but the oversimplification of American schoolbook history, with a natural and in a sense excusable dramatization of the events of the Revolution, making the embattled farmers the heroes and the redcoats the villains of the piece, has obscured the truth—to the peril of the world's peace and freedom. Professors Allan Nevins and Henry Steele Commager in their *History of the United States* wrote:

It was not true that the British colonies suffered from tyranny. By and large they enjoyed a political freedom that in the seventeenth and eighteenth centuries was unequaled in any other part of the globe (pages 18-19).[1]

Such a statement—as I happen to know from contacts with American university students—comes as a complete shock to those whose history has not got beyond the episodic heroes versus villains picture of the elementary schoolbooks. As to certain declarations coming from some of the Founding Fathers, reproduced below, I have more than once had the experience of American students branding them out of hand as "obvious forgeries."

The survival and maintenance of that form of society in America which most serious American historians now declare to be the freest then existing anywhere in the world depended upon Britain maintaining her struggle with Spain, with France of the monarchies, later still with France of Napoleon, with the monarchies of the Holy Alliance, and later still, of course, with Germany, the whole forming one connected fight lasting over three hundred years. If Britain had been defeated in those struggles, the form of society developed in the United States would have been replaced by one less free and less democratic. The contest was a world struggle. If Britain had been defeated by the French in India, and France had been able to draw upon the resources of India to fight British power, that would certainly have had an effect on the struggle against France in North America—in Canada, the Ohio valley, and Louisiana.

[1] De Tocqueville, in his *Democracy in America* (published in 1835), wrote: "The English colonies (and this is one of the main causes of their prosperity) have always enjoyed more internal freedom and more political independence than the colonies of other nations. . . . The general principles which are the groundwork of modern constitutions, principles which in the seventeenth century were imperfectly known in Europe and not completely triumphant even in Great Britain, were all recognized and established by the colonial laws of New England: the intervention of the people in public affairs, the free voting of the taxes, the responsibility of the agents of power, personal liberty, trial by jury were all positively established without discussion."

The struggle of the colonists which began in 1776 for the defense of rights asserted in the Declaration of Independence was a struggle which was also going on in Britain itself. As Professor Shotwell has pointed out, the Declaration of Independence "is both a reaffirmation of the rights of Englishmen and an indictment of the king and government of that day for having violated them in the treatment of the colonists." Professor Shotwell adds that one is prone to forget the very fundamental fact "that unless English colonists had been schooled in freedom the protest . . . might have remained unwritten."[2] The Englishman now attempting to explain the nature of the power struggle at work would wish that, had he lived at the time of the Revolution, he might have sided with the Revolution; but that his descendants would do their best to forget it, as wise Americans on both sides of the Mason and Dixon line try to forget the war between the states, in which struggle more Americans, many times more, were killed by Americans than were killed by the king's troops in the Revolution. That it is thought a part of good citizenship (which it is) to forget the much more recent and much bloodier conflict of the Rebellion (in which men still alive took part) but permissible, desirable, a part of patriotism to keep alive artificially and by some measure of historical distortion the memories of a much less bloody and much more ancient conflict, can only be explained by the kind of nationalism the Atomic Age would do well to shed.

As a matter of simple historical fact, the American and the British peoples, despite the Ancient Grudge, continued to co-operate and combine their power—often unobserved—against the pressure of totalitarianism, and for the expansion of United States territory and power, very little uninterrupted by the Revolution.

This was illustrated by a certain circumstance of the Louisiana Purchase, that step which enabled Jefferson to double the area of the nation. It will be recalled that Spain had long held the country west of the Mississippi, with the port of New Orleans near its mouth.

[2] It is sometimes forgotten by Americans who write of Tom Paine as "the soul of the American Revolution," the "typical American voicing the aspirations of the new American society," that Paine was a working-class Englishman who never saw America until approaching middle life, and that the ideals which inspired him he must therefore have acquired in England.

But soon after Jefferson came into office Napoleon forced the weak Spanish Government to cede the great tract called Louisiana back to France. The moment he did so intelligent Americans trembled with apprehension and indignation. New Orleans was an indispensable port for the shipment of American products grown in the Ohio and Mississippi valleys. Napoleon's plans for a huge colonial empire just west of the United States, balancing the Anglo-Saxon dominion in North America, menaced the trading rights and the safety of all the interior settlements. Even feeble Spain had made a great deal of trouble for the southwestern country. What might not France, the most powerful military nation in the world, do?[3]

What did Jefferson, author of the Declaration of Independence of Britain, then do in order to secure the future of the United States? Almost instinctively he turned to the power of Great Britain as the force in the world which could save the situation for America, as against the thrust of less democratic forces. He instructed Livingston, his Minister in Paris, to notify Napoleon that the day the French occupied New Orleans the United States "would marry itself to the British nation and the British fleet," and that the first cannon shot fired in a European war would be the signal for the march of an Anglo-American army against New Orleans. Napoleon was impressed, the historians tell us, "by the certainty that the United States and Britain would strike."

There can be no doubt that it was Jefferson's shrewd use of British power which enabled him to double the size of the United States, to leave it in control of the whole central river system of the continent, so that, as Lincoln said later in the Civil War years, "the Father of Waters went unvexed to the Sea."

But this was no isolated experience of the United States' use of British power for its own security.

It is indeed strange to reflect that the foreign policy of President Truman (in the matter of aid to Greece and Turkey) was an extension of the Monroe Doctrine, regarded favorably by Monroe himself, was urged still more definitely by his predecessor in the presidency,

[3] *The Pocket History of the United States*, by Allan Nevins and Henry Steele Commager, 1943, pages 159, 160.

Madison, and was implicit in advice proffered to Monroe by still another former president, Thomas Jefferson.

It has thus taken a century and a quarter to put into political practice a principle which three American presidents—one of them the author of the Declaration of Independence, another having led his country into war against Great Britain—were disposed to approve in 1823. The fact should surely prompt us to ask the why and where-fore of such a time lag. For if the form those elder statesmen favored had been adopted in their time, instead of 124 years later, many wars, including probably two world wars, might have been avoided and civilization might be in better shape than it happens to be at the moment.

The thing becomes the more disturbing when we reflect that the forces which defeated those earlier leaders were of the kind which a century later were to defeat still another American president, Woodrow Wilson, who so strongly urged his country to give, with Britain, that Anglo-American guarantee to France which Clemenceau so urgently sought and which, by deterrence of Germany, might have prevented the second World War.

Certain facts, so often ignored or unknown, need recalling.

When Monroe received Canning's offer of British support in resist-ing any design of the Holy Alliance to reconquer the Spanish colonies, the President immediately consulted with his predecessors, Madison and Jefferson. Madison took a line which in effect was this: "Of course, we must accept the proposal of the British Government, but we ought not to limit the principle of the policy to the Western Hemisphere. Let us declare now, in company with Britain, that a weak nation, anywhere in the world, threatened by a powerful neighbor, shall receive our support in defense of its right to life." And he went on to cite, please note, the case of Greece, then resist-ing Turkey, as a case in which help should be given to enable a small state to defend itself against the pressure of a more powerful neighbor.

Madison wrote:

With the British power and navy combined with our own, we have nothing to fear from the rest of the world, and in the great struggle of the epoch between liberty and despotism, we owe it to ourselves to sustain the former.

Jefferson expressed his views in a long letter, far too little known, dated Monticello, Oct. 24, 1823, which might almost be regarded as a last political will and testament and in which the general principle of avoiding the "entanglements and broils" of Europe is qualified by some very suggestive conditions. They are, however, conditions in keeping with the policy which Jefferson as president was quite ready to adopt twenty years earlier in handling the Louisiana situation.

Even then, in 1803, Jefferson saw the desirability, in dealing with Bonaparte, of forecasting "a closer connection with Great Britain," with a view to the holding of the Western world "in sequestration for the common purposes of the united British and American nations." The point at that time, as Jefferson doubtless saw, was that the maintenance of relations in which an Anglo-American alliance remained always a possibility rendered it unnecessary for the alliance actually to come into being.

By 1823 this general conception of American foreign policy had become stronger still in Jefferson's mind. In his letter to Monroe he urged acceptance of Canning's proposal, pointed out its relevance to the world struggle between despotism and freedom, and seized upon the same point as Madison—that the issue was a much larger one than the defense of the newly born Latin-American republics against reconquest by Spain. Jefferson wrote:

Nor is the occasion to be slighted which this proposition [i.e., Canning's] offers of declaring our protest against the atrocious violations of the rights of nations by the interference of anyone in the internal affairs of another so flagitiously begun by Bonaparte and now continued by the equally lawless alliance, calling itself Holy.

The reasons which prompted even then the "larger view" of the Monroe Doctrine have been too readily forgotten, though they have disturbing resemblance to present problems. The Holy Alliance, initiated and headed by Russia, had become a sort of Axis or international of the dictatorship powers carrying on a crusade against parliamentary and constitutional movements. The Russian ruler had an almost mystical conviction that dictatorship was the divinely appointed form of government. (Thus the "Holy.") Russia had, very late in the struggle against Napoleon, become one of the allies, and by the resistance to him on Russian soil had contributed greatly to his defeat. As one of the victors Russia's power spread westward. Russian troops were in Paris, as they are now in Berlin.

Russia was also at that time an American power. She had territory and a sphere of influence in the Western Hemisphere far beyond what is now Alaska. In 1821 the czar issued a ukase extending Alaska to the fifty-first parallel, well within what is now Oregon, and declaring *mare clausum* the waters thence to Bering Strait, thereby denying American fishing rights in those waters. Russian trading posts, which were also forts, had already been established in California, then held by a very weak government. All this had to be considered in addition to the contemplated recovery of the Spanish colonies.

In his letter to Monroe, Jefferson hints that one event could render the Holy Alliance a really appalling menace to the United States. That event would be for Britain to join or support the alliance. But if, goes on Jefferson,

We can effect a division in the body of the European powers, and draw over to our side its most powerful member, surely we ought to do it. . . . I am clearly of Mr. Canning's opinion that it would prevent instead of provoking war. With Great Britain withdrawn from their scale and shifted into that of our two continents, all Europe combined would not undertake such a war.

The passages in Jefferson's letter which seem to represent a final summing up of his thought are these:

The question . . . is the most momentous which has ever been offered to my contemplation since that of independence. That made us a nation; this sets our compass and points the course which we are to steer through the ocean of time opening on us. . . . Our endeavor should surely be to make our hemisphere that of freedom. One nation, most of all, could disturb us in this pursuit. She now offers to lead, aid, and accompany us in it. By acceding to her proposition we bring her mighty weight into the scale of free government and emancipate a continent at one stroke, which might otherwise linger long in doubt and difficulty. Great Britain is the nation which can do us the most harm of any one, or all, on earth; and with her on our side we need not fear the whole world. With her then we should most sedulously cherish a cordial friendship.

Thus wrote the reputedly Anglophobe Jefferson. Since his day the relative power positions of the two countries have been reversed. Britain was able to sustain the fight against Napoleon without aid from the New World. She could not have won the fight against Hitler without that aid, by herself. But she could have lost it by herself, and lost it perhaps for others as well.

John Latane, in his *History of American Foreign Policy*, remarks that the opinions of Monroe, Jefferson, and Madison "in favor of a broad declaration against the intervention of great powers in the affairs of weaker states in any part of the world, have been severely criticized by some historians and ridiculed by others." But, adds Latane, "time and circumstance bring some changes," and many, even after the first World War, wondered whether the three elder statesmen were not right, and Adams and Clay, who successfully opposed them, were not wrong.

We cannot alter the past. But we may use the past as a guide to shape our future.

Because the simple historical facts concerning the genesis of the Monroe Doctrine are so often in dispute, it may be useful to recall a detail or two.

Britain had been asked to join the Holy Alliance, but held back. Canning was of the opinion that the reconquest of the Latin-American colonies would give to the states of the Holy Alliance a power that would upset the continental balance in a way dangerously hostile to constitutional government. He decided, therefore, to "call in the New World to redress the balance of the Old," and in an unofficial and confidential letter to Rush (the American Minister in London), dated August 20, 1823, asked if "the moment had not arrived when the two governments might come to an understanding in regard to the Spanish American colonies."

In his letter to Jefferson of October 17 President Monroe said:

Many important considerations are involved in this proposition. 1st, shall we entangle ourselves, at all, in European politicks, and wars, on the side of any power, against others, presuming that a concert, by agreement of the kind proposed, may lead to that result? 2nd, if a case can exist in which a sound maxim may, and ought to be departed from, is not the present instance, precisely that case? 3d Has not the epoch arriv'd when G Britain must take her stand, either on the side of the monarchs of Europe, or of the U States, and in consequence, either in favor of Despotism or of liberty and may it not be presum'd that, aware of that necessity, her government has seiz'd on the present occurrence, as that, which it deems, the most suitable to announce and mark the commenc'-ment of that career.

My own impression is that we ought to meet the proposal of the British govt. and to make it known, that we would view an interference on the part of the European powers, and especially an attack on the Colonies, by them, as an attack on ourselves, presuming that, if they succeeded with them, they would extend it to us.

I have found myself repeatedly challenged even by informed Americans when making the statement that Britain in fact initiated the Monroe Doctrine and used her power to make it feasible. This bit of history is not affected by the fact that Monroe's Proclamation emerged as that of the United States alone, and that British support did not take the shape of a formal treaty; nor indeed by the fact that Cleveland invoked the Doctrine against British action in the Vene-zuelan incident. The Madison-Jefferson correspondence above-re-produced should surely settle the question of the Doctrine's origin. But that correspondence does not stand alone. A quarter of a century later Calhoun gave a very precise account of the events which led up to and followed the proclamation of the Monroe Doctrine in a speech delivered in 1848, just after the popular movements of that time had seen the end of the despotic governments against whose policy the Monroe Doctrine was directed. He confirmed the account above given, of the circumstances which led to the establishment of the Doctrine, and speaking of Canning's proposal said:

It was received here with joy; for so great was the power of the alliance that even we did not feel ourselves safe from its interpositions. Indeed, it was anticipated, almost as a certain result, that if the interference took place with the governments of South America, the alliance would ulti-mately extend its interference to ourselves. . . .

That very movement on the part of England, sustained by this declaration, gave a blow to the celebrated alliance from which it never recovered. From that time forward it gradually decayed, till it utterly perished. The late revolutions in Europe have put an end to all its work, and nothing remains.

The fact which caused the objections of Adams to a dual Anglo-American declaration to prevail was the hesitation of Britain in making immediate recognition of the South American colonies. Canning wished to avoid immediate recognition of the colonies in order not to give unnecessary offense to Spain and the Allies. He urged Rush to agree to the joint declaration on a promise of future recognition. Rush refused to accede to anything but immediate acknowledgment of independence, "and so the matter ended."

The declaration when it came was warmly welcomed by liberal England. Sir James Mackintosh said:

This coincidence of the two great English commonwealths (for so I delight to call them and I heartily pray that they may be forever united in the cause of Justice and Liberty) cannot be contemplated without the utmost pleasure by every enlightened citizen of the earth.

PART V

Russia and the West

CHAPTER XVII

The Russian View

IT IS well to restate the alternatives in the relations of the West with Russia. We can learn to live with her at peace by agreeing to differ: two differing systems living side by side, as differing religions do in the West, though for so long the respective theologians declared this to be a moral impossibility. Such is one alternative. But if different systems cannot live together one must conquer the other, and uniformity be brought about. This need not necessarily involve war: one can become like the other by persuasion, peaceful penetration, each perhaps surrendering something to the other. But the continuance of such a process without war will almost certainly depend on how much one has to concede to the other. It is conceivable that Europe might have accepted the hegemony of, say, Germany, as some twenty American republics of the Western Hemisphere have accepted the hegemony of the United States, if the exercise of German power held out the prospect that the nations of Europe would enjoy the degree of internal autonomy which the nations of Latin America have on the whole enjoyed. But twice in a single generation the attempt of Germany to establish domination in Europe has been resisted by nearly all its nations at unimaginable costs in devastation and misery. Yet that this resistance would indeed be the common policy of the nations was so little realized in the interwar years that the early attempts to organize it, and make it plain to Germany that she would meet resistance, were resented as provocative and likely to lead to war. That aspect has been discussed in the preceding pages.

It is clear that if we are to demand some degree of freedom as well as of peace as the condition of agreement with Russia, we must know something of Russia's views, what she is likely to demand, what concede, what, in other words, the terms of agreement with her can be. What, for instance, does she really regard as essential to her security? Does she in fact believe that the best hope of peace in the world (and Russia's own security) is the spread of communism? And that this is most likely to come by the breakdown of parliamentary capitalist democracy, or social democracy? How may we of the West make such a conviction—if it is a prevailing conviction among Soviet rulers—compatible with peaceful and friendly relations?

Many such questions arise and about most of them Russia's rulers and spokesmen have made positive, categoric, unqualified statements. But we in the West have all but completely ignored these statements of policy. We have done so, in part because of an assumption that peace will best be served by ignoring them; that they don't mean what they appear to mean; that the Russian rulers are not sincere in these declarations. Curiously enough this last plea is made most frequently by those who somewhat noisily proclaim themselves the friends and defenders of Russia.

But even the decision that the statements of policy are not to be taken at their face value is worthless unless we know what they are.

It is here suggested that we shall make no headway toward agreement with the Russian leaders until we assume that they mean what they say, especially when what they say is not a mere casual opinion of this or that leader, but a deeply rooted philosophy of life and politics, constituting the political religion of Russia, instilled during a generation by every device known to modern propaganda into the whole of the Russian people. Statesmen and writers continue to talk of Russian policy as an enigma, a mystery, whereas of all the countries of the world the policy which has been most clearly and unmistakably stated is that of Soviet Russia. It has been stated again and again, by Stalin, by other Russian statesmen associated with him; by approved Russian writers; and by the friends of Russia in the West. As Mr. Max Eastman—who has lived much in Russia, who was an early friend of the Russian Revolution, who speaks Russian with fluency, is familiar with Russian literature, has translated Russian books—says in a recent article:[1] "Only a person who is unable to

---

[1] In the *American Mercury*, September, 1946, to which I am indebted for many of the quotations from the Russian here made.

read has any excuse for ignorance—or for the slightest doubt—of what Stalin is up to. It is explicitly written down in a book signed by him, currently revised by him, and translated by his authorization into all civilized languages, selling in millions of copies and adhered to as a textbook and campaign book by his followers in every corner of the globe. It can be read through and digested in one afternoon, and summarized in about ten propositions."

Stalin's statements certainly do not lack clarity. Here is one from his book, *Problems of Leninism*:

It is inconceivable that the Soviet Republic should continue to exist for a long period side by side with imperialist states—ultimately one or the other must conquer.

"Imperialist states," Mr. Eastman reminds us, "means us."

This is not ancient history, dating from the early days of the Revolution, or before the pact with Hitler, or before the war. It is what Stalin is saying now in thirty languages (including an excellent English translation) to hundreds of millions of people.

The international significance of our revolution lies in this, that it is a . . . first step in the world revolution and a powerful base for its further development. . . . What *is* our country as it builds socialism but a base for the world revolution?

That is Stalin's answer, Mr. Eastman insists, to those in his own party who imagine that in purging his old Bolshevik colleagues he abandoned their plan to promote chaos in "bourgeois" nations, to engineer the "breakdown of capitalism," and to achieve a communist transformation of the world. "He is very happy to have our diplomats believe that legend, but not his followers—they must know the truth," and know that it is "going to be a bloody, violent undemocratic and lawless job." To quote again from *Problems of Leninism*, which, together with Stalin's *History of the Communist Party*, Mr. Eastman (himself an historian of some aspects of the Russian Revolution) says may be regarded as the *Mein Kampf* of world communism:

Can such a radical transformation of the old bourgeois system be achieved without a violent revolution, without the dictatorship of the proletariat? Obviously not. . . .

The scientific concept, dictatorship, means nothing more nor less than power which directly rests on violence, which is not limited by any laws or restricted by any absolute rules. . . . Dictatorship means unlimited power, resting on violence and not on law.

Stalin is here, of course, setting before his people what were the doctrines of Lenin, and insisting that they are as valid for the conditions of today as they were in Lenin's time. How truly he interprets Lenin's view that the supreme moral goal of mankind was the establishment of communism in all nations and that all means to this end were justifiable may be gathered from what Lenin himself has written in *The Infantile Sickness of "Leftism" in Communism*. In Chapter 6 of that pamphlet Lenin wrote:

It is necessary . . . to use any ruse, cunning, unlawful method, evasion, concealment of truth. . . .

and follows with a passage which is pretty well word for word that used by Stalin in the first quotation above. To it, however, Lenin added this:

We are living not merely in a state but a system of states . . . a number of terrible clashes between the Soviet Republic and the bourgeois states is inevitable.

In order that there should be no mistake that these Leninist views still dominate Russian policy, they were confirmed twenty-five years after Lenin wrote them by Stalin's deputy, Andrei Vishinsky, who has so often represented the USSR abroad, in a speech in Moscow, a speech, moreover, translated into English by the Russian authorities and published by the Soviet Embassy in Washington in its Bulletin for November 17, 1945. Mr. Vishinsky's speech contained this passage:

Lenin purged the teachings of Marx . . . and exposed the sweet-sounding nonsense about a calm and smooth development of bourgeois society into socialism—nonsense to the effect that it is not in the fires of battle, not by means of revolutionary struggle, but in reconciling and smoothing out class contradictions that the socialist transformation of the state is to be effected.
Lenin developed the teachings of Marx on the important question of "smashing the bourgeois state apparatus."

If we are to do justice to the Russian Government and people—and keep our own tempers—in quoting statements of policy such as those here made, there are certain facts about our own attitudes we should keep in mind. The British say sincerely that they want peace. Yet twice in this generation they have gone to war without being attacked because they put their security above peace. Having gone to war for security, they applied in their relations with the enemy a moral code no whit different from that which Lenin and Stalin alike apply to what they regard as their implacable enemy, the capitalist world—implacable because their study of history has convinced them first that capitalism is by its very nature aggressive and will be pushed by impersonal forces to expansion of power, and second because no two such systems as capitalism and socialism can live in the same world together. It is true that Stalin has recently seemed to recant in some degree on this point, expressing the view that he sees no reason why the two systems should not live together side by side. But we are compelled to consider this in the context of what he and Lenin regard as justifiable tactics in the midst of the unfinished war of the working class, very similar statements made at the time of the Stalin-Hitler Pact and in the context of statements such as the following:

Every time treaties are made concerning the realignment of forces for a new war, these treaties are called treaties of peace. Treaties are signed defining the elements of a future war, and always the signing of these treaties is accompanied with a lot of claptrap about peace.[2]

On February 9, 1946, at the close of a year during which hardly a week had passed in which Russia had not been concerned with some effort toward international co-operation, Stalin calmly announced in a speech to his own people that "under a capitalist system of world economy" wars are unpreventable.

Carefully reminding them that he was still a "Marxist," he explained, in straight, unaltered, unqualified Marxian terms, the inevitability of wars under capitalism:

"It would be wrong to think," he said, "that the second World War was a result of the mistakes of any particular statesman. . . ."

[2] Fourteenth Congress All-Union Communist Party, December, 1925.

(Which lets out Hitler somewhat.) "Actually the war was an inevitable result of the development of world economic and political forces on the basis of monopoly capitalism." And so long as capitalism lasted, Stalin continued, this would happen periodically—the competition for markets and raw materials would result in "the splitting of the capitalist world into two camps and war between them." With that by way of introduction, Stalin based his essential program for a fifteen-year development of the Soviet economy on the prospect of another war.

The "two armed camps" into which Stalin sees the capitalist world dividing for the next war can only be captained by Great Britain and the United States. Russia's diplomacy, so long as it rests on Stalin's Marxism, will have that eventuality constantly in mind. And astute statesmen, both American and British, comments Mr. Eastman, will as constantly remember that Stalin's "ally" throughout this development, whatever his temporary maneuvers, is neither of these nations but *the conflict between them.*

That this is his view has been made clear by statements without number—as indeed it is part of the Marxist dogma he reiterates. At the Thirteenth Conference of the Communist Party of Moscow in 1925 he said:

We have an ally, implacable, impersonal, but in the highest degree important—that is, conflicts and contradictions between capitalist countries. Undoubtedly the greatest support of our power and our revolution is strife, conflict, and war among our enemies. These, I repeat, are our greatest ally.

Lenin, Stalin, and Trotsky have all alike freely predicted an "inevitable" war owing to commercial rivalry between the United States and Great Britain. This war would come, be it noted, not because the United States was capitalist and Britain socialist, but because capitalist governments by their very nature had to come into conflict with each other, which incidentally seems a little in conflict with the theory of "capitalist encirclement of the USSR." In his *History of the Communist Party of the Soviet Union,* of which twenty million copies were distributed before the war and which has just been reissued to the number of eleven million, Stalin explains the relationship between the policy of socialism in one country *and* world revolution. He writes:

> The victory of socialism in the USSR, as expressed in the abolition of the capitalist economic system . . . could not be considered a *final* victory, inasmuch as the danger of foreign armed intervention and of attempts to restore capitalism had not been eliminated. . . . To destroy the danger of foreign capitalist intervention, the capitalist encirclement would have to be destroyed. . . . It followed from this that the victory of the proletarian revolution in the capitalist countries was a matter of vital concern to the working people of the USSR.

Thirty-one million copies of this work circulated or to be circulated—one for each literate family in the Soviet Union.[3]

Incidentally at an earlier date[4] Stalin said:

> I think the moment is not far off when a revolutionary crisis will develop in America. And when a revolutionary crisis develops in America, that will be the beginning of the end of world capitalism as a whole.

His attitude toward reforms in general, whether of the New Deal or the Fabian type of British labor, is stated in *Problems of Leninism* as follows:

> To a reformist reforms are everything . . . To a revolutionist, on the contrary . . . reforms serve as instruments that disintegrate the regime . . . as strongholds for the further development of the revolutionary movement.

This attitude toward reforms would seem to represent the general communist tactic: bring the "bourgeois" world to chaos and then seize power. Use reforms for purposes of "disintegration" and as a "stronghold for the further development of the revolutionary movement."

That the motive forces behind so much of Russia's foreign policy —forces which will have to be taken into account in our relation with Russia—are indeed of the general character indicated by the above quotations has of late received confirmation in an unexpected quarter.

[3] The figures were given in the *Bolshevik* for December 1945.
[4] Speech to the American Commission of the Praesidium of the Executive Committee of the Communist International, May 6, 1929.

In the first part of this book attention is called to two passages from Professor Laski's writings, one implying that Soviet communism, or "the central idea of the Russian Revolution," is likely to furnish to our generation an inspiration and an impulse such as that which Christianity furnished to the generations which saw the breakup of the Roman Empire, and the other describing the kind of moral code which commonly guides the behavior of communists. The second passage was taken from his pamphlet, *The Secret Battalion*, written as Chairman of the Labor Party to support that party's rejection of the Communist Party's request for affiliation. He describes at the outset the nature of the Communist Parties everywhere, their doctrinal foundations, thus:

Communist Parties all over the world have accepted the theory and practice of Moscow as the only valid philosophy of socialism. They have argued that only a violent revolution can overthrow even a democratic bourgeois regime, and establish a socialist society in its place. They have insisted upon the need for a highly centralized party, with iron discipline and led by professional revolutionaries, mingling with the toiling masses, educating them, organizing them, leading them. When the hour of destiny arrives, the Communist Party will lead the workers to the conquest of the state-power. They will establish the dictatorship of the proletariat and thus repulse the counterattacks the bourgeoisie is certain to make upon the communist determination to consolidate the party's hold on power. By suppressing all opposition, if necessary by a revolutionary terror, by breaking the machinery of the bourgeois state, and replacing its police and defense forces by men and women who are loyal to the communist ideal, they will prepare the conditions in which the transition from capitalist society to socialist society becomes possible.

It will be noted that the first sentence of this passage testifies to the fact that Communist Parties all over the world accept "the theory and practice of Moscow as the only valid philosophy of socialism," which means that the description of communist doctrine and practice which follows must also therefore be in large part a description of the policies, attitudes, and ethics of the Russian Government, which is either the instrument of the Communist Party in Russia—or its master. His analysis, therefore—particularly since it comes from one so deeply sympathetic to the Russian cause as to deem it a sort of inspirational successor to Christianity—should throw light on the question how far the extension of Russian power can be met by conciliation and accommodation or even nonresistance; and how far noncommunist governments, in order to get co-operation, must have power behind them when they pit their view of life and politics as against Russia's.

Lenin supports the communist view expressed in the above quotations. He wrote:[5]

It is an illusion of the petty-bourgeois democrats, and of their chief representatives at the present day, the "socialists" and the "Social Democrats," to imagine that the toiling masses under capitalism can attain to such a degree of class-consciousness, such strength of character, such penetration and breadth of political outlook, as to enable them to decide by merely voting, or generally to decide in advance, without long experience and struggle, which class or which party they shall follow. . . . Only the proletariat, therefore, can lead the toilers from capitalism to communism. . . . This circumstance the devotees of "consistent democracy" constantly lose sight of. They imagine that serious political questions can be decided by voting. As a matter of fact, such questions, when they have been rendered crucial by the struggle, are decided by civil war.

The situation in France, where communist influence has been so much greater than in Britain, gives a clearer picture than does the situation in Britain of the effect of communist policy and Russian influence.

Arthur Koestler, the ex-communist novelist who has made so deep a study of communist and Russian psychology, wrote recently[6] that "what France needs most urgently is a kind of spiritual retreat; a few years of security and peace to rethink her problems, to ruminate and crystallize her new values." This is made impossible, he thinks, mainly by the fact that the numerically strongest party in France today is a party which "openly confesses its loyalty and allegiance to a foreign power whose interests and traditions are alien to the interests and traditions of France. The pride and stronghold of Latin tradition through two thousand years has become the

[5] *The Elections to the Constituent Assembly,* article of December 29, 1917. In *Selected Works* (London, 1936), page 476.

[6] *New York Times Magazine,* January 5, 1947.

advance post of the influence of Byzantium." Koestler does not raise in this connection the merits or demerits of Stalinite rule. "The situation would be equally tragic for France if she had happened to fall under the sway of a Chinese—or Mexican—sponsored party."

The core of the "repressed complex" which as yet the average Frenchman does not dare to face is that the French state has lost its sovereignty internally, in the sense that the executive has no longer the real power to control the country. More precisely, no French Government could maintain itself in power even for a few days against a general strike of the CGT, the all-powerful, centralized labor union under communist control. Koestler shows how this particular trade union so controlled can paralyze the life of the country. The public actions of the Communist Party in France, he insists, are but a façade for the underground activities of a revolutionary movement "with an old conspiratorial tradition, a neo-Machiavellian philosophy and a clear grasp of the power factors that really matter." He goes on to describe how, in the chaotic days when the German administration had collapsed and no new one taken its place, the communist elements of the underground succeeded to a considerable degree in purging the police and *Garde Républicaine* of their most prominent anticommunist elements "partly by physical liquidation as collaborationists, partly by defamation." He writes:

If the French Communist Party had the brazenness to ask in public for the invalidation of the parliamentary seats of Daladier and Paul Reynaud as "traitors"—because in 1939 they arrested communist leaders who had preached nonresistance to the nazis and sabotage of the "imperialist war" —then one can imagine how ruthlessly they get rid of political opponents when unobserved by the public eye. About this dark chapter in the history of the Liberation little is as yet known abroad; as little as about the vanishing into thin air—at the rate of one or two cases per week—of prominent emigrés from Russia or Russian-controlled countries.

Infiltration has proved even more effective than intimidation. "The honeycombing of the administration, of police, army, editorial offices, etc., with caucuses of secret party members or sympathizers is one of the oldest, most efficient methods of disruptive policy, which the nazis copied from the Comintern."

But spectacular as the success of the fifth-column infiltration was in Holland, Belgium, and France, it was child's play compared with the potentialities of this third column, heir to the officially disbanded Third International, with its reservoir of five million native communist voters, and with more than a hundred thousand disciplined party members; a third column in official control of a number of important ministries and of the workers' unions. If in 1940, despite twenty years of preparation against German aggression and despite the antinazi *mystique* of the left, France collapsed in six weeks, it would be optimistic to assume that she could resist a new invasion, supported by a revolutionary *mystique*, even for six days.

Koestler gives detailed evidence of the way in which the tactics of the Communist Party in France are integrated with the larger European strategy: now quiescent and biding its time, now pushing forward, now perhaps joining in government, now opposing it, but all the time continuing "their patient underground termite work to undermine the last vestiges of sovereign government in France." He goes on:

> Every chess player and strategist knows that an implied threat is more paralyzing than the open attack. And thus the political scene in France will become more eerie and unreal, for in all the brilliant speeches and editorials, just the one basic truth will be left out with everybody's tacit consent. France has become a Troy, with the wooden horse standing on a pedestal in the market place; the children pat it on the nose, and the grown-ups, who know better, do the same, with an embarrassed laugh, pretending not to hear the ominous noises in its belly.

And Koestler is an expert on underground conspiracy, as on open revolution.

But if the Soviet influence acting through Communist Parties is of the kind described by Koestler in France, that influence on the other side of the world in China is not less noteworthy and is even more immediately related to actual and visible shaping of events. Testimony on this point of authoritative and official character comes in the report made by Secretary of State Marshall of his efforts to bring some sort of peace to China. He states the issue in China simply and bluntly:

> On the one hand, the leaders of the government are strongly opposed to a communistic form of government. On the other, the communists

frankly state that they are Marxists and intend to work toward establishing a communistic form of government in China, though first advancing through the medium of a democratic form of government of the American or British type.

Marshall's report is rendered the more impressive by the fact that he does not hesitate to condemn in severe, unqualified terms the reactionaries in the National Government and the Kuomintang Party, nor to face the fact that the two are virtually one organization. He also expresses the belief that among the communists are some liberals who can be persuaded to work loyally with the government, adding, however, that "this view is vigorously opposed by many who believe that the Chinese Communist Party discipline is too rigidly enforced to admit of such differences of viewpoint."

The picture becomes a familiar one in areas of communist activity when the general reports:

The dyed-in-the-wool communists do not hesitate at the most drastic measures to gain their end as, for instance, the destruction of communications in order to wreck the economy of China and produce a situation that would facilitate the overthrow or collapse of the government, without any regard to the immediate suffering of the people involved.

Equally familiar and in striking accord with the communist psychology as sketched by Professor Laski is the following observation of Secretary Marshall:

However, a very harmful and immensely provocative phase of the Chinese Communist Party procedure has been in the character of its propaganda. I wish to state to the American people that in the deliberate misrepresentation and abuse of the action, policies and purposes of our government this propaganda has been without regard for the truth, without any regard whatsoever for the facts, and has given plain evidence of a determined purpose to mislead the Chinese people and the world and to arouse a bitter hatred of Americans.

It has been difficult to remain silent in the midst of such public abuse and wholesale disregard of facts, but a denial would merely lead to the necessity of daily denials; an intolerable course of action for an American official.

In the interest of fairness, I must state that the Nationalist Government publicity agency has made numerous misrepresentations, though not of the vicious nature of the communist propaganda.

Incidentally, the communist statements regarding the Anping incident which resulted in the death of three marines and the wounding of twelve others were almost pure fabrication . . .

Again the technique is familiar as revealed in the following passage:

The communists by their unwillingness to compromise in the national interest are evidently counting on an economic collapse to bring about the fall of the government, accelerated by extensive guerrilla action against the long lines of rail communications—regardless of the cost in suffering to the Chinese people.

Marshall's task in China was to help in the setting up there of a government as truly representative as possible of the Chinese people, and not merely of either a Kuomintang or a Communist Party. He has described the obstacles he encountered in the shape of the Communist Party and its intrigues in China. But communist activities in the United States have also had a bearing upon the task Marshall assumed. It could hardly have been rendered any easier by a persistent agitation for withdrawal of all American forces from China, and a return, so far as the United States in the Pacific area is concerned, to a policy of neutrality and isolationism. In that agitation the Communist Party of the United States has played no small part.

The examination of the activities, motives, and methods of Communist Parties throughout the world is indispensable if we are to appreciate the nature of Russian foreign policy. That the connection between national Communist Parties and the headquarters in Moscow is still close and intimate, despite the dissolution of the Comintern, has just recently been abundantly demonstrated by evidence such as that revealed in the recent Gouzenko incident in Ottawa.

It has been suggested by Mr. Edgar Snow,[7] a foreign correspondent familiar with the Russian scene, and sympathetic to Russia, that we could come nearer to a *modus vivendi* if we understood that all Russian diplomats have to talk with two voices:

One is the language of Soviet nationalism, slowly integrating itself within the deep forces of Russian history. The other is still the language

[7] In the *Saturday Evening Post,* February 15, 1947.

of social revolution. . . . This dualism was long personified by the Soviet Government's efforts to maintain collaboration with capitalist states and at the same time to give haven to a Comintern pledged to overthrow them.

He goes on:

Because Marxism-Leninism remains a guiding philosophy behind Soviet domestic policy, outside politicians and observers—including American communists—continue to confuse the vital interests of Russia as a state and going concern with what are often purely theoretical abstractions or propaganda aims.

Thus, says Mr. Snow, when Molotov and Vishinsky and such people spit out common words like fascism, imperialism, feudalism, dictatorship or collaborator and purr over favorites such as socialism and democracy and communism, they are not only talking Russian but simultaneously using a second language which is rarely translated for the American newspaper reader. They are speaking in Marxian:

They know that everything they say will be checked, compared, interpreted and annotated by the Red professors, and that they must be prepared to reconcile their utterances with classical doctrine. They are often less concerned that their Anglo-American colleagues should understand them than they are that they should not be misunderstood by the magistrates at home.

Mr. Simeon Strunsky, dealing with this explanation, observes that it is of some use to know that when a Moscow politician addresses the outside world he may be speaking normal language, or Marxian language, or Russian patriotic language, or a combination of all three. "For instance, if an official Moscow statement says that everybody in Poland is free and happy, all that our people in the State Department have to do is to decide whether everybody in Poland is normally free and happy, or Marxianly free and happy, or free and happy in the patriotic Russian sense."

The important question for the West is whether all this adds up to a possibility that Russia may modify her doctrinal intransigence and accept the principle that communist and capitalist states can live in peace in the same world. Mr. Snow's testimony, perhaps unwittingly, is to the effect that official Russia still demands rigid adherence to Marxian doctrine. Both Stalin and Molotov have recently, however, indicated a modification of Marxian orthodoxy. Nevertheless, remembering Mr. Snow's warning about the several languages Russian diplomats are compelled to talk, were they just talking "Western" as opposed to "Marxian"? And how are these more conciliatory statements to be reconciled with those of different temper and quite recent date quoted earlier in this chapter? And with actual policies in Eastern Europe and in dealing with Communist Parties, as shown by the Ottawa spy revelations?

And are Western Communist Parties to be more royalist than the king? Is a French Communist Party to be encouraged to block all forms of Western unity, save the communist form, using Russian power as a threat in the background?

The greatest hope for accommodation between Russia and the West lies in persistent presentation of the facts. Mr. Snow seems to feel this. "Everybody who has followed Soviet politics knows that the evolution of the war and its outcome presented Marxist theorists with thorny new questions which have never been answered in a finished thesis." The simple outstanding fact of the war as bearing on Marxian theology, as these pages have insisted with very necessary repetition, is that the "imperialist" states did not perform as prophesied. "The world bourgeoisie consciously rejected their one great opportunity to unite and destroy the one socialist state. Instead, the Socialist Fatherland was saved from destruction by an alliance that endured with the most advanced capitalist powers of the earth." This flatly contradicts basic theories of Marxism-Leninism. Is there a possibility that the fact should be sufficiently recognized to bring about some revision of communist doctrine? Mr. Snow says he asked General Scherbakov, then head of the Red Army political department and a member of the Politburo, whether the fact that the greatest capitalist power had come to the aid of socialist Russia did not introduce an entirely new stage in world history, one quite unforeseen by Lenin's classic *The Imperialist War*. The general agreed that it did; things had happened which Lenin could not foresee. Mr. Snow hopes that the theory of the "inevitable" clash between capitalism and socialism can be laid to rest like Marx's prophecy of the "withering away of the state" under socialism.

But if it is to happen it might be suggested that it begin in the West; that until the socialists of the Western Democracy admit this possibility of co-operation between different systems and doctrines we can hardly expect the Russians to do so. Yet many Western leftists still shout the old slogans, still insist that "capitalism" leads straight to war; that the sole road to peace is through "socialism," though we are not agreed as to what socialism is; and though the quarrel of Russia with the West is not only with its capitalists but its socialists, the social democrats. So long as emotion-creating doctrines are so very immune to plain fact, we cannot build secure peace.

CHAPTER XVIII

The War of the Myths

TO THE question raised in the last chapter: "Is it possible for socialism and capitalism to live together in peace?" we have seen that a great part of the intelligentsia of our generation replies with a resounding "No." Capitalism by its "innate contradictions" has within itself the seeds of imperialism and war. Quotations given in the preceding pages show with what tenacity and obduracy this doctrine is held. Any hope that there can be a middle way, any compromise between the two systems, is, says one of the Great Lights of the Left, "a satanic illusion." His view is the common one.

But this raises, also as we have seen in the preceding pages, a further question: Which socialism? Which is the kind that has none of the compromise which would be so dreadful an illusion? Those who make up the labor government of Great Britain believe themselves to be socialists. But Moscow laughs this to scorn. And there are a good many leftist critics of the labor government who are convinced it falls very short of the real thing. A writer who attempts to explain Russia to America and America to Russia points out that the Russians believe that all the bourgeois democracies of the West live under a form of dictatorship and he quotes Lenin in explanation. Lenin wrote: "The forms of bourgeois states are extremely varied. But in essence they are all the same. In one way or another in final analysis, all these states are inevitably the dictatorship of the bourgeoisie." What Moscow desires, it would seem, is that the West should be rescued from dictatorship.

This deep disagreement as to what is the true socialism is not confined by any means to disagreement between the Russians on the one side and the social democrats of the West on the other. It keeps recurring between Russians and Russians. The great purges in Russia were not purges of capitalists and of the bourgeoisie: they were purges of communists, many of them pioneers of the Russian Revolution. But they had "deviated" as to the methods and to some extent, perhaps, as to the real purpose of socialism.

So when we argue that only socialism can give us peace, we must know which of the many kinds of socialism. Because if it is the wrong kind, it will not suffice for that peace with Russia which we all desire. The proof of that, of course, lies in the bitter conflicts going on all over the world, not between socialists and capitalists, but between socialists of one kind or another on one side and communists on the other. Yet communists, too, are socialists. We are drifting to a war of doctrines, as the world has so often done before. And we may discover, after the war, as we discovered after the religious struggles, that we were mistaken as to the vital nature of the differences between us; that heretic and orthodox could live together in the same state.

I suggest as a contribution to understandings and agreements which might as well come before the war as after, that there is no such thing as "complete" or "absolute" socialism or absolute and integral capitalism, any more indeed (as previous chapters have attempted to show) than there is such a thing as absolute national independence, or absolute freedom, or absolute democracy. The very existence of freedom, or national independence, or democracy, depends upon their limitation. The survival of freedom and democracy will depend, not on the application of an impossible absolute, but upon a good political judgment of the particular freedoms which must be surrendered to secure the preservation of more important ones; how far we shall consent to live under governments that do not represent us in order to have any representative government at all; to what extent a nation may surrender its sovereignty and independence in order to prevent a condition in which it will have none. Some similar synthesis has to be made between the need for controlling certain economic processes and the rightful desire of the individual to dispose of his life as he thinks best in the form of free activity which he prefers.

We shall see the facts more clearly, perhaps, if we keep in mind the nature of that social evolution which has taken place even in the lifetime of living men.

When land transport in Europe or in America was mainly by horses and wagons, a man bought a team of horses or oxen and a wagon and could transport his neighbors' goods or persons as a natural and proper piece of private enterprise. Except as to the payment of tolls at bridges and on the roads, the government and the community had little cause to intervene in any arrangements that the carrier might make with his customers.

But what happened when railways came along? First, note that this form of "property" could not exist at all until the community, the government, had given its consent by a franchise. Some early public opinion was greatly opposed to railroads at all. Even in America they were regarded at times as impious, hostile to the public welfare. The Duke of Wellington in the House of Lords bitterly opposed their introduction into Britain on the ground that it would enable "the lower orders to go running about all over the country, escaping all proper control." (It was a true forecast.) But the intervention of the government to the extent of granting the franchise was only the beginning of a profound modification in the concept of private property. When the old-fashioned landlord—as happened time and again—refused to allow puffing billies to desecrate his estate, the community did not say, "We must respect private property, which is the foundation of our social and economic system, and accede to the wish of the landowner." It did nothing of the sort. It evoked the right of eminent domain, condemned the property, and put the railroad through whether the owner of the private property involved liked it or not. In order to assemble the required capital, the commonly accepted relationship of debtor to creditor had to be modified. In the early nineteenth century a partner in any corporation was liable in all his property for the payments of the debts of that corporation or partnership—thus the stories in early Victorian novels of a man of wealth having a small share in some bank that went bankrupt and finding his whole property involved in the collapse. So the principle of the share of limited liability was introduced. But this in itself involved a great extension of the control by the government of the financial organization of "free enterprise."

But the changes in economic and social structure did not stop there. The government fixed prices. What a railway could charge was fixed by Act of Parliament or Act of Congress—more in the former case than in the latter. Yet price fixing belongs characteristically to socialism.

What is true of the railways is broadly true of most forms of public utility: water works, gas, telegraphs, telephones, power. None of these is a private enterprise in the sense of existing or being able to exist uncontrolled by government. And what is true of the forms of public utility just mentioned is still truer of banking, which, beginning with the safekeeping of bullion and valuables by goldsmiths, who lent it out to customers for commercial purposes on the assumption that it would not all be called for at once, has developed into an immensely intricate and elaborate system which long since ceased to be an unregulated, uncontrolled matter of free enterprise. Similarly with a score of other private-enterprise concerns, such as insurance. When we take stock of the vast body of railway, public utility, insurance, banking legislation which has grown up since the industrial revolution, we see at once that not a year passes without some new form of control by the government of the economic activities of the community within a characteristically capitalist economy. There is no economically civilized country in the world that does not adopt, year after year, increasing doses of what our forefathers would have condemned as pure socialism.[1]

Years before the nationalization of the Bank of England by the socialist government, Maynard Keynes had pointed out in his pamphlet *The End of Laissez-Faire* that the conception of the Bank of England as a piece of private property owned by its shareholders

[1] Mr. E. A. Whitman a year or two since pointed out in connection with certain American legislation that the notion that the owners of railway stock own the railroads is a complete misconception. "The shareholders own the shares, but the public own the roads, which cannot be built, mortgaged, leased, discontinued, without the public's consent. The railroad corporation is invested with governmental power to take private property against the will of the owner. In some states the roadway is exempted from local taxation. The reason for this is manifest. The public welfare, nay, the existence of our present civilization, is dependent upon the existence and maintenance of railroads. A stoppage of railway transportation today would quickly bring starvation to millions and the destruction of inland industries. The railroads, therefore, are not merely clothed with a public interest, they are the public interest itself."

was complete nonsense. It had become a public concern, whose directors managed it with a view to the country's financial welfare along principles which might be right or wrong, but which were certainly not dictated merely by a consideration of the profits of the shareholders. It was agreed on all hands when nationalization took place that in actual practice little was altered: the relations between the bank and the treasury would continue about as they had been previously, the same people managing the affairs of the bank, and that, though it was conceded that the added powers conferred by the new legislation could be useful in certain contingencies, the motive behind the legislation was possibly much more one of satisfying the claims of socialist doctrine than of responding to any practical need.

Indeed, it is possible to go further. During the war there took place in England an economic revolution, in the sense of the practical dispossession of the well-to-do classes. When you get a condition in which there are not in a country like England a hundred persons with net individual incomes of more than five thousand pounds a year once the tax-gatherer is through with them, you have a transfer of wealth certainly as complete as anything that could be achieved by means of guillotines and barricades. But this dispossession had been carried out by a government under the leadership of the head of the Tory Party, Winston Churchill. In other words, the revolution brought about for the purposes of war by a coalition government, dominated (at least in the view of the Labor Party) by the conservatives, had already taken place before the Socialist Party came to power. It may be their office to make it permanent. But much of it would have been permanent in any case. A great part of the legislation of the Labor Party would have been enacted even if the coalition government had remained in power. (It explains in part the failure of the opposition to resist with any degree of insistence much of the legislation which has been passed.) But apart from that, the present socialist government is authority for the statement that some 80 per cent of the business and industry of the country will be left unnationalized and in private hands. It has assured us, moreover, that it will not control for the purpose of control.

There are very few indeed in England who do not recognize the simple truth that the immensely difficult problems which confront that country, dependent as it is upon exports to countries all over the world and imports from countries all over the world, cannot be solved merely by waving a magic wand called nationalization or socialism.

In recognizing that fact, Britain has been wise enough to benefit from the experience of Russia itself. The story of the Russian experiment is marked by no straight line of advance toward a communist state. As we know, it has been a story of applying in the first instance sweeping theories of communism, finding that some of them don't work, retreating from the first position, introducing new economic policies, trying new roads of approach to the peasants, the city workers—applying, that is, the very gradualism of which the pioneers of communism like Trotsky were so contemptuous. Yet the revolutionary pioneers had the enormous advantage of a state in which only rudimentary capitalism had been developed, had, that is to say, something resembling a clean slate upon which to write the new economic constitution. Furthermore, the new dictatorship was prepared to use on behalf of that new order a degree of ruthlessness which has always marked the history of government in Russia, but which it would be extremely difficult to impose upon a Western people.

Political and social discussion is peculiarly subject to the fallacies which arise from too literal an acceptance of labels and categories. Historians warn us against dividing history into neatly cut periods: the fall of Rome, the feudal age, the Renaissance, the Reformation, the industrial revolution, insisting that there are no such sharp divisions, that they often merge one into the other. We create myths of another kind when we personify nations and insist upon a national character and personality. Similarly with our "classes"—the working class, the bourgeoisie, the petty bourgeois, the upper class, the middle class . . . In attributing to a nation a special character and a definite collective responsibility, we have helped to build up nationalisms which have been murderous and productive of appalling evil. Let us not bedevil the solution of our economic problems by the introduction into them of a similar fallacy of watertight divisions between a nonexistent absolute capitalism and a nonexistent absolute socialism.

CHAPTER XIX

An Outline of the Problem

THE outstanding facts of the Russia-West problem are these:

1. "Russia wants peace." So did Britain in 1914 and again in 1939, but found that she wanted security for her institutions and way of life more than she wanted peace; and deliberately without waiting to be attacked, went to war to forestall the danger to those things involved in the continued expansion of an alien power pursuing purposes which might threaten them. The United States somewhat later made the same choice of security before peace.

2. Neither the British nor the Americans realized that this was truly their choice until the danger was on top of them and aggression had obtained such momentum that resistance meant war. If both had fully realized earlier than they did that they would resist, then the power which they finally used to make war might have been used as a means of preventing it, deterring the aggressor by making plain beforehand that he would have to meet the forces he did meet. Both Anglo-Saxon powers in peacetime followed the contrary course, one by neutrality, the other by appeasement. Their future action was so uncertain and unpredictable as to constitute a temptation to the aggressor to take a gambler's chance that he would not be resisted. There is a growing danger that we may repeat this mistake by uncertainty of our future policy, delaying decision until aggression has gained such momentum that resistance, when it is made, will mean war.

3. Neither Great Britain nor the United States regards the power of the other as a threat to itself. The United States is an outcome of British power dating from the time when the defeat of the Armada made the first settlements possible, down to co-operation in two

world wars of the present century. There is sufficient agreement on the principles which should govern the intercourse of nations and on the rights which power would be used to maintain to make co-operation instead of competition possible, despite considerable difference in the political and social systems of the two unions. (The nonfortification of the United States—Canadian frontier was agreed upon when Canada was still of colonial status, ruled by a monarchical government, and the base of British military and naval power.) The underlying agreements are sufficient to offset the differences and make a combination of power for the defense of common interests possible. Our purpose should be to find out what body of commonly accepted principles and interests Russia will accept as the basis of an international society which she, in common with other powers, will defend.

4. Russia's view of her security—expressed both by what she has said in a long-sustained propaganda and by what she has done—demands "friendly"[1] governments in the countries on her borders; "friendly" meaning government by parties which accept the theories and policies of her own one-party system, communist or near-communist. A Russian foreign policy so guided is implicit in the creed or doctrine (which is the ideological basis of the Russian state much as a Bill of Individual Rights is the basis of democratic states) to the general effect that capitalist governments are by their nature aggressive, that capitalism must in the end produce war, and that Russia therefore lives in a condition of constant danger so long as "capitalist" states exist. This theory—an important fact in the situation—is also held by Socialist Parties of Marxist complexion in the Western nations and frequently expressed by them. While this state-theory need not, and should not, be accepted as the last word in the discussion, it should be accepted as the first word and taken seriously, since peace would not be likely if a preliminary condition were that all the world had to become socialist in the Russian sense, or that all countries had to become capitalist in, say, the American sense.

[1] "Russia must be 100 per cent certain that the governments of her immediate neighbors are definitely friendly and have no vestige of fascism left in them. . . . The USSR cannot permit the existence on her borders of states with semifascist or anti-Soviet governments." *Anglo-Russian News Bulletin* (issued by the Anglo-Russian Parliamentary Committee), October 8, 1945.

5. There are welcome signs that the Soviet rulers may be willing to modify their doctrine that the very existence of capitalist states is a danger to Russia, and that they may yield something of doctrinal orthodoxy to the fact of the event: the fact that in the sternest struggle of history the victory of communist Russia was made possible by aid given by the most completely capitalist state in the world; and that "imperialist Britain" declared war on fascism at a time when Russia found it possible to make an accommodation with it. It should not be impossible now to persuade the Soviets to accept as a principle of international intercourse that each nation has the right to live under the system it prefers and which is best suited to its circumstances, especially now that the capitalist states have made war to defend, among other things, the right of Russia to remain communist. Russia's difficulty in accepting this principle will be with her own people. In agreeing that nations of different political, economic, and social institutions can live together in peace and co-operate for common ends (just as in Western democracies parties of opposed theories can live under the same constitution making gradual adjustment of differences), Russia would, in her relations with foreign states, be applying principles she refuses to apply at home to Russians. But recent declarations by Molotov and Stalin (quoted in a previous chapter) indicate that there is hope of agreement along this line.

6. This hopeful tendency will not be helped by the continued insistence of leftist parties in the West that the older Russian view that "capitalism inevitably leads to war" is correct and that the United States is bent on plans of aggression against Russia, and, generally, that American imperialism is the great threat to future peace. Such a view is in any case incompatible with a policy of strict neutrality: it is in effect a subscription to the Soviet view of foreign policy. The extension of its influence would create in Britain a situation similar to that which exists in France in which though the communists are a minority they have sufficient power to make it difficult to pursue any policy which may not be satisfactory to Moscow.

7. The fact that Russia insists upon the right of "friendly" governments in all territory which might be a base of operations against

her would make it extremely difficult for Britain to maintain a position of neutrality in the event of a Russian-American conflict. In the event of such a war, it is likely that Russian forces would be in occupation of the territory of France with the acquiescence of a communist government, which would probably come to power in the event of such conflict. Russia would, in that case, have some serious grounds for fearing the occupation of British ports and territory by American forces. Especially as anticommunist feeling in Britain—strong at present in the Labor Party as in the Conservative Party—would look favorably upon American assistance in resisting absorption by Russia or resisting the establishment of a communist dictatorship in Great Britain. This last event would, in the imagined circumstances, be regarded by Russia as the sole satisfactory guarantee of "neutrality." The setting up a government of collaboration with Russia against the United States would have behind it the same kind of force which brought about the establishment of a Vichy French government, collaborating with Germany against Great Britain. "Neutrality" would almost certainly develop into collaboration with either Russia or with the United States, and in the early stages of the struggle Russian collaboration might be the only available means of saving the population from destruction by air warfare. Any real neutrality would be impossible.

8. The power behind the political changes taking place in Europe is not the power of the atomic bomb. The fate of peace, the chances of avoiding the bomb, depend upon the direction of changes made during the next ten or fifteen years—changes which will not be made through the instrumentality of the bomb. So far in the Western nations Russian influence—acting through Communist Parties—has been that of a revolutionary ideological appeal to minorities who are able to impose their policies upon majorities because the majorities are divided (again as in the French situation).

9. Heretofore the Western democracies have not been able to duplicate the communist influence in this respect, largely because the political freedoms which would be valued so highly if we did not have them happen to be to a great extent already in our possession. The goods we do not have but are promised for the future are usually more highly valued than those we have today.

10. This advantage will not always lie with Russia and its communist allies. Already in Poland, the Baltic, and the Balkan States which have known a bourgeois society, the people are beginning to be skeptical of the virtues of communism and to be attracted to the policy which the United States is beginning to develop: a policy of material aid to those states possessing a noncommunist majority disposed to resist communist pressure. This kind of resistance to Russian expansion and communist penetration gives promise of being effective. It is quite unlikely to provoke Russia into military action within the next ten or fifteen years, by which time stable political democracy may have established itself firmly in Western Europe and a *modus vivendi* with Eastern communism brought about.

11. In the promotion of this policy the British Commonwealth can be of substantial, indeed indispensable help, provided it is willing to accept the conditions already indicated.

12. The fears which are aroused by the idea of dividing the world into two blocks arise largely from confusion. A hopelessly divided Western Europe is bound to be at the mercy of minorities, much as a nation with a multiplicity of parties usually drifts to minority government and is usually marked by instability. The two-party state is not either less peaceful or less stable than the one possessing, say, twenty parties. If the United Nations is to become a political reality, embodying the Parliament of Man, that parliament will reflect the division of the world into different economic and political systems. The division exists. The best hope of a *modus vivendi* is not to pretend that it does not exist or to insist that no international institution shall take cognizance of it. We must start by facing the fact of difference, and then find means of peaceful existence despite it. A Western Europe incapable of common action would constitute a standing temptation to Moscow to dominate it by the methods she applies to her own people where divisions of that kind are not tolerated. Russia could be persuaded more easily to adopt an attitude of negotiation, looking to agreement with a West that presented unitedly the Western point of view, than she could with one hopelessly divided, with some of it leaning to her own interpretation of things. In the latter situation she would be almost compelled to

impose her own solution with the help of her own allies existing within the Western lines.

As an addendum to the above points a little historical note may be appropriate. Over a century ago—one hundred and twelve years to be precise—de Tocqueville, a Frenchman who knew Europe and had made a firsthand study of America, wrote this:

There are at this time two great nations in existence which, proceeding from different points, appear to be advancing toward the same end. I mean the United States of America and Russia.

All the other nations seem to have reached very nearly the bounds which nature marked out for them and have nothing further to do but to keep what they already possess. These two only are still in progress. These alone are marching forward rapidly with giant steps in a career to which the eye can as yet discern no limit.

The American depends chiefly on self-interest to effect his objects, and leaves the individual to act almost without direction. The Russian concentrates in one man the whole power of society. The main principle of the former is *liberty*; of the latter, *despotism*.

Their respective points of departure are different; they move in opposite directions; but each seems to be called, in the secret designs of Providence, to hold in its hands at some future day the destinies of half the world.

An observer of the international scene, writing to describe it more than a hundred years after de Tocqueville wrote, would not have to alter much of the above, although Russia has meanwhile gone through a revolution which many have described as the most profound change in the structure of human society that has ever occurred, and America has had a great civil war and has changed the face of the New World. It indicates most strikingly the strange permanence of certain underlying characteristics and forces that shape the course of nations.

PART VI

Conclusion: The Ultimate Issue

Conclusion: The Ultimate Issue

LET US summarize.

The control or abolition of atomic weapons (or worse) demands a world authority of some kind. Its establishment comes into conflict with the feeling of nations for independence, with "sovereign rights" which have heretofore rallied the deepest moral passions. Its effective working is also hampered by doctrinal conflicts concerning the right form of economic and political society, as in Eastern Europe and in China, and in lesser degree in France; by religious or racial conflicts as in India and Palestine.

Since the breakup of the Roman Empire, Europe has never managed to achieve by voluntary co-operation the unity which it possessed under that authority. If to the disintegrating force of nationalism we now add the fanatical passions of rival social and economic doctrines within each nationality, we may drift to a condition of chaos in which the choice will be between the risks of atomic war and the burden of an authority based on force and coercion.

Russia is showing the possibility of establishing such authority. Not only is her government at home more secure than government in, say, France, Italy, Greece, China, and even Britain; not only has her government a much freer hand in the shaping of foreign policy than the government of any democracy, but she has brought into subjugation or obtained great influence in a long list of nations wherein, less than ten years ago, she had no power at all: Esthonia, Latvia, Lithuania, Finland, Poland, Rumania, Bulgaria, Yugoslavia, Albania, Czechoslovakia, a large part of Germany and some of Austria.

Russia's power lies where Hitler's lay: in the disunity of those who would like to oppose her but cannot agree upon the method and policy of so doing. Hitler would have been powerless to commit his aggressions if non-German Europe (to say nothing of the world) had been a unit in opposing him before his aggressions began. The aggressions would never have been attempted if Hitler had been reasonably sure beforehand that his victims would resist with the power that in the final event they had to use.

The conviction of Russia's rulers is that owing to the nature of the economic system to which most of the democracies adhere, a Western unity sufficient to constitute resistance to Russian expansion is impossible, that Western civilization is on the eve of collapse and that the Russian system must be substituted for it. Many leftist parties in the West share this view.

Only a demonstration by the event that the Western democracies can unite for mutual defense is likely to shake Moscow's deep-rooted conviction and predispose the government there to a co-operative relationship. Western unity is not inimical to a One World or a strong United Nations; it is the indispensable condition precedent of both.

Peace will depend less upon ambitious plans of world organization, promulgated without reference to existing differences between the nations, than upon the day-to-day conduct of policy which will reduce those differences and replace them by increasing co-operation. Such matters as the civil war in China, the conditions of the loan to Britain, the conflicts within India, certain conditions in Russia, cannot at this stage be handled by the United Nations; but mismanagement of them outside can undermine the success of that institution.

The best chance that public opinion shall help and not hinder governments in the pursuit of sound policy whether in China, or Greece, or Turkey or Palestine, or Anglo-American relations, or help to Europe, is in the development of an increasing sense of responsibility for avoiding sweeping judgments rooted in emotional partisanship, whether of the old nationalist or racial or religious kind or of the kind which is associated with the advocacy of class war and violent revolution as the proper means of social betterment.

It is not true that the passions which so easily flare up over differences in international adjustments or in political and social theory are "inevitable manifestations of human nature." They result, in large part at least, from moral and intellectual attitudes which can grow in some periods (as in that of the religious wars in Europe) and diminish in others, as the passions which provoked the religious wars have diminished in our time. Ways of thought, which mean also ways of feeling, can vary from age to age, though fundamental human nature, the physical foundations of it, that is, remain the same. Those ways of thought and feeling vary as between nations. The standards of moral and intellectual conduct common in Germany under Hitler were not so common in neighboring nations of the West, nations often of the same racial stock and of the same physical make-up as the Germans.

An indispensable element in the development of sound public judgment in democracies is a greater sense of individual responsibility for the acts of government; which involves a sense of responsibility for the rightness of our own judgments, a sense of "the moral obligation to be intelligent."

In no age so much as in this Atomic Age has the need for that particular sense of responsibility been greater. If the element of reason and reasonableness can make no headway against group emotion and passion in the conflicts of our time, if we are the puppets of circumstance which our individual wills cannot effect, then we are probably headed for extinction and we can do nothing about it.

But the decision that we are thus puppets is the very decision which deprives us of the sense of responsibility which might save us. It may not be true that where there is a will there is a way; it is certainly true that where there is no will there is no way.

It is a grim coincidence that the discovery of means of almost universal destruction should synchronize with a determinist philosophy, popular and fashionable, which insists that the individual, his ideas, his moral behavior are the product of external circumstance he can do nothing to control. In so far as men are guided by such fatalism it undermines their sense of responsibility to get at truth and to see that it guides policy. It undermines the very basis of democracy, which is that the opinion of the individual is all-important and the foundation of government. It is no accident that Marxist communism is associated with dictatorship.

While some changes in the purposes and methods of education for democracy are urgently called for, we do not have to wait for it to ensure improvement. The temper and the climate of opinion where the press is free can change rapidly. Isolationism of the kind expressed in the Neutrality Acts is probably dead in America. Yet those acts were passed barely ten years ago.

To reshape the education of Western peoples in the direction which the new age calls for, we must be guided by a recognition of past failures of public judgment. We must have an answer to the question: "Where did the public mind go wrong? And why?" We shall then have some basis in experience for making the necessary changes. Much of this book has been devoted to showing, in the light of the event, where public judgment erred.

"Education" in the sense of "a wider dissemination of knowledge" will not of itself help us. The Germans were the most educated people in Europe, perhaps in the world—past masters in the making of theories about life and the universe. The Japanese were the most literate people in Asia, and the most Westernized. The communist leaders in Russia and throughout the world are almost always highly educated men, spending their lives in the discussion of human society and behavior. This generation as a whole is the most educated of which we have any record, and the one most likely grievously to hurt itself with instruments of its own devising.

The facts do not help us unless we have learned how to interpret them aright. Nor does understanding between peoples come necessarily with closer contact. When the Germans indulged in theories about the Jews and the Ayrian race (which later the non-German world came to look upon as the ravings of madmen) they had the "facts" beneath their noses in the shape of Jewish people who had lived among them for two thousand years. The "facts" about Moslems are known to Hindus, and about Hindus to Moslems, since they live their lives together in the same village or city. Not a year passes but the killed and wounded in the clashes between them are numbered by tens of thousands.

Without education and knowledge we cannot solve our problems; they are indispensable tools. But they are tools which, ill-used, can make the case worse instead of better, as a surgeon's instruments which, properly used, can save life, can also, in the hands of a reckless or irresponsible practitioner, cause death; or, in the hands of a passionate or unbalanced man, become the means of murder or of suicide.

Men can acquire new skills in the use of the instrument of the mind, as the Greeks did; and can lose those skills, as the Greeks did. We have mechanical means of knowledge which the ancients did not possess. We must use them to a better understanding of our own natures, realizing that the barriers to peace are not physical obstacles but reside in the minds and hearts of men.

We hold within our hands the material means of preserving those freedoms we fought two wars in this generation to defend. They are means largely in the hands of the English-speaking peoples, whose communities now encircle the globe. If, yielding to disruptive and divisive impulses, we fail in the necessary co-operations, we shall not be able to blame the Russians or the communists. Once more we shall have been turned from the better course and from the means of salvation, by those baser forces of the human spirit which it has been the purpose of this book to render visible.